# The Myth of the Global Market



Capitalism is often held to be the best of all possible worlds, or even the only possible world, in which the market is underpinned by the highest principles of rationality, efficiency, and compatibility with democracy. These truths are backed up by economists, a group who present themselves as impartial experts capable of operating independently of ideology or political intrusion.

This book questions these "scientific truths". It discusses the ideological foundations of neoliberalism and the value judgements, often kept implicit, in economic theory. It analyses the claims of the key pillars of neoliberal economics – the neoclassical and Austrian schools of economic thought – and the myths which they propagate about markets. It is shown that there is a deep division between the theoretical market – the fair market, the free market, the market of equal opportunities, the market as a producer of wealth, the market as a forum for discovering and sharing information – and the reality. This is not a simple problem of realism. The problem also concerns the perfect market idealized by these theories, which is subjected to criticism through a process of demystification that reveals the true ideological content hidden behind the market myths. There have been various attempts by heterodox schools of economics to move beyond this flawed view of the market. However, these have struggled to gain mainstream attention because of the cultural and political dominance of the neoliberal mindset which is claimed to be objective and neutral. Ultimately, the book argues that neoliberalism needs to be countered with an alternative based on a progressive decommodification of social relations to reduce the real and imagined significance of the market.

This book is essential reading for those interested in Marxist political economy, heterodox economics, and critiques of neoliberalism, capitalism and markets.

**Giulio Palermo** is a researcher in Political Economy at the University of Brescia (Italy). He was formerly an official at the Italian Ministry of Economy and Finance. His publications deal with Marxism, critique of neoliberalism, relations between economics and ideology, ontology, methodology, and power relations.

## Routledge Frontiers of Political Economy

**Economics as Rhetoric**
The Thought of Bernard Maris
*Anne Isla*
*Translated by Aude Di Paolantonio*

**Inequality and Stagnation**
A Monetary Interpretation
*Capraro, Panico and Torres-González*

**Political Economy of Post-Capitalism**
Financialization, Globalization and Neofeudalism
*Richard Westra*

**The Political Economy of Mediterranean Europe**
A Growth Models Perspective
*Luis Cárdenas and Javier Arribas*

**Economics for Humanity**
Integrating Well-being, Community, and Practical Philosophy
*Mitsuaki Okabe*

**Sustainable Economic Development**
Perspectives from Political Economy and Economics Pluralism
*Edited by Giorgos Meramveliotakis and Manolis Manioudis*

**The Myth of the Global Market**
A Marxist Critique of Neoliberalism
*Giulio Palermo*

For more information about this series, please visit: www.routledge.com/Routledge-Frontiers-of-Political-Economy/book-series/SE0345

# The Myth of the Global Market

## A Marxist Critique of Neoliberalism

**Giulio Palermo**

Routledge
Taylor & Francis Group
LONDON AND NEW YORK

First published 2025
by Routledge
4 Park Square, Milton Park, Abingdon, Oxon OX14 4RN

and by Routledge
605 Third Avenue, New York, NY 10158

*Routledge is an imprint of the Taylor & Francis Group, an informa business*



*British Library Cataloguing-in-Publication Data*
A catalogue record for this book is available from the British Library

ISBN: 978-1-032-72612-0 (hbk)
ISBN: 978-1-032-72617-5 (pbk)
ISBN: 978-1-032-72616-8 (ebk)

DOI: 10.4324/9781032726168

Typeset in Times New Roman
by Apex CoVantage, LLC

# Contents

# About the author

**Giulio Palermo** is a researcher in Political Economy at the University of Brescia (Italy). He was formerly an official at the Italian Ministry of Economy and Finance. His publications deal with Marxism, critique of neoliberalism, relations between economics and ideology, ontology, methodology and power relations.

# Foreword

In this book, the Marxist critique of political economy is actualized in relation to classical analysis in economic thought. It is, therefore, a search from within economic science, a precise and tenacious demystification of the very figure of classical political economy, of its claimed neutrality and its presumption to present itself *super partes* as an objective and necessary indication, unquestionable therefore, of the mechanisms regulating the economy.

Giulio Palermo counters market culture by, first of all, demonstrating the inconsistency of its scientific foundations. The market's alleged rationality, efficiency, desirability and necessity actually have an ideological and biased content that severely conditions scientific thinking. Methodological individualism and the ideology of individualism are inextricably mixed: hence the slide of individualism towards consumerism, the deduction of absolute morality in the market game, the denial of class struggle and the sanctification of 'free' market rules. But the game of the market, its efficiency, shows a series of growing limits, not only objective, from the point of view of the functioning of the market itself and its structure, but also subjective, from the demand side, in the complex and never resolved relationship between individual preferences and the common good. It is here, on these subjective and objective margins, that the issue of the struggle against exploitation is defined based on the contradictions that the capitalist system shows.

Palermo's book is therefore highly critical, not only of the assumptions of classical political economy but, consequently, of all those on the left who make market principles their own: it is, in fact, only from the rejection of the logic of exchange values as an expression of rationality and social efficiency, that in line with Marxist thought, a criterion of rationality based on use values and democratically determined social priorities can be determined.

This is the central axis of the book. The linear development of the argumentation naturally also opens up, in its course, parentheses on the risks of developing the theoretical investigation along mined roads that, while detaching from and criticizing the hard core of the classical theory, do not question its presuppositions. The annotations developed on the radical theory of Bowles and Gintis, among others, as well as those that Palermo makes from time to time on so-called 'analytical Marxism', seem very important to me. Another interesting part is the one concerning the so-called market failures and the form in which classical theory remedies them.

We could continue by insisting on other important points for the analysis. Rather, it is worth insisting once again on the internality of the critique to its object. It is from within that classical political economy must be dissolved. The author bites, in many cases leaving the mark of a critique that always wants to reveal the anxiety of reconstruction. In fact, this is also a pedagogical book, useful for every reader: it is concluded by a glossary of the terminology of classical economics, in its now more than secular development, which at the same time clarifies and sometimes demystifies certain concepts and/or methodological stereotypes that fill the language of economists.

It remains, however, that the fundamental character of this book is political. The realization of democratic principles, in a context in which the limits of the market are recognized, is affirmed through four interdependent conditions: a definition of absolute democratic procedures, the expansion of the economic space regulated through the conscious instrument of planning, the progressive affirmation of the principle 'from each according to his abilities to each according to his needs', the progressive decommodification of our lives. These are elements that no innovation in Marxism, no going beyond Marx, can get out of the way. Thanks to the author for reminding us.

by Toni Negri

# Preface

This book weaves together economic, political, ideological and moral issues. It is, however, first and foremost a book on economics or, more precisely, critical economics. In contrast to the approach that dominates economic theory today, the book makes no claim to universality, nor does it aspire to provide a unanimously agreed view of existing economic and social relations. On the contrary, it is based on the assumption that capitalist economic relations are by their nature conflictual and that there is, therefore, no point in claiming the superiority of any particular worldview, nor in seeking theoretical solutions that can be considered unanimously satisfactory.

This theoretical position openly clashes with the self-proclaimed scientific neutrality of mainstream economic theory. Indeed, the latter clearly rejects the introduction of value judgements, considering them incompatible with the very scientific nature of economics. This is why economists do not like to talk about value judgements and the role of ideology in economic theory. The problem is that avoiding explicit discussion of the values on which political economy is based is not sufficient to remove value judgements from economic theory and only serves to pass off as neutral scientific prescriptions with necessarily ideological content.

The purported objectivity that characterizes bourgeois economics is therefore rejected and explicitly challenged on a theoretical level. This, of course, does not mean that the critique I develop is only valid if one espouses a particular ethical or political position. In fact, the critique is developed through a process of demystification of the theoretical positions of bourgeois economics aimed at exposing the economic interests it reflects and the political conveniences hidden behind its normative prescriptions. This work does not require the adoption of any particular moral sphere or ideological approach. It is simply a matter of making explicit the guiding values of economic and political action that, for reasons of convenience or incompetence, are kept implicit by stakeholders and so-called 'experts' in their economic and political discourses.

Having rejected the presumed objectivity of economic theory, in the parts of this book with the most proactive content, although I will limit myself to considering the proposals aimed at overcoming the criticisms developed, I will not, however, make any effort to conceal my value judgements and political convictions, nor will I hesitate to discuss explicitly the different moral value systems and political positions that confront and clash today in parliamentary halls, international fora and, above all, in the streets (but, alas, less and less in scientific debates). As the Swedish economist Gunnar Myrdal argued, objectivity in social research can never be absolute and universal since it necessarily reflects, if only in the definition of the problem to be analysed and in the choice of instruments of analysis (but sometimes also in the theoretical conclusions), the convictions and values of the theorist, who, in a world of conflicting interests, can in no way be considered above the parties (Myrdal, 1969). Faced with this situation, all one can do on the level of methodological correctness is to address the discourse of values explicitly, stating one's motivations and specifying the theoretical implications arising from the different ideological premises.

It is obvious that, in the debate on the construction of a social and economic system that better responds to the moral principles deemed most appropriate, there is no reason to expect a unanimous moral or political consensus. On the contrary, it is entirely desirable that the different conceptions and the different concerns and aspirations of political actors be openly confronted. From this point of view, I certainly do not expect that the moral and political reflections I will introduce here and there will be immune to criticism from different approaches. However, this does not affect the general process of demystification that is intended to be the real scientific contribution of this book: the critique of the existing economic and social system and its mystified representations does not, in fact, depend in the slightest on the adoption of a particular moral sphere. This makes demystification safe from the criticism encountered by purely ideological attempts to moralize society, the effectiveness of which remains subordinate to adherence at the outset to a particular ideology. In some ways, therefore, from a political point of view, the present work has only a minimal goal consisting in bringing to light the values that guide economic and political intervention, as an indispensable premise for a more general rethinking of the capitalist logic of social interaction.

In explicitly addressing the discourse of values, perhaps the greatest obstacle is the superficiality with which ideological and moral philosophy issues are treated in the political and economic debate. From this point of view, neoliberal thinking, with its appeals to unquestionable values such as, indeed, *freedom*, today constitutes the most advanced form of mystification of the ideological and moral discourse.

On a philosophical level, the liberal doctrine in no way implies the defence of a world in which everything is permitted, in which all rights are placed on an equal footing. On the contrary, the defence of certain rights considered fundamental necessarily requires the imposition of constraints, of restrictions on anyone's freedom of conduct. There are values that can be questioned and others that instead, according to liberalism (but also according to other ideological approaches), must be considered of a higher order and must therefore be treated as inviolable and inalienable. In this sense, the reference to *freedom* as a fundamental value, without specification or contextualization, means nothing. The freedom to kill cannot be placed on the same level as the freedom to stay alive. The freedom of a state to militarily occupy the territories of other peoples is not the same as the freedom of a people to defend its own territory. The freedom to buy and sell products in the market is not the same as the freedom to profess one's political or religious beliefs in society. There is a hierarchy of values and rights on which it is logical for there to be disagreement and political confrontation but which it would be absurd to deny. The confrontation between different moral systems goes through the discussion of different priorities in values and rights, but one cannot reason as if the different forms of freedom all have equal moral dignity. First, because in a world of complex interactions, one's freedom is the constraint of another. Second, because the guarantee of certain freedoms is only achieved by setting norms, rules and constraints that necessarily restrict other types of freedom.

But the real paradox is that in the economic sphere, it is precisely freedom in market relations that leads to the trampling of all rights, even those that, on reflection in terms of values, one would consider inviolable and inalienable. With the transformation of every social relationship into a market relationship, rights, even those considered morally inalienable, receive a price at which they can be indeed alienated. Health, according to many, has no price. Yet when a market for hospital care or medicine is created, a price for health is set, and those who cannot afford to pay it are de facto deprived of their right to health. The freedom (of some) to make profits increases, and that (of others) to grow up healthy or to die with dignity decreases. The transformation of liberal philosophy into a market-driven economic doctrine, therefore, incorporates a profound contradiction that I believe is worth returning to. By elevating economic freedom to an absolute value, neoliberalism simply ends up trampling all other spheres of individual freedom underfoot.

Many of the criticisms of neoliberal theories focus on the fact that they are based on assumptions far removed from real market systems. Such criticism, this being an undeniable fact, is certainly pertinent. However, it is sometimes forgotten that the problem with neoliberal schemes lies above all in their underlying injustice, concealed behind the pretended goal of the common good. In other words, it would almost seem that the true problem is to make real market systems more closely resemble the models of neoliberal theory. The point is, however, that even if one were to succeed in creating a world in the image of the neoliberal models, everything could be said except that such a world would be unanimously desirable, as we are led to believe. This is why it seems important to me to discuss neatly the different theoretical levels on which it is possible to criticize the neoliberal proposal.

My critique of neoliberalism does not only concern the theories that prescribe the widening of the sphere of market relations but touches more generally on the whole set of theories that take the rationality of the market system as given (even if only in its idealized form), that is, that set of theories which ultimately coincides with bourgeois economics and which certainly includes the hegemonic theory on the scientific level – the neoclassical theory – and the Austrian heterodoxy (which takes the liberal doctrine as its explicit philosophical presupposition), but also large slices of the heterodoxy which is not explicitly neoliberal, but which accepts, in some cases only as a theoretical challenge, the methodological approach and world view of the neoclassical theory.

It could be observed that when faced with a set of theories that do not work, it is enough to focus the criticism on the most disruptive aspect, on a pillar that is sufficient to bring down the whole edifice. Certainly, criticism of realism is very effective, given the abstractness of the assumptions of the models of neoliberal theory. However, the critique of the theoretical model remains, in my view, necessary because it shows us that the pillars that are unable to support the neoliberal theoretical edifice are numerous and placed at different levels of the theoretical structure. Therefore, it becomes important to understand the theoretical consequences of the demolition of each pillar and to determine which of the conclusions of the neoliberal theory collapse as the various pillars collapse. The importance of this process of systematic critique is twofold: first, it helps us to think about what we want; second, it shows us the way to overcome the limitations of the existing economic model.

Obviously, then, insofar as the theoretical frameworks used are so abstract as to become representations of a world that is not our own, it is also worth questioning the true objectives pursued through such frameworks. Thus, in both the critique of realism and the critique of the theoretical model, the watchword is one only: demystification.

My basic critique of the principle of market rationality lies in the fact that it takes on a very particular meaning in economic theory, certainly different from its common meaning and highly questionable from the point of view of moral philosophy. And yet, once this principle is accepted in the academic world, it enters fully into common sense, taking on new meanings capable of evoking emotions and provoking reactions under the illusion that everything rests on a rigorous scientific foundation.

The book is primarily aimed at an audience interested in the problems of economic theory and their impact on political affairs. The treatment does not presuppose any specific knowledge of economic theory and should, therefore, also be accessible to the uninitiated. Today, in fact, the greatest difficulties in accessing economic discourse derive not so much from the complexity of the subject (which, admittedly, is anything but simple) but from the technical and mathematical obstacles that modern economic theory imposes. My attempt, therefore, is to provide a critical review of the state of economic research by breaking down the technical and mathematical barriers that confine the economic discourse to an expert audience and that effectively prevent democratic participation in economic and political debates.

It is, however, to professional economists that I would like to issue the challenge by questioning the general foundations of their science, leaving aside, for once, the usual technicalities concerning the latest mathematical tool discovered and its economic applications.

## Reference

Myrdal, G. (1969) *Objectivity in social research*. New York: Pantheon Books.

# Acknowledgements

My deepest thanks go to Marisa and Ivan Palermo, who are actually my mother and father, besides having been a much-loved high school teacher and a great historical and political journalist, for the decisive help they gave me in resolving the contrast between the demands of scientific rigour and expositional clarity that continually reemerged in the various versions of this scientific contribution of a divulgative nature. Their critical remarks and requests for clarification have been a real guide to my writing.

The very need to write this book, however, did not arise in family relationships but in political activism. I have discussed the themes of this book with many militants engaged in social and political struggles, participated in assemblies, occupations, demonstrations and street battles, and tried to contribute, with my limited tools, to the development of a class consciousness without which the radicalism of struggles can remain only a façade.

I have also received many comments from critical economists, or supposedly so, which have forced me to define a strategy of systematic critique of both mainstream and heterodox economics that leave no illusions about the bourgeois nature of even those theories that pretend to be radical but which in fact take for granted the rationality of the capitalist world and the mystified representation of it provided by bourgeois economics.

I wrote this book while Nico was coming into the world; the first Italian edition came out while Maïa was born, and in the meantime, also Laura has arrived. It would, therefore, be spontaneous for me to dedicate this work to my children. Recently, I have also lost, in a very sad way, my father and my sweet sister Francesca, the lawyer with the biggest heart on earth, always on the front line in the defence of women victims of violence, which fuels my anger against the hypocrisy of our society, in which the right to live and the right to die are both hostage of religious and economic Gods.

However, in all humility, I prefer to dedicate this book to all the comrades who study and fight, even in the hardest and saddest times, in the conviction that only the critique and the struggle can challenge the absurd principles of our society and show the way also to Nico, Maïa and Laura and to all those who, like them, inherit a world of privileges and discriminations.

# Introduction

The liberal tradition of thought arose in England and Holland towards the end of the 17th century as a political-philosophical reaction against the feudal residues existing in society. It brings together feelings of revolt against religious intolerance, political absolutism and hierarchy in social relations, feelings that largely reflect the changed economic and political relations, which had shifted decisively in favour of the bourgeois class. In the economic field, liberalism takes the form of a stream of thought that sees the market as the institution best suited to the free manifestation of individual interests and preferences.

In the course of the history of economic thought, the liberal school has developed various theoretical models, which have, however, been the object of fierce criticism. The first influential inspirer of liberalism is the Scottish economist Adam Smith, who lived in the 18th century and is regarded by many as the very founder of the classical school and of political economy as a whole. According to Smith's theory, the desirability of the market as a mechanism of social interaction depends on the possibility of achieving social outcomes beyond the conscious design of single individuals. The individual who solely pursues his own interests in the market, says the Scottish economist, is guided by an 'invisible hand' that leads him to promote social ends beyond his/her own intentions. The so-called anarchy of markets is thus not the source of economic disorder, as one might think, but the real engine of economic and social growth (Smith, 1776).

Throughout the period from the 18th century to the present day, classical liberal thought has been hotly debated. The harshest critique is undoubtedly that of Karl Marx and Friedrich Engels, elaborated during the 19th century and then developed by different thinkers, both in the strictly economic field and in the philosophical and political fields. Indeed, Marx's own critique of the capitalist system and its representation by bourgeois economics does not have a purely economic dimension. In capitalism, as in any other mode of production, the economic sphere is intimately linked to the social, juridical and cultural spheres. In this dialectical relationship between the different forms of social action, Marx believes that capitalism is characterized by the increasing importance of the economic dimension over all the others, with the consequent imposition of the logic of economic accumulation on the other spheres of social life as well. Marxian theory is thus not an economic

DOI: 10.4324/9781032726168-1

theory in the strict sense: instead, it is a conception of the history of society as a whole.

As the hegemony of the economic dimension in all social relations grows, so does the need to represent capitalism as the expression of the highest economic rationality. Bourgeois economics takes up this demand. The problem, according to Marx, is that it is precisely the internal laws of functioning of the capitalist system that are the real cause of the instability of the process of capital accumulation and the recurrent economic crises to which capitalism is subject. The anarchy of markets, which for Smith is a source of economic and social growth, is, for Marx, the root cause of capitalism's internal contradictions. By elevating the pursuit of profit to the sole true economic objective, the law of the market prevents the organization of the economic system according to the needs of the population and instead subjects the population to the needs of capital reproduction and valorization.

For Marx, the critique of political economy is not only an instrument for scientifically questioning the liberal political convictions of his time but also an instrument for demystifying the capitalist system itself, that is, a system in which the essence of the relations of exploitation of man over man and the impossibility of true emancipation of the individual are concealed behind an appearance of formally equal relations between juridically free subjects.

Although the Marxist tradition of thought played a primary role in the political debate of the 20th century, inspiring socialist revolutions and profound institutional changes in about half of the planet, academically it has never achieved the status of dominant school of thought in capitalist countries. Certainly, in some academic circles, the Marxist school has gained important spaces. With the political and institutional crisis in the countries of the socialist bloc, however, Marxist theory has decisively lost positions almost everywhere, in universities as well as in the general economic and political discourse.

From the point of view of the history of economic thought, the theoretical turning point that allowed a new wave of liberal doctrines to impose itself academically dates back to 1870. In this period, two schools of thought strongly inspired by liberal economic principles emerged: the neoclassical school and the Austrian one. These two schools of thought come into being with the almost simultaneous publication of the works of three economists of different nationalities, Léon Walras (1874), French, Stanley William Jevons (1871), English (founders of the neoclassical school) and Carl Menger (1871), Austrian (founder of the homonymous school), who quickly become the new theoretical references in economic studies, supplanting the Ricardian and Marxian approaches, then widely diffused. The radical change in method, in the perspective of analysis and in the very foundations of economic theory compared to the classical and Marxist tradition leads to characterizing this theoretical shift as a scientific revolution, known today as the marginalist revolution.

The term 'marginalist' refers to a particular way of approaching and solving economic problems through so-called 'reasonings at the margin', which, from a mathematical point of view, are represented as problems of differential calculus. However, according to one of the most important historians of economic thought,

Joseph Schumpeter, what the neoclassical and Austrian schools have in common is above all the proposal of a subjective theory of value as a radical alternative to the objective theory of value of the classical economists and Marx, and the idea that all economic propositions must be constructed from postulates concerning individual rules of behaviour (methodological individualism), which deprives all concepts of a social nature (such as social classes) of any scientific content, concepts that instead constituted the methodological foundations of classical and Marxian economics. Indeed, the use of differential calculus as the instrument par excellence for solving economic problems is only developed by the neoclassical school, while the Austrian school not only rejects this instrument but, more generally, maintains a critical stance towards mathematical formalism. From this point of view, again according to Schumpeter (1954), it would be more correct to speak of a 'subjectivist revolution' rather than a 'marginalist one'.

The reasons for the affirmation of the subjectivist approach can be traced, on the one hand, to some internal problems encountered by Ricardian and Marxian theories, and, on the other, to the political implications of these two theories, especially the latter, which, on the basis of a theory of value of commodities based on the labour involved in their production, lead to revolutionary conclusions at the level of economic and political relations in capitalism. In fact, in the decade 1870–80, several European countries (France, Great Britain, Germany and Italy) and the United States were torn by harsh social struggles, followed by violent repression. In this climate, academic circles linked to the bourgeoisie immediately show sympathy for the new approach based on the outright rejection of the objective theory of value and the related Marxian concepts of exploitation and class struggle. This evidently does not mean that the three protagonists of the marginalist-subjectivist revolution are all fully aware of the political significance of the theoretical turn they are involved in. As Maurice Dobb notes, of the three economists only Jevons is fully aware of the political significance of the new approach (Dobb, 1973).

After an incubation phase in which the methodological differences between the neoclassical and Austrian schools remain largely latent, from the 1930s onwards, the two schools took divergent methodological paths: while the neoclassical school defined its research programme by identifying mathematical formalism as a decisive aspect of its methodology of scientific investigation, the Austrian school distances itself from the formalist project, criticizing it harshly for its inapplicability to social sciences. At the same time, the Austrian school takes its subjectivist conception to extremes, going far beyond the neoclassical conception. In this process of theoretical characterization, the two schools of economic thought often find themselves on opposite sides in some of the most important methodological controversies. At the same time, however, the common neoliberal ideology emerges as a strong element of affiliation to the new economic research programme initiated with the marginalist revolution.

With this brief historical reconstruction, it is possible to appreciate the complementarity of the theoretical contributions of the two schools of thought in the process of the affirmation of neoliberal ideology at an academic and cultural level. In fact, it is as if a sort of scientific division of labour existed between the neoclassical school, which today constitutes the orthodoxy at the academic level, even though it remains substantially obscure to those without a degree in economics, and the Austrian school, confined to narrow academic circles, but with a strong cultural impact.[1]

Neoclassical theory uses a complex mathematical language reserved to experts and makes logical-deductive rigour the real strong point of the entire theoretical construction. The attempt to analyse every economic problem in strictly mathematical terms and the consequent need to set economic problems in a way that is compatible with existing mathematical techniques leads neoclassical economics to invest decisively in mathematical research, in some cases becoming the most advanced front of mathematical research itself. At the same time, however, while the technical toolbox becomes richer, neoclassical theory progressively moves away from any question of economic realism, with the consequence that the highest mathematical rigour ends up, in many cases, being applied to models that are decidedly distant from the economic reality they wish to explain. The inaccessibility of the analysis and the high degree of technical sophistication mean that neoclassical theory is now firmly rooted at the academic level (where mathematical skill is considered the true marker of an economist's goodness), but completely alien to economic discourse as it develops outside universities, in culture and in society in general.

The Austrian theory, instead, uses easily accessible language and develops its arguments mainly on an intuitive level, often relying on simple common-sense considerations that reflect a market conception well rooted in popular culture. Indeed, on the one hand, it simply reflects the beliefs and convictions typical of bourgeois culture (e.g. the perception of the market as a spontaneous and natural mode of social interaction); on the other hand, it is particularly appealing on a scientific level due to the relative simplicity of its arguments. Despite the difficulties encountered in gaining adequate representation in the academic framework, the radicalism of its theoretical and political positions has allowed the Austrian school to establish itself as a protagonist in some of the most important theoretical controversies in the history of economic thought. From the point of view of the affirmation of market values, the importance of Austrian theory probably lies in its ability to move in parallel, both in the strictly scientific domain and, more generally, in that of the dominant culture.

As an example of the complementary relationship between the two schools, let us consider the transition process to capitalism that took place in the countries of the former Soviet bloc. In these countries, it was the ideas of Friedrich August von Hayek, one of the leading exponents of the Austrian school, that imposed themselves in the economic and political debate. Freedom of enterprise and the exaltation of the market as an instrument of individual liberation were the ideals that captured people's imagination, not the mathematical theorems of neoclassical theory on market efficiency. However, when the transition process was initiated, the economic advisors were all selected from the neoclassical camp, based on the academic prestige they received in the West.

As a result of the contrasting developments in theoretical research, neoliberalism, as it appears today in the panorama of existing schools of economic thought, certainly does not constitute a monolithic block. On the one hand, ideas from the old classical liberalism re-emerge and are inserted into a body of theoretical knowledge that has, in the meantime, been enriched; on the other hand, new theories that depend heavily on modern techniques of economic analysis, based on the massive use of mathematical tools, take shape. Between these two fronts also emerge a number of attempts at synthesis between the different theoretical approaches that try to exploit and recompose the intuitions matured within the different traditions of liberal thought.

It is clear, however, that insofar as the methodological approaches of the various liberal/neoliberal theories are incompatible with each other, any attempt at their synthesis is risky. In fact, by changing the methodological assumptions, the same terms on which a theory is based take on different meanings and the same proposition may be valid in a given theoretical context but not in another. Likewise, the defence of liberalism according to a certain theoretical perspective may be incompatible with the defence of liberalism developed according to a different theoretical perspective. This means that in discussing and criticizing the neoliberal political project one must clearly specify the theoretical perspective adopted and the very meaning that the neoliberal proposal takes on in that perspective. This is the fundamental methodological assumption to which I will adhere in the course of the book.

The book is structured in eight chapters. In the *first chapter*, I criticize the bourgeois view that sees the market as the utmost expression of rationality and efficiency, clarifying the particular meanings these terms take on in the scientific discourse and showing their strongly ideological content. This view is shared by all neoliberal approaches. The focus, however, is on the dominant economic theory, the neoclassical one.

In *Chapter two*, I discuss the relationship between democracy and the market, arguing that they are actually contradictory. In particular, I highlight the anti-democratic character of market interaction and criticize the method of bourgeois economics for its surreptitious ideological content and its idealized (and false) view of the market.

In the *third chapter*, I consider some of the main market myths (the myth of the fair market, the myth of the free market, the myth of the equal opportunity market, the myth of the wealth-producing market, and the myth of the market that discovers and manages information), criticizing them both on a level of internal consistency and on a level of realism. These myths are not actually a peculiarity of economic theory. On the contrary, they are widely rooted in society and are an integral part of today's dominant culture. In the academic field, it is mainly the Austrian school that attempts to provide scientific support for them.

The *fourth chapter* explores the relationship between theoretical and real markets and the logical leap that occurs when constructing a normative theory of markets from models based on unrealistic assumptions. The analysis focuses on neoclassical theory and, in particular, on the general economic equilibrium model, which constitutes the most important organic contribution developed by this school of thought in its attempt to explain and evaluate the functioning of an entirely market-based economic system.

Given the importance of the neoclassical school at the academic level, in *Chapter five*, I focus on some of the most important scholarly contributions that attempt to develop the neoclassical conception beyond the confines of the highly abstract general economic equilibrium model. In particular, I analyse the efforts of the neo-institutionalist, neo-Keynesian and part of the radical school to reinterpret in a neoclassical fashion the 'old' institutionalist, Keynesian and Marxist theories, which are today relegated to academic heterodoxy. My goal is to show how such appendices of neoclassical theory, which in the specialist literature are referred to as post-Walrasian economics, not only distort the conceptions of the old heterodox schools (which are decidedly critical of the market) but also fail to offer solid scientific support for the supposed virtues of the market. Ultimately, from the most explicitly conservative contributions to those that would pretend to be radical, this strand of research is just a modern version of what Marx called 'vulgar economics'.

Despite the problems highlighted so far, in *Chapter six*, I argue that bourgeois economics, with its various internal streams and schools of thought, scores a major success in imposing market values at the cultural level, making them appear objective and neutral.

Starting from this set of critical considerations, in *Chapter seven*, I address the problem of 'what is to be done' to counter this tendency towards the market's totalizing domination of social relations, proposing a counteroffensive based on the progressive decommodification of social relationships.

In the *eighth chapter*, I rearrange the various criticisms and draw some conclusions.

## Note

1 The term 'Austrian' no longer has any connection to the nationality of the economists belonging to this school of thought. It only remains to indicate the historical origins of this ultraliberal school, which originated in Vienna at the end of the 19th century. In fact, modern Austrian economists are mostly American.

## References

Dobb, M. (1973) *Theories of value and distribution since Adam Smith. Ideology and economic theory*. Cambridge: Cambridge University Press.

Jevons, S. W. (1871) *The theory of political economy*. London: Macmillan.

Menger, C. (1871) *Grundsätze der Volkswirthschaftslehre, Erster, Allgemeiner Theil*. Wien: Wilhelm Braumüller. English translation: *Principles of economics: first, general part*. New York: Free Press.

Schumpeter, J. (1954) *History of economic analysis*. London: George Allen and Unwin Ltd.

Smith, A. (1776) *An inquiry into the nature and causes of the wealth of the nations*. Amsterdam: MetaLibri. Available at: www.ibiblio.org/ml/libri/s/SmithA_WealthNations_p.pdf

Walras, L. (1874) *Éléments d'Économie Politique Pure ou Théorie de la Richesse Sociale*. Lausanne: L. Corbaz & cie. English translation (2013). *Elements of pure economics*. London: Routledge.

# 1 The 'rationality' of the market

## Market rationality, economic efficiency and social desirability

In economic theory, the discussion of the social desirability of a particular economic policy or, more generally, of a particular mode of organizing the economy is based on the concepts of rationality and efficiency. Rationality and efficiency are not absolute concepts. They only take on meaning within a context in which the objectives to be pursued are made explicit. A given instrument can be efficient in the pursuit of particular goals and be completely inefficient in the pursuit of different goals. A boat is an efficient instrument for travelling on water but is completely inefficient for travelling on land. Consequently, a boat transport system may be a rational solution to the problem of connecting the different islands of an archipelago, but it may be completely irrational as an answer to the problems of land transport.

The same applies when considering the overall efficiency or rationality of a system. Consider, for example, the healthcare system. An AIDS strategy that does not minimize suffering, contagion and deaths can hardly be considered efficient or part of a rationally organized health system when assessed against the objectives of prevention and treatment of the patients. However, if the same strategy fits into a context of repression and punishment of drug users (as indeed happened in the 1990s in Italy), then a few more contagions among drug addicts may not necessarily be 'inefficient' or 'irrational'. It is all a matter of specifying the objectives against which the efficiency of the AIDS strategy and the overall rationality of the health system are assessed.

A distorted or even partial specification of the objectives actually pursued necessarily generates ambiguities and misunderstandings in the economic and political debate. In the case of AIDS, in fact, in addition to the sensitivity of the subject, the existing divergence on the objectives to be pursued has generated a profound incommunicability between the actors most involved in the health economics debate. On the one hand, the local health units (now transformed into local health enterprises) most attentive to the phenomenon and most present in the territory harshly criticized the national strategy against AIDS, considering it to be totally inefficient, and tried by all means to pass on to the highest ministerial levels all those prevention experiments based, for example, on the supply of sterile syringes or simple sterilization products, such as bleach, in the hope that they could be

DOI: 10.4324/9781032726168-2

encouraged and generalized throughout the country. On the other hand, in a context in which drug addiction also implied clandestinity, instead of being listened to and taken as a model, they ended up encountering increasing obstacles, attracting the criticism of those who saw in these pragmatic prevention strategies only ways of making life easier for delinquents.

This means that the same AIDS strategy could be regarded as inefficient when assessed in relation to certain (strictly medical) objectives, and efficient (or at least significantly less inefficient) when assessed in relation to different political goals. Actually, according to the advocates of the absolute priority of the strategy for combating drug addiction (and drug addicts), it was precisely the pragmatic strategies for combating AIDS that had to be considered utterly contradictory and inefficient: to what rationality criteria does a system respond if, on the one hand, it wants to put an individual in prison for taking drugs and, on the other, it helps him/her to take drugs, even providing him/her with a clean needle?

If the discourse is framed in terms of values, rights and general legal principles, the answers to such a question can obviously be many. One can argue, for example, that the principle of punishability of drug addiction should not override the right to health, or one can argue, more generally, that the goals of the health system should be independent of those of repression. In any case, the fact remains that that same national strategy, which was evidently contradictory and inefficient with respect to the objectives that the local health units were attempting to achieve, was far less irrational and inefficient when assessed with respect to different objectives. Ultimately, therefore, it is only a question of goals: what is efficient for one purpose is useless (or even harmful) for another.

One of the biggest problems when trying to form one's own ideas about economic matters is that economists speak of economic efficiency and the rationality of the economic system as absolute values, without making explicit the objectives against which efficiency and rationality are defined. In fact, when economists discuss the overall rationality and efficiency of an economic system, these concepts tend to be presented as synonymous with social desirability, as if there were such an obvious convergence on the objectives defining rationality and efficiency that their very discussion becomes superfluous. However, it is clear that the terms of the problem do not change. If, in order to talk about rationality and efficiency, it is necessary to specify the objectives pursued, the overall desirability of the economic system itself depends on the objectives against which rationality and efficiency are defined. Only to the extent that the goals against which rationality and efficiency are defined can be considered socially acceptable does it make sense to associate a concept of social desirability with them. A society in which people die of thirst or starvation, with low literacy rates and large-income inequalities is absolutely inefficient and irrational in relation to the goals of decency of life and equal opportunities and is therefore undesirable when measured against these goals. But if the goal against which society is assessed is instead profit maximization (of one part of the population), then misery and poverty (for the other part of the population) are perfectly compatible with economic rationality and efficiency; indeed, they may even be a necessary condition for it. In this case, therefore, poverty is not at all socially undesirable (simply because the good of society has been identified with the profit maximization of one part of the population). It is all a matter of clarifying which objectives are actually pursued. Changing the objectives also changes the assessment of rationality and efficiency, and hence of social desirability. And so, conceding that indeed the capitalist system is rational and efficient in some sense, it becomes important first to clarify what are the social objectives on which the concepts of rationality and economic efficiency are based. Only in this way is it possible to reason openly about the actual social desirability of the economic system in which we live and that of other possible worlds.

## The allocative rationality of the market

As we were saying, bourgeois economists claim that the market is a rational, efficient, desirable or even necessary allocative mechanism. But, rational according to what logic? Efficient in what sense? Desirable for whom? Necessary for what?

Bourgeois economists' answers are straightforward:

1. The market is *rational* according to the logic of allocating scarce resources (i.e. according to the only logic they conceive, that of the market).
2. The market is *efficient* given the distribution of resources.
3. The market is *desirable* for all.
4. The market is *necessary* for the satisfaction of the needs of individuals according to their preferences.

But the proposition that the market is rational and allocates resources efficiently (which makes it desirable and necessary) is just a mystification of the neoliberal theory. The reality is quite different, and one only has to observe it. Is it rational for medical resources to go into advanced biotechnological researches that will benefit perhaps 1,500people in the world, when every year 1.5 million people (mostly children) die of dysentery just because they have less to spend overall than the first 1,500people (World Health Organization, 2020)?

The theoretical expedient is simple and explicit: rationality, efficiency and desirability are all expressed from given demand curves. An individual's demand curve, as we shall see better later, depends on two things: the economic means at his/her disposal and his/her preferences. Thus, anyone who has no monetary resources to demand goods or services on the market does not exist from an economic point of view and has no right to be taken into account by the bourgeois economist when talking about rationality, efficiency etc. What counts is in fact not the demand understood as the set of goods and services that each individual wishes to have in order to satisfy his/her needs, but the solvent demand, that which is expressed money in the hand. Needs that cannot be expressed on the market for lack of money do not in fact exist according to the definition of efficiency of bourgeois economics. In other words, in the discussion of the rationality and economic efficiency of capitalism, individuals are only taken into account to the extent that they are able to buy and consume. This principle constitutes the fundamental reference of all normative economics to the extent that, according to bourgeois economists, the consumer must be considered as the true 'sovereign' of the economy.

The principle of 'consumer sovereignty' states that the assessment of the functioning of an economy should depend solely on the degree to which consumer preferences are satisfied. This principle is, in fact, a special case of the principle of the 'sovereignty of the individual'. The latter, in turn, is based on a twofold assumption: 1) the individual is the best judge of his/her needs (and preferences) and of the means best suited to satisfying them (which excludes paternalistic attitudes in the definition of social criteria for evaluating the functioning of the system); 2) social evaluations must be based solely on the evaluations expressed by individuals (which excludes ethical attitudes other than individualism). The principle of consumer sovereignty restricts the sovereignty of the individual to the act of consumption, which, of course, depends on the different spending capacities of individuals. In this way, the ability of a system to satisfy individual preferences expressed in (solvent) demand curves becomes the sole normative objective of economic theory, and individuals who do not have the resources to express their preferences in the market are implicitly excluded from theoretical analysis.

It is on the basis of this principle (at the very least questionable from the point of view of moral philosophy) – consumer sovereignty – that bourgeois economics defines rationality, efficiency and social desirability. And, of course, once consumer sovereignty has been assumed, it follows that all that matters is to satisfy the sovereign-consumer, so that the market, that is, the mechanism that ensures the best satisfaction of the sovereign, is even presented to us as necessary (. . . who knows why the task of a people should be to organize itself in such a way as to satisfy its sovereign!). But if it is easy to understand why such a principle is defended by the sovereign himself (and his epigones: the bourgeois economists), it is not easy to understand why even those whom we might call the 'subjects', that is, those without sufficient monetary resources to express their needs on the market, should be convinced of the absolute importance of satisfying the sovereign.

Here then is the explanation of the bourgeois economist: in capitalist society there is no single sovereign, in fact, we all demand, and we all consume (otherwise we would die). And, indeed, one would have to answer, in reality many people die (precisely because they cannot even demand). But, apart from the extreme cases of individuals who, having no economic means to demand, are not even considered by the bourgeois economist (extreme cases that affect several hundred million people on this planet anyway), the general principle remains that *an individual's importance in society is given by his/her purchasing power*.

The principle of consumer sovereignty together with its corollary that individuals only count if they have economic means to consume give the concepts of market rationality, economic efficiency and social desirability very special meanings.

The *rationality* of the system comes to depend on the presence of mechanisms that allow sovereign consumers to express and see their preferences fulfilled.

*Economic efficiency* is defined on the basis of the inviolability of the consumer's desires: not, of course, of an abstract consumer, that is, a generic individual who needs to consume in order to live, but of a very concrete consumer, the one who pays cash. In modern economic theory, the virtually unanimously accepted concept of efficiency is that of Vilfredo Pareto (the Italian economist and sociologist who lived between the 19th and 20th centuries), which can be defined as follows: 1) a 'Pareto improvement' (or 'Pareto move') is a change that improves someone's situation without making anyone's worse and 2) a 'Pareto-efficient' situation is obtained when Pareto moves are no longer possible. In other words, a situation is Pareto-efficient when every attempt to improve an individual's position makes someone else's worse (Pareto, 1906).

The transition from the determination of Pareto efficiency conditions to the determination of *social desirability* conditions is subtle and must be analysed carefully. First of all, let us recall that since the Pareto criterion is based on the principle of consumer sovereignty, it is only valid within individualistic logic. This, in itself, means that those who do not identify with individualistic morality (or, simply, who accept that society may be inspired by values other than individualism) have no reason to consider Pareto efficiency as an economic goal. For example, if one attaches some importance to economic equality, a Pareto move might well be socially undesirable if it only improves the position of those who are already well-off simply because such a change would only exacerbate inequality. This is already enough to show that the Pareto criterion is by no means unanimously acceptable, nor can it be considered neutral in terms of value judgements. But, in addition to the acceptance of individualistic logic, the transformation of efficiency-ist questions into normative questions requires the introduction of further moral assumptions. Indeed, as pointed out in the debate on the use of Pareto efficiency in normative economics, in reality, the Pareto principle does not directly provide any normative criteria (Archibald, 1959; Hennipman, 1976). In order for Pareto efficiency to be associated with some form of social desirability (on the basis of which normative positions can be derived) it is necessary to introduce the ethical principle of so-called 'minimal benevolence'. This principle can be stated by saying that 'it is good that people are better off'. With the addition of this minimal ethical principle, effectively all propositions of positive economics aimed at identifying the conditions of Pareto efficiency can be transformed into as many propositions of normative economics, thereby validating the normative principle that Pareto efficiency is socially desirable (for a critical discussion of the role of minimal benevolence in the transition from positive to normative economics, see Blaug (1992), Hausman and McPherson (1996)).

The use of the Pareto criterion in the normative field would thus derive its strength – in addition to the presumed universality of individualistic morality – from the minimality and benevolence of the ethical principle that serves to transform Pareto efficiency issues into issues of social desirability. Indeed, this principle seems entirely innocent and shareable: only envy and malice could lead one to argue the opposite, namely that 'it is good that someone is worse off'.

However, on closer examination from the perspective of moral philosophy, it turns out that the principle of minimal benevolence is not benevolent at all, nor is it minimal, and indeed it is even contradictory, for the simple fact that it is possible to get better while being bad. In fact, in the case where someone who was bad gets a little better as a result of a Pareto improvement, the much-innocent principle of minimal benevolence ends up providing an ethical endorsement of the fact that he/she continues to stay bad. Consider this example: individual *A* is hungry and thirsty but has neither food nor drink; individual *B*, on the other hand, lacks nothing, has a full fridge and bathes in a pool of drinking water but longs for the latest model of Ferrari. Thanks to a Pareto move, the economist gets a bowl of rice to *A* and the Ferrari to *B*. Unfortunately, however, without water, *A* dies of thirst. This, according to economic theory, is Pareto-efficient and socially desirable. If, on the other hand, we had taken a glass of water out of *B*'s pool to give it to *A* this would have violated *B*'s sovereignty and would therefore have been socially undesirable. But then that apparently benevolent principle we thought we were inspired by (claiming that by realizing Pareto efficiency the economist pursues the good of all) is in fact not benevolent at all, because it amounts to saying that it can also be a good thing if someone is bad, which is a completely different thing from pursuing the good of all.

A more acceptable ethical principle might perhaps be, if anything, that 'it is good that people are well' and, once it has been ascertained that everyone is well, that 'it is better that people are better off'. But to say that 'it is good that people are better off' is in fact a statement that is anything but minimal and benevolent; on the contrary, it is very strong ethically and, as we have seen, also potentially malevolent.

This, which perhaps seems a truism, is instead considered an unacceptable criticism: according to mainstream economics to say that it is good for people to be well is to introduce value judgements that are anything but agreeable since they imply the need for radical changes that would inevitably benefit some (those worse off) to the detriment of others (those better off), and this, again according to mainstream economics, is scientifically indefensible (which simply demonstrates that the prescriptions of economic theory, presented as neutral and impartial, only serve to preserve acquired privileges by preventing any radical change).

Of course, it is of no importance here to establish the superiority of one kind of value judgement over another: I think it is good that people are well, and economists think it is good that people are better off; but when it comes to value judgements, it is perfectly permissible to think differently. The strange thing, however, is that that particular value judgement according to which no one can be harmed – an innocent value judgement only in appearance – is the only value judgement admitted in the scientific field by mainstream theory (to the extent that many economists forget that this is also a value judgement), while the introduction of any other ethical principle is condemned theoretically because it is considered incompatible with the scientific nature of economics.

Whatever the case may be on an ethical level, social desirability is defined by juxtaposing Pareto's efficiency criterion – which, as we have seen, is based on individualism and consumer sovereignty – with that of minimal benevolence, so that the sole judges of the system's desirability turn out to be the sovereign consumers who are given absolute veto power over any changes that might harm them.

But then let us see how things really are behind the mystifying veil of economic theory:

1. The market is *rational* in the sense that it rationalizes the problem of getting as many resources as possible to the sovereigns (i.e. to those with monetary means) and because it allows them to get precisely those bundles of goods that our sovereigns prefer.
2. The market is (Pareto) *efficient* because, given the distribution of resources (i.e. given the impossibility of questioning the purchasing power of the various sovereigns), it is better for each sovereign to be very well rather than simply well, and if someone is bad because of his/her limited sovereignty (his/her little money), it is better for him/her to be a little less bad, even though he/she will still be condemned to be bad!
3. The market is *desirable* to all who have the means to buy and, of course, the desire to have a society in which everything can be bought on the market is all the stronger the greater one's purchasing power.
4. The market is *necessary* to allow the current sovereigns to remain so and thus perpetuate a world of sovereigns and subjects.

## The theorist of the sovereign and the 'successes' of capitalism

Of course, all this is well known to economists (or at least it should be). It is somewhat less so to the layman, who hears the theses of rationality, efficiency etc. repeated without being told the particular meanings these terms take on in the theoretical context in which economists operate and thus end up believing one thing for another. Let us then consider some figures on the great economic and social successes of capitalism in the concrete realization of these high principles of rationality and efficiency.

On our now almost entirely capitalist planet, access to resources presents significant asymmetries. About one-third of the world's population has no access to sources of drinking water. In low-income countries, this share is close to three-quarters of the population. The lack of safe water sources causes 2.3 per cent of the world's total deaths. In the countries of Central Africa this percentage exceeds ten per cent (World Health Organization and United Nations Children's Fund, 2024).

According to data from major international organizations presented by Our World in Data (2024), there are one billion people without access to electricity, again concentrated in Africa and low-income countries.

On the food needs front, ten per cent of the world's population is undernourished. This is certainly not because of the insufficient production of foodstuffs, which is constantly growing worldwide, but because of inequalities in the distribution of purchasing power: in the United States and Europe, the percentage of the population undernourished is 2.5 per cent, in Africa it reaches 50 per cent.

While most of the world is starving, obesity rates are rising steadily in the highest-income countries. The highest rate of obesity is in the United States: 37.3

per cent of people over the age of 18 are obese. In 1975, the percentage of obese people was 11.7, an increase of 219 per cent. However, obesity deaths are concentrated in Africa and Asia, in countries with lower obesity rates but worse economic conditions. It is estimated that around five million people died prematurely in 2019 as a result of obesity.

Among those most exposed to socio-economic asymmetries are, of course, children. Around six million children under 15 die every year from perfectly treatable diseases, simply because of poverty.

Despite being curable and preventable, 1.6 million people died from diarrheal diseases in 2017; one-third were children under 5 years old. Diarrheal diseases are the third leading cause of child mortality globally, falling just behind pneumonia and preterm birth complications.

Naturally, the more severe the socio-economic conditions, the greater the push to incorporate children into the labour market. According to the International Labour Organisation (2013), in the world, there are around 265 million working children (aged between 5 and 15 years), almost 17 per cent of the worldwide child population: 18.1 per cent for boys and 15.2 per cent for girls; 11.8 per cent for children between 5 and 14 years and 33.0 per cent for those between 15 and 17 years. The highest prevalence of child labour is in sub-Saharan Africa. In Cameroon, the percentage of working children reaches 33.4 per cent: practically one child out of three is in labour.

There is also no reason to think that the other two children are doing any better and that they, at least, can enjoy the right to school, which is in fact denied to their companion. More likely, they are, in fact, unemployed children, waiting to relieve working children, depending on the needs of (foreign) capital and its (local) bosses.

Considering first and secondary education, around 260 million children are not in school. Of the world's 787 million children of primary school age, 62.8 million do not go to school (8.0 per cent). Most of them are in sub-Saharan Africa (36.3 million children) and South Asia (15.0 million children).

This disparity in access to essential goods and services produced in the world is symmetrically accompanied by a disparity in the destruction of the planet's resources and its ecosystem. Considering carbon emissions, the top ten per cent of emitters are responsible for close to 50 per cent of all emissions, while the bottom 50 per cent produce 12 per cent of the total (World Inequality Database, 2022).

Inequalities are marked both between and within countries. The bottom 50 per cent of the population of East Asia emits around three tonnes per year per person. In North America, the bottom 50 per cent emits around ten tonnes. These figures increase significantly when considering the most polluter top ten per cent: 39 tonnes in East Asia, and 73 in North America. As we can see, despite the green agenda imposed by richest countries on the whole world, so far, climate policies such as carbon taxes have had a strong impact on lower- and middle-income people, while leaving the consumption habits of richest unchanged.

All this regards the social asymmetries between those who benefit the most from capitalist interaction, while imposing the greatest costs on society, and those who receive only duties and unfavourable conditions from the world, without even having the time or means to pollute, while generally living in the most polluted places, under the fiction that it is the subjects of the former group who are concerned about those of the latter. But let us now move on to economic data.

In 2021, global income amounts to 122 trillion dollars, while global net wealth amounts to six times this value, 723 trillion dollars. In terms of purchasing power parity, used to compare the absolute purchasing power of the countries' currencies, an average adult individual earns 23,380 dollars per year and owns 102,600 dollars in real and financial activities. These averages, of course, mask wide disparities both between and within countries.

The richest ten per cent of the global population takes 52.0 per cent of global income, whereas the poorest half earns 8.5 per cent of it. On average, an individual from the top ten per cent of the global income distribution earns 122,100 dollars per year, whereas an individual from the poorest half makes 3,920dollars per year.

Wealth inequalities are even more pronounced. The richest ten per cent of the global population own 76 per cent of all wealth. On average, they own 771,300 dollars each. In contrast, the poorest half of the population only owns two per cent of the total, an average of 4,100dollars per adult.

Of course, the aggregate comprising the poorest half of the population is very heterogeneous within itself, in terms of both income and wealth. But it is clear that with these average values, large segments of the population live below the poverty line and their wealth is negative, that is, they are essentially in debt.[1]

Moreover, current trends do not suggest any levelling out of incomes and wealth. The gap between the average incomes of the top ten per cent and the bottom 50 per cent of individuals within countries has constantly increased since the 1980s from 8.5x to 15x, so that inequalities within countries are now even greater than the already significant inequalities observed between countries.

Over the past several decades, global multimillionaires have captured a huge share of global wealth growth: the top one per cent took 38 per cent of all additional wealth accumulated since the 1990s, whereas the bottom 50 per cent captured just two per cent of it.

Since 1995, the share of global wealth possessed by billionaires has risen from one per cent to over three per cent. The steepest increase in global billionaires' share of wealth is recorded in 2020. After all, Covid has not been such a tragedy for everybody. While statistics speak of millions of people dying and workers losing their jobs due to 'anti-pandemic' measures, billionaires were making profits and taking over an even bigger slice of the world.

The neoliberal policies started in the 1980s have also transformed the ownership structure of real and financial wealth, with a general transfer from the public to the private sector. Countries have become significantly richer, but their governments have become significantly poorer. In rich countries, the share of net wealth held by the public sector is now close to zero or negative, meaning that all wealth has been transferred into private hands and the state is left with nothing but debts. This trend has been magnified by the Covid crisis, during which, in many countries, governments borrowed 10–20 per cent of the GDP in a single year, mainly from the private sector.

Finally, despite much talk about feminism and women's rights, women's share of total incomes from work is less than 35 per cent (in a gender-equal world, women would earn 50 per cent of all labour income).

Some commentators are horrified by this data and think that then there is something wrong with this system. They are unaware, however, that this is precisely the efficiency of capitalism, at least according to the conception developed by bourgeois economic theory, which assigns no importance to the distribution of income and to the satisfaction of the objective needs of the population (but rejoices in the fact that, under capitalism, each individual can choose 'freely' how to spend his/her income according to his/her subjective preferences). In the case of economists, instead, the peaceful acceptance of this absurd approach passes through theoretical mystification, academic indoctrination and personal convenience. In fact, those economists who play the game, by setting aside the critique and developing theories that suit the sovereign, are not only adequately rewarded through recruitment mechanisms in power positions, but also become sovereigns themselves, in the sense that they are also rewarded economically, which obviously increases their incentive to do their duty well: to serve the sovereign.

If it ended there it would not be so bad: there is nothing strange if those in power seek to preserve and increase it. Nor is there anything strange if the theorist of the sovereign universalizes the good of his/her sovereign by making it coincide with the good of society. Instead, the problem is the acceptance of this approach by those who are critical of this way of organizing society, that is, by those who would like to 'improve things'. The problem is substantial because, in order to improve things, one must clearly identify what is wrong. So, we have to go back to the starting point, to the general hypothesis of the theoretical framework, which defines the market mechanism as a rational way of regulating society. It follows that the reality of capitalism – made of luxury for some and misery for others – is also rational. Therefore, it is hard to see why it should be changed. Conversely, if someone sees something illogical or unjust in the existing state of affairs, then inevitably the theoretical rationalization provided by bourgeois economics must be revised.

Of all the properties of the market discussed so far, it is on the principle of efficiency that the (bourgeois) economists most sceptical of the supposed virtues of the market (virtues that at this point it would be appropriate to simply call features) have concentrated their greatest efforts. Thus, a whole strand of research was born and developed aimed at demonstrating that the market is not always efficient and that it is neither desirable nor rational to imagine a society based solely on the market because certain forms of state intervention could eliminate some market inefficiencies. This line of research gives rise to the so-called 'market failure' theory.

The demonstration of market Pareto efficiency (as we shall see in more detail in Chapter four) presupposes particular assumptions concerning technology, individual preferences, the distribution of resources and the properties of the goods produced. The theory of market failures emphasizes the impossibility of Pareto-efficient situations when these assumptions are not met (which, moreover, is the rule, not the exception, in reality). At the normative level, the theory of market failures prescribes that economic initiative be left to the market in those cases where the market is Pareto-efficient and instead be entrusted to the state in those cases where the market is Pareto inefficient. Modern textbooks, after the presentation of the theory of market failures, hasten to discuss the so-called 'state failures' (mostly due to bureaucratic inefficiencies), also capable, under certain assumptions, of preventing Pareto efficiency. In this way, the market regains some of the ground lost in theory, since state failures may turn out to be even more serious than market failures. In other words, compared to an abstract and highly unrealistic pure market model, the theory of market and state failures takes a step in the direction of realism by making the normative discourse more articulate and questioning the conception of the market as a universal remedy to all economic problems.

The problem is that according to the singular language of economic theory, both the more extremist one in favour of the market and the more balanced one that allows a residual role for the state, the fact that entire populations live and die in misery does not constitute a market failure. The market failures that economists deal with only concern the impossibility, under certain circumstances, of achieving Pareto efficiency; but poverty and inequality, as we have seen, are perfectly compatible with Pareto efficiency. Thus, we fall again into the mystified representation of capitalism proposed by bourgeois theory, according to which market prices are the maximum expression of rationality, and their only limit is given by the technical problems of what economists consider to be market failures (i.e. the situations in which the market does not realize Pareto efficiency). And this happens, to a large extent, precisely because of the use of strong words such as efficiency and rationality, which are presented as universal references of normative analysis, as if they were completely objective criteria unrelated to ideologies and value judgements, whereas, on the contrary, these terms take on meanings in economic theory that are anything but neutral.

In this way, even the economist who is sceptical of the market, instead of questioning its principles, ends up serving them even better, by re-establishing efficiency and rationality (defined, as we have just seen, according to the parameters of individualism and consumer sovereignty) where the market is inefficient and irrational, thus fully accepting bourgeois logic and forgetting that efficiency and rationality are not social goals, but partisan goals, the goals of the sovereigns.

## Limited and absolute sovereignty

What is more, the bourgeois economist (sceptical or trusting of the market), in elevating the consumer as its sole sovereign, enters into contradiction with the founding principles of most capitalist democracies. Just one example: Article 1 of the Italian Constitution states (still) that 'Italy is a democratic republic, founded on work', not on consumption, and this obviously places a limit on consumer sovereignty (strictly speaking, it should cancel it altogether, assigning the title of sovereign to the worker). But this does not matter, because economic theory based on the universal principle of market rationality serves precisely to correct human errors dictated by emotional impulses and contingent circumstances (anti-fascism, resistance, catholic solidarism, socialism, communism).

Thus, our economist turns from a conservative ideologue into a subversive troublemaker, suggesting that society should be changed so as to better serve the interests of the only sovereign he/she recognizes (the consumer), even in violation of the law, since the legitimacy of the sovereign-consumer, even in a world almost entirely dominated by the market, is in fact still limited. After having defended the market through the construction of a theoretical model that made the market society appear as the maximum expression of human rationality, the economist now goes on the attack: he/she implicitly recognizes that the real world is not like that of his theoretical model, but at the same time calls loudly for the world to finally conform to his/her model, cancelling the institutional residues that put limits on consumer sovereignty.

In the name of efficiency and rationality (which are good only for those who have economic resources), all other categories of subjects are overshadowed: people count only because they consume and any specific rights won by individuals as workers, unemployed, citizens, black, women, immigrants, sick, children, aged etc., being extraneous to consumer sovereignty, appear, in the scheme of bourgeois economics, as inefficient and irrational and, therefore, to be eliminated.

## The distributive rationality of the market

The attempt of bourgeois economics to portray the market system as rational and desirable does not stop at the analysis of the market as a mechanism of resource allocation in the productive sphere but also extends to the analysis of the market as a mechanism of income distribution. According to the distributive rationality of the market, intellectuals, managers and all those occupying the most important social positions receive high incomes – significantly higher than those of workers, miners or clerks – as a due reward for the investment in 'human capital' made during the years of education and training. University professors, journalists, lawyers, notaries, and managers all feel that they have made their own way. It was thanks to their fortitude and perseverance that they were able to study, graduate and specialize, whereas their peers preferred to enter the labour market at the age of 14 (or much earlier), and it is, therefore, logical and fair that, now that the long training course is complete, they receive high incomes to compensate for all those sacrifices at school and university.

Indeed, if things are assessed according to the parameters of market rationality, those years of study were indeed years of sacrifice (in terms of lost income). However, the argument holds only because each individual compares his choices with the others available to him/her (the actual notary's sacrifice may have consisted of having sacrificed one of his/her weekends sailing for the benefit of study), not with the material situation of other individuals (for many of whom a free afternoon to devote to study is still a hard-won prize). In the latter case, it would be obvious that the life of the university professor, executive or notary is just a progressive acquisition of new privileges: when they were young, they sacrificed themselves at their school desks while their miner and worker peers could not give up an immediate income (the one that allowed them to get by from day to day); then, in their university days, when, if only they had wanted to, they could have already earned respectable incomes, our willing students continued their life of sacrifice and abstinence, and so on until they entered the world of work, immediately ready to manage, command and get paid with interest for all those sacrifices made. And while they sacrificed themselves, their peers meanwhile stayed in the factory or the mine making a good life (or a bad death). There is no instant in which the life of the university professor was more sacrificed than that of the miner peer, and yet, according to the parameters of the market, the one who sacrificed was the former, not the latter (and it is the university professor himself/herself who teaches us this with his/her economic theories).

If economic rationality had even a tenuous connection to the moral sphere, hard and dangerous work should be better remunerated than light and risk-free work; according to market rationality, however, the opposite is the case. Faced with this situation, bourgeois economics does not set out to find ways to change reality in the direction of greater rationality, not based on the market, but on more morally decent principles; instead, it mobilises all its efforts to theoretically justify the paradoxical reality of the market, calling *rational* what is in reality simply *immoral*.

I do not know whether it is harder to work in a nice office on the hundredth floor of a skyscraper, with a good cigar in the mouth, or to work two hundred metres underground, with the lungs full of toxic dust. What I do know is that those who work in skyscrapers do not even have the curiosity to go on a guided tour in a mine, while those who work in mines will never waste their hard-earned money to go and see the view from the Empire State building. And if the economist assures me that all this is rational, I expect the miner's salary to be at least a hundred times that of the executive. Otherwise I do not see how two free individuals could choose to do such different jobs.

Incidentally, on the question of risk, it is precisely bourgeois economics that has theorized that the capitalist's profit is the just reward for risk-taking in productive activity. Frank Knight (1921), in particular, in an attempt to ethically justify the profit, argued that it serves to reward the capitalist for the risk he/she incurs in investing his/her capital in activities whose return is inherently uncertain. But clearly this only applies to the capitalist's risk, certainly not to that of the miner or construction worker.

Faced with the fact that the laws of the market crush the weak and reward the strong, all the bourgeois economists can do is construct theories that make this moral paradox appear economically rational. The miner's wage and the executive's wage – we all know this – have nothing to do with moral issues; they are just the result of market laws. But to be unable to find an economic justification for the phenomenon that the harder, humbler and more dangerous a job is, the less it is remunerated would be to question the very desirability of the market as an allocative mechanism. Only the bourgeois economist could succeed in this feat by inventing absurd normative principles capable of making appear even such a moral paradox as rational.

## Note

1 *World Bank*'s data on poverty are subject to harsh criticism from the point of view of methodological correctness. In particular, criticism has focused on three factors: the definition of the poverty line, the calculations of the purchasing power of different currencies (necessary to make international comparisons) and the very accuracy of the *World Bank*'s calculations. According to this critique, these three sources of error lead to an underestimation of the scale of poverty and allow *World Bank* officials to argue that the world is nevertheless on the right track in the fight against poverty (see, e.g. Chossudovski (1997, 1999) and Reddy and Pogge (2002)).

## References


Archibald, G. C. (1959) 'Welfare economics, ethics, and essentialism', *Economica*, 26, pp. 316–327.

Blaug, M. (1992) *The methodology of economics*. 2nd ed. Cambridge: Cambridge University Press.

Chossudovski, M. (1997) *The globalization of poverty. Impact of IMF and World Bank reforms*. London: Zed Books.

Chossudovski, M. (1999) 'Global falsehood: how the World Bank and the UNDP distort the figures on global poverty', *Transnational Foundation for Peace and Future Research (TFF)*. Available at: www.transantional.org

Hausman, D. and McPherson, M. (1996) *Economic analysis and moral philosophy*. Cambridge: Cambridge University Press.

Hennipman, P. (1976) 'Pareto optimality: value judgment or analytical tool', in Cramer, J. S., Heertje, A. and Venekamp, P. (eds.) *Relevance and precision: from quantitative analysis to economic policy*. Amsterdam: North-Holland.

International Labour Organisation (2013) *World report on child labour*. Available at: www.ilo.org/wcmsp5/groups/public/–ed_norm/–ipec/documents/publication/wcms_178184.pdf

Knight, F. H. (1921) *Risk, uncertainty and profit*. Boston: Houghton Mifflin.

Our World in Data (2024) Available at: https://ourworldindata.org

Pareto, V. (1906) *Manuale di Economia Politica con una Introduzione alla Ricerca Sociale*. Torino: Einaudi. English translation (1971). *Manual of political economy*. New York: Augustus Kelley.

Reddy, S. G. and Pogge, T. W. (2002) 'How not to count the poor', *Technical papers*. Columbia University. Available at: www.socialanalysis.org

World Health Organization (2020) *The top 10 causes of death*. Available at: www.who.int/news-room/fact-sheets/detail/the-top-10-causes-of-death

World Health Organization and United Nations Children's Fund (2024) *WHO/UNICEF joint monitoring programme for water supply, sanitation and hygiene (JMP)*. Available at: https://ourworldindata.org/clean-water

World Inequality Database (2022) *World inequality report 2022*. Available at: https://wid.world/news-article/world-inequality-report-2022

# 2 Market and democracy

## The market as a mechanism for collective decision-making

As we have just seen, bourgeois theory states that the free expression of individual preferences in the market is reflected in prices and the demand for a good reflects the social preference for that good relative to other goods, given the relative scarcities of different resources (and given their distribution among the agents of the system). If a nation consumes the basket of goods *X*, it is because basket *X* represents the efficient result of a rational process of aggregation of citizens' preferences (a basket of goods is a collection of different goods in given quantities). It is the citizens themselves who, by buying the goods they each prefer, determine the collective decision to consume basket *X*.

One of the criticisms of collective decision-making mechanisms based on conscious and democratic control of the decision-making process, however, concerns the impossibility of deriving the 'objective function' (i.e. the set of objectives to be pursued and their relative weight) of the public decision-maker through a procedure of preference aggregation that is both rational, Pareto-efficient and compatible with the democratic principle. According to the 'impossibility theorem', formulated and demonstrated by Kenneth J. Arrow, it is in fact logically impossible to derive an order of social preferences 1) that is defined solely from individual preferences, 2) that respects certain elementary principles of rationality and morality, and 3) that gives rise to Pareto-efficient outcomes (Arrow, 1951).[1] In the case of strictly economic choices, the impossibility of deriving an order of social preferences implies, as a special case, the impossibility of expressing a social preference for one basket of goods over another. This means that any attempt to define the social preference for the basket *X* through a democratic voting procedure is incompatible with Pareto efficiency or other criteria deemed reasonable and desirable.

Yet we have seen that this is exactly what the market does every day, aggregating the preferences of all participants and giving each one what he/she demands. In some ways, in fact, the market is also a voting mechanism: if in the market system, the basket of goods *X* rather than *Y* is produced, it is because through aggregate demand, society votes for basket of goods *X* and against basket *Y*. And what is aggregate demand if not the aggregation of the demands of the different individuals participating in the market process?

DOI: 10.4324/9781032726168-3

Just as a public decision-maker can determine that basket *X* is preferable to basket *Y*, the market can make the choice between the two baskets by letting individuals express their preferences through individual consumption choices. The strange thing is that while in the first case Arrow's theorem affirms the impossibility of deriving the social preference for basket *X* from a democratic vote, in the second case the implicit vote via the market seems to erase the problem. And, indeed, in the formal representation provided by the mathematical models of neoclassical theory it would seem that the market mechanism is precisely the ideal voting system for deriving social preferences from individual preferences, respecting the will of all and in a manner compatible with Pareto efficiency.

But how is it possible that what cannot be done through conscious, democratic control is instead possible through the impersonal mechanism of the market? The answer is simple: because the market is not democratic (which charges the concept of rationality with that morally absurd meaning, according to which individuals count in proportion to the thickness of their wallets, a concept that bourgeois economists instead present as morally neutral).

Democracy works through the principle 'one head, one vote', the market through the principle 'one dollar, one vote' (see, e.g. Dobb, 1955). In aggregating individual preferences, through aggregate demand, the market assigns different weights to different individuals: with one dollar, one can choose whether to buy one packet of sweets or one bus ticket; with ten dollars, one can choose whether to buy ten packets of sweets or ten bus tickets. So, when we interpret the choice of a market society to consume *n* packets of candy and make *m* bus journeys as a rational choice of direct democracy defined by the citizens themselves eating candy and travelling by bus, we should remember that one citizen voted once, the other ten times. In general, therefore, whenever we say that 'the market respects the will of all', we should always add 'according to their purchasing power'. And we should also remind ourselves that never in the history of mankind have inequalities been so pronounced as in capitalism (which, however, according to a conception as widespread as it is unfounded, continues to be considered synonymous with democracy).

Paradoxically, however, Arrow's impossibility theorem is generally discussed in the context of planned systems, not in the context of market systems. More specifically, it is presented as an element against planned systems because planning itself requires a clear definition of the objectives to be pursued. It would then seem that, given the possible incompatibility between democracy and Pareto efficiency, planned systems are doomed to dictatorship or inefficiency (according to the Pareto criterion). According to bourgeois economic theory, however, in the case of the market, the problem does not even arise: economic democracy (the distribution of voting rights in society) is a matter of political discussion and economic theory must simply stay out of it.

## Value judgements and scientific neutrality

The apparent disappearance of the voting problem in the market is related to the scientific attitude of mainstream theory according to which value judgements must be kept away from economic discussion because they are incompatible with the neutrality of science (Pareto, 1906; Robbins, 1932; Mises, 1949). If the problem of voting seems to disappear in the market, it is because the economist, unlike the politician, believes he does not have to (or, indeed, cannot) impose any minimal ethical principles on the criteria for aggregating preferences in the definition of collective choices. Faced with Arrow's theoretical result that Pareto efficiency and democracy are incompatible, economic theory chooses to deal only with efficiency, regardless of the fact that this implies a violation of democracy. The extraneousness of the economist to value judgements thus translates into the conscious violation of the minimal ethical criteria that create so many problems for scholars of voting systems.

The violation of the 'one head, one vote' rule, as we have seen, occurs systematically in the market, but this is a problem that does not concern the bourgeois economist. He/she does not deal with ethics, he/she solves technical problems. For the economist, the distribution of voting rights (the initial distribution of resources) is exogenous to the model. It is external to the theory, not a fact to be reasoned about, so the problem of its justness cannot be posed. If individual *A* has an expenditure capacity of ten and individual *B* has an expenditure capacity of 1, this is not a problem for the economist to explain, but the datum from which to start. It does not matter whether this datum is itself the result of market interaction; the point is instead to show how market interaction harmoniously recomposes the preferences of *A* and *B* without trampling on either (but assigning ten voting rights to the former and one to the latter).

Therefore, it is no wonder that it is so difficult to resolve disputes in the political arena respecting (within certain limits) the interests of all parties, while it is so easy to resolve the problem through the market (with the imposition of the interests of the richest): it is simply the violation of the most elementary democratic principles that allows the bourgeois economist to draw conclusions on efficiency by avoiding an open discussion of the problem of value judgements. But, in so doing, he/she does not eliminate value judgements from the theory, he/she simply accepts them without making them explicit (also because, once explicit, he/she would perhaps find it difficult to defend them). In choosing to remain extraneous to the problem of values, the bourgeois economist thus does not affirm his/her *neutrality*, but rather his/her *disinterest* in the ethical assumptions on which he/she implicitly bases his/her theory.

## The economist's ex post rationalization

The lover of theoretical speculation will now point out that the problem could be solved simply by ensuring similar spending capacities for all. This, in itself, would certainly be revolutionary, but since it is a purely theoretical speculation, he/she will not even bother to provide the details of how this could actually be achieved, through appropriate processes of expropriation (obviously without compensation) and redistribution. Nor will he/she feel the need to remind the reactions of the capitalist centres in those historical cases in which this was actually achieved (just to give an example, the US coup d'état in Chile, 11 September 1973, against the democratically elected government of Salvador Allende who, faced with the grave socio-economic situation, had launched a plan of nationalizations, without compensation, a plan unpalatable to the United States of President Richard Nixon and the then Secretary of State Henry Kissinger, Nobel Peace Prize winner in 1973, strenuous defenders of North American private capital wherever it is located). Rather, in pursuing his abstract reasoning, he would prefer to note that, without having to resort to any real expropriation, it is enough to imagine that at some point in history equal spending capacity really has been the rule, and here we also find an ethical justification for people's differing spending capacity. With this interpretation, even the *unequal* distribution of voting rights in the market (the fact that *A* has ten and *B* only one) would be somehow *just*, as a due reward for past efforts (if *A* has ten it is because of his/her propensity to save and his/her skill in market interaction, if *B* has one it is because of his/her propensity to consume and his/her inability).

This theoretical attitude of inventing a history that makes the present appear rational and just has been abundantly criticized by historians. Unfortunately, for some reason, economists consider themselves above history and therefore believe they can rewrite the past at will. From a philosophical point of view, this is the persistence of the speculative method of idealist philosophy abundantly criticized (in my opinion, convincingly) by Marx and the entire Marxist tradition. But Marxism is now out of the centres of official knowledge: it has almost disappeared from university teaching (where the tendency is to divide political economy courses into microeconomics and macroeconomics modules, cutting out any voice of dissent that cannot be framed within these narrow meshes) and all that remains of the Marxist critique of bourgeois theory and society is a great deal of ignorance. Modern economics has thus been able to return to pre-Marxian positions without any attempt to overcome that criticism. Marx (1844, First manuscript, ch. 4) wrote about the economists' attitude to history in his early studies:

> Do not let us go back to a fictitious primordial condition as the political economist does, when he tries to explain. Such a primordial condition explains nothing. He merely pushes the question away into a grey nebulous distance. He assumes in the form of fact, of an event, what he is supposed to deduce. . . . Theology in the same way explains the origin of evil by the fall of man: that is, it assumes as a fact, in historical form, what has to be explained.

The mystified story of the functioning of the market makes it all appear upside-down: the rich man, according to the story of bourgeois economics, has a greater weight in the social decision-making process because he has abstained from consumption in the past or because, thanks to his/her skill, he/she has managed to get a good placing in the competitive game; the poor person, on the other hand, must have done something wrong in the competitive struggle. The fact that the market is not born out of the Eden of equal opportunities, but is the result of a historical process that, in the words of Marx (1867, ch. 26), remains 'written in the annals of mankind in letters of blood and fire' is considered secondary:[2] the important thing is not to explain what is happening and what has actually happened, but to interpret the existing reality as the result of a logical and just process, even if it did never happen.

Historians, in attempting to explain the present as the result of past processes, arrive at a representation of reality made up of contradictions, conflicts, convergences and divergences. Economists, by contrast, assume that the present is the expression of a coherent set of principles and then invent a story whose logical, rational and just epilogue is precisely the existing reality. Thus, what for historians are contradictions or compromise solutions, become for economists the conditions of consistency. This obviously implies that the historians' and economists' stories are different and go in opposite directions, from the past to the present in one case, from the present to the past in the other: the former explain history, understood as a critical interpretation of the past, the latter tell a story, understood as a fairy tale whose happy ending is the present.

## The freedom-coercion dichotomy

In this clumsy attempt at *ex post* rationalization of the present, the story of neoliberal theory is made up of spontaneous interactions between free subjects, who, thanks to the market, find a way to express their subjective preferences and, thanks to the expansion of markets, see the domain in which their preferences can actually be realized expand. This further mystification is operated in economic modelling through the double assumption that individual preferences and endowments are given, which implies (tautologically) that any transaction is the product of free choices on the part of all participants (if a transaction is not mutually desired, it is in fact not realized). In the specific case of market interaction, the tautology states that any exchange is necessarily desired and intentional, since the market is by definition the arena in which one exchanges only if one wants to.

Like any tautology, this proposition is also logically true. The problem, however, is that the tautology is arbitrarily truncated: market interaction does not simply express individual preferences (as the neoliberal apologetics claims), but rather depends on existing preferences and constraints. And it is not difficult to realize that if the rich financier George Soros and I express different demands on the market, it is not so much because we have different tastes (which may even not be true) but because we have different endowments. All this is, of course, well known, but who knows why, when we talk about the functioning of the market, we identify demand with preferences and not with constraints (and this makes us mistakenly see the market as a pure instrument of freedom, when at the same time it is also an instrument of oppression).

In economic language, there is also a tendency to surreptitiously load the market with ideological values by using the expression 'free market'. Asking what exactly this expression means sounds only provocative. In fact, it is not only part of everyday language, but is also found, sometimes obsessively, in economics textbooks and in the speeches of experts. Personally, it is not clear to me what it means for an *institution* to be *free*. Freedom may be of the people, not of the institutions that regulate their interactions. Perhaps free market means the principle that the market mechanism is left free to operate. But then, I do not understand what is the point of making a normative issue out of it, given that the price to be paid for the freedom of the market is precisely the lack of freedom of the subjects that interact in it. Or another possible interpretation is that it is precisely the subjects interacting in the market that are free. But, as we have seen, this can only be asserted if we take their decision-making constraints (their economic endowments) as given. However, if constraints are taken as given, any action is free, by definition. So why not also speak of 'free jails'? After all, even a prisoner is *free*, as long as one takes bars, surveillance and all other restrictions imposed on him/her as given.

The freedom-coercion dichotomy, on which neoliberal economists insist so much by attempting to associate with it the market-state dichotomy or, more generally, the market-hierarchy dichotomy (Williamson, 1975), is in reality meaningless. There are only constrained choices, both in the market and in the other spheres of social interaction and, precisely as such, they are both free and coerced: free insofar as they are chosen, coerced insofar as they are constrained. Therefore, the relevant question is not freedom in an absolute sense, but that of the types of constraints within which individual freedoms can be guaranteed.

Incidentally, the definition of the economic problem as a 'constrained optimum' problem is considered by mainstream economists as the most important step forward in economic science. According to the neoclassical approach, which is widely dominant in economics today, 'economics is the science that studies human conduct as the relationship between ends and scarce means applicable to alternative uses' (Robbins, 1932). Mathematically, this approach leads to representing any economic problem as an optimizing choice problem within a set of constraints. The free character of choice is thus expressed in the decision-maker's objective function (which defines the goals to be pursued and their relative weights, derived from the preferences of the decision-maker itself), while its coercive character is expressed in the functions describing the existing constraints (i.e. the limited means available to realize the set goals).

Neoliberal economists, however, prefer to insist on freedom when referring to market interaction and on coercion when referring to all other forms of economic interaction, with the contradictory result that in interpreting market exchanges as the product of free and intentional interactions, one of the two pillars on which the whole of modern economic theory rests, that of constraints, is set aside, giving the (mistaken) impression that everything depends on preferences.

If I travel in second class and you in first, according to bourgeois mystification, it is because, evidently, you prefer to travel comfortable, while I prefer something else. Thus, it would then be normal to expect that I have a nicer car than you or that I go on holiday somewhere nicer. And instead, when we get off the train, me from second-class and you from first-class, everyone knows that the nicer car will be yours, just like the holiday place. And this is because in decision-making, constraints count first and only within constraints is there room for the expression of preferences. One does not need to be an economist to understand this truism, but it is thanks to the economist and the authority of his/her science that the truism is transformed into a half-truth, remaining logically unassailable, as being the product of a tautology, but being at the same time false, like any half-truth.

If there were no classes on the train, we would all travel under the same conditions, and this would obviously limit the freedom to travel comfortably of those who can afford it (but would increase the probability of finding a seat for those who cannot). Obviously, however, this would be inefficient according to bourgeois theory. The conditions of allocative efficiency, so dear to economists, are in fact expressed in the equality between willingness to pay and price, and the willingness to pay of a rich person is certainly greater than that of a poor person (regardless of their preferences for train travel, cars and holidays). The point, however, is that an individual's willingness to pay cannot be defined independently of his/her budget constraint: there is no point in asking how much one is willing to spend on a certain good if one does not know one's overall spending limits. It is thanks to this simple omission of the question of constraints (which of course are heterogeneous in reality) that the market can be described as the home of economic freedom. But the fact remains that this home for some is a villa, for others a cell.

## The market-democracy dichotomy

Extending the space of market relations means introducing 'classes' into ever larger areas of our lives and allowing those with the economic means to grab the best while leaving others the rejects (if any). What is the point of charging a 'ticket' to take the train, to go to school or to receive health care if not to keep those who cannot afford it out of trains, schools and hospitals? And what is the point of having different tickets according to the quality of service if not to prevent second-class citizens from mixing with first-class ones? If one really wants to meet people's needs (or if one simply wants to reduce inequality) then let us all travel in the same class, let us all go to the same schools and let us all go to the same hospitals.

But then, one will object: you want to restrict the citizen's right of choice! As if this were not already the case: how many are there who cannot even attend school or afford a train journey and, when they can afford it, they certainly do not consider the problem of choosing which class to travel in? Marx and Engels (1848, ch. 2) wrote about private property:

> You are horrified at our intending to do away with private property. But in your existing society, private property is already done away with for nine-tenths of the population; its existence for the few is solely due to its non-existence in the hands of those nine-tenths. You reproach us, therefore, with intending to do away with a form of property, the necessary condition for whose existence is the non-existence of any property for the immense majority of society. In one word, you reproach us with intending to do away with your property. Precisely so; that is just what we intend.

And so, if it is objected to me that I want to restrict the citizen's right of choice, my answer is yes: if for you citizens are only those who have the problem of choosing a private school, a clinic, and a class in which to travel, yes, they will have to give something up; if by citizens we also mean all others, then no, the freedom of the latter can only increase. If technology and existing resources allow comfortable first-class trains, then let us make first-class trains for everyone; if existing resources do not allow it, let us make them second-class or intermediate class. But let everyone be guaranteed the right to transport.

The equality that the market brings is purely formal. It is true that the law of the market is equal for all, but it is we who are not equal in the market. The principle of formal equality is thus transformed into the very premise of the existence and perpetuation of substantial inequality: in the abstract, in the market, all men are equal, but in practice, it is only those with adequate spending power who ultimately enjoy the goods and services produced by society and this makes men different. This contradiction between formal equality and substantive inequality in the market implies that the wider the sphere of economic and social relations regulated by the market, the narrower the sphere of relations in which principles of real democracy and substantive equality can be enforced.

The very assertion that variety in the quality of goods and services offered by the market is a positive normative fact is only valid for those who enjoy the right to choose, and this right in the market is proportional to wealth. For those who do not have sufficient wealth, variety is only an instrument of discrimination. And, more generally, this discrimination increases as market relations expand. All this in the guarantee of the highest efficiency.

## Notes

1 The problem of the impossibility of obtaining a coherent ordering of social preferences from individual preferences had already been identified, if only intuitively, at the end of the 18th century by Marie G. A. N. de Caritat Condorcet (1785). With the publication of Arrow's book (1951), the literature on the subject developed considerably, giving rise to the so-called 'social choice' school, which makes heavy use of formal analysis and is, from this point of view, not easily accessible to the 'layman'. Articulate expositions rich in bibliographical references are provided by Arrow (1987) and Sen (1987).

2 The quote is taken from a long chapter in *Capital* in which Marx reconstructs the historical conditions that led to the advent of the capitalist mode of production. The topic of pre-capitalist conditions and social phenomena related to the establishment of market society is much discussed by economic historians even outside the Marxist tradition. A classic on the resistance of society against the establishment of market relations as a mode of regulation of society is Karl Polanyi's (1944) book, *The Great Transformation*.

## References

Arrow, J. K. (1951) *Social choice and individual values*. New York: Wiley.

Arrow, J. K. (1987) 'Arrow's theorem', in Eatwell, J., Milgate, M. and Newman, P. (eds.) *The new Palgrave dictionary of economics*. London: MacMillan Press.

Condorcet, M. G. A. N. (1785) *Essai sur l'Application de l'Analyse à la Probabilité des Décisions Rendues à la Pluralité des Voix*. Paris: Imprimerie Royale.

Dobb, M. (1955) 'Economic theory and the problem of a socialist economy', in Dobb, M. (ed.) *On economic theory and socialism. Collected papers*. London: Routledge and Kegan Paul.

Marx, K. (1844) *Economic and philosophical manuscripts of 1844*. Available at: www.marxists.org/archive/marx/works/1844/manuscripts/preface.htm

Marx, K. (1867) *Capital. A critique of political economy, Book 1, The process of production of capital*. Available at: www.marxists.org/archive/marx/works/1867-c1/index.htm

Marx, K. and Engels, F. (1848) *Manifesto of the communist party*. Available at: www.marxists.org/admin/books/manifesto/Manifesto.pdf

Mises, L. von (1949) *Human action. A treatise on economics*. London: William Hodge and Company Limited.

Pareto, V. (1906) *Manuale di Economia Politica con una Introduzione alla Ricerca Sociale*, Torino: Einaudi. English translation (1971). *Manual of political economy*. New York: Augustus Kelley.

Polanyi, K. (1944) *The great transformation*. New York: Ferrar & Rinehart.

Robbins, L. (1932) *An essay on the nature and significance of economic science*. London: Macmillan.

Sen, A. K. (1987) 'Social choice', in Eatwell, J., Milgate, M. and Newman, P. (eds.) *The new Palgrave dictionary of economics*. London: MacMillan Press.

Williamson, O. E. (1975) *Markets and hierarchies: analysis and anti-trust implications. A study in the economics of internal organization*. New York: The Free Press.

# 3 The market and its myths

## The myth of the fair market (the market as an incentive mechanism)

Let us now return to the myth of the bourgeois economist who, in order to present the market society as the result of an efficient, rational and just process, invents a zero time in the past, in which all individuals stand on equal footing at the starting blocks, with more or less equivalent endowments. This is in fact a popular myth that only historical ignorance can keep alive. For their part, economists, so fond of the speculative method, certainly do not contribute to reducing such ignorance. We have already seen how this myth clearly conflicts with the history of the origins of capitalism. Let us now examine the theoretical contradictions that lie behind it. Let us therefore try to follow the historical fantasies of our economist and those who believe that the past can simply be hypothesized, rather than studied, and imagine that this idyllic time zero actually existed. But then again, shouldn't we reset everything every time a new individual is born? Why should someone who has not even had time to learn his/her own name be responsible for the mistakes (or merits) of his/her parents or great-great-grandparents? But then the right to inheritance would have to be abolished; and then, for the sake of consistency, the right to donations would also have to be revised; and to be really rigorous, the very concept of private property would have to be redefined, which would end up conferring much more limited rights than those that exist. And then, once the right to inheritance and the right to donations have been revised, what would happen to the resources belonging to the individual who dies? They should be allocated to the state (perhaps only pending allocation to a new unborn child). But then this is not a market economy model, but one of socialist economy, with public ownership and allocation of resources on a centralized basis. And, if so, what room is left for the market?

How is it possible not to see that the myth of the fair market is a contradiction in terms? Even assuming that the market is in itself desirable and that the only problem is that of the equal distribution of endowments (the same value of endowments for all), the arrangements necessary to make the fair market operational would be such as to prevent the market mechanism itself from functioning. We are in fact faced with a substantial contradiction: if the market is considered fair because of the system of rewards and punishments that it inflicts on the good and the bad, it cannot be equitable at the same time, otherwise the system of rewards and

DOI: 10.4324/9781032726168-4

punishments would lose its effectiveness: if with the same endowments, individual *A* starts a successful business and individual *B* embarks on a failing enterprise, is it not fair (at least according to meritocratic logic) that *A* gets rich and *B* gets poor? And what sense would it make to ensure the same remuneration for both? But then, if the market to be fair must be inequitable (in that the good must be rewarded and the bad punished), what sense does it make to invent a time zero of perfect equality? And how is it then possible, after time zero, to talk about redistribution without undermining the market's incentive system?

If one accepts inequality as a necessary condition for market fairness, one must also accept as fair the misery, degradation and lack of opportunities for emancipation that characterize most market societies. If, on the other hand, these effects of market interaction are seen as undesirable and unfair (because one recognizes that success and failure depend not only on the merits and demerits of individuals, but also on the starting conditions, or even because one does not believe in meritocracy as a yardstick of justice), one would have to continually intervene to rebalance these conditions. But this would end up impeding the very functioning of the market's incentive mechanism. Therefore, if fairness is conceived more broadly, including the distribution of resources, it can only be achieved by altering the market's incentive system. In short, the only way to make the market fair is to hinder its functioning.

## The myth of the free market (the market without power relations)

According to the representation provided by mainstream economic theory, the market is a place of voluntary and paritetic interaction in which individuals compete freely and are rewarded or penalized according to their successes and failures in the competitive process. All this in contrast to other contexts of social interaction regulated instead by power relations or even authoritarian and hierarchical relations. In this way, the market is presented as an arena of freedom that, by expanding, takes away space from the coercion of bureaucracies and organizations. The champion of neoliberalism, Hayek, Nobel Prize winner for economics in 1974, presents the issue in the following terms:[1] 'It is, as Adam Smith already understood, as if we had agreed to play a game, partly of skill and partly of chance' (Hayek, 1978, p. 186).

But, apart from the fact that we never decided to participate in such a game, but were forced to, the point is that the game at hand is not governed at all by skill and luck, but primarily by economic power relations. As economists know, the subject of power is kept away from economic schemes. Power, authority, domination, are all topics considered extraneous to the market, at least in its perfectly competitive form. Two distinct issues arise here: first, perfectly competitive markets are certainly not the norm; second, power relations exist even in markets of perfect competition.

On the first point, there is not much to be said at the theoretical level, the question is rather resolved empirically. In fact, history shows with great evidence that the spontaneous tendency of capitalism is towards capital concentration, certainly not towards atomistic competition between a multitude of infinitesimally small enterprises. And this alone would be enough to cast doubt on the validity of the schemes that defend the market by associating it with the perfectly competitive form.

On the second point, economists will have a reaction of rejection, considering me a heretic who has stepped outside the canons of official culture, based on the now age-old conviction that competition and economic power are incompatible.[2] Yet, it would suffice to recall the issue of legal, institutional, budgetary constraints to show that social relations, including market relations, are power relations and that, within power relations, economic power plays a primary role. To stick to the constraints that appear explicitly in the economist's theoretical scheme, at least two forms of economic power deserve attention: purchasing power and market power.

The assumption that the budgetary constraints of the players in the competitive process are heterogeneous implies the existence of economic power relations, if only because the more stringent the budgetary constraint, the narrower the 'purchasing power'. And without purchasing power, one cannot compete: I could be a very skilled financial market strategist and I do not think it is simple bad luck if I do not succeed in establishing myself globally alongside the 'big three' multinational investment companies – *Blackrock*, *Vanguard* and *State Street* – who together manage assets worth 20 trillion dollars and control 40 per cent of all listed companies in the United States; I simply do not have the means to try.

Obviously then, economic power goes far beyond its specific form of purchasing power, calling into question even the cardinal principle of the neoliberal ideology of consumer sovereignty: in a world where advertising is a substantial corporate expenditure chapter, the assumption that consumer preferences are exogenous to the model (or even innate) and that the consumer is the best judge of himself/herself is at best extravagant (Dobb, 1955). But purchasing power as a form of economic power is already sufficient to prevent the competitive game from being won by the most skilful or the luckiest, since it will instead be won (other things being equal) by the strongest in terms of economic means.

The invention of the perfectly competitive scheme allows at most for the exclusion of cases of direct power relations between two subjects: under conditions of perfect competition, it is in fact not possible to impose disadvantageous conditions on the counterpart of the exchange compared to those ensured by the market because the counterpart would immediately find another subject with whom to carry out the transaction. But who said that the conditions assured by the competitive market do not express power relations? Certainly, under conditions of perfect competition, anyone who tried to sell a pair of shoes for 1,000dollars when the competition sells it for 100 dollars would find his/her warehouses full and his/her coffers empty. But on what basis can one say that 100 dollars for a pair of shoes is a 'correct' price and that the correct price for a kilo of rice is one dollar? How much does the farmer have to work to buy a pair of shoes? In what sense can a competitive price be considered free of power relations?

Under monopoly conditions (or at any rate under imperfect competition) it becomes possible to sell the same product at a higher price than would be the case, other things being equal, in a market of perfect competition (which provides, according to neoclassical theory, a measure of the monopolist's 'market power'). But price depends not only on the form of the market, but on a whole range of other factors. Thus, for example, if in market *X*, of monopoly, shoes are priced at 200, it is by no means certain that in market *Y*, of perfect competition, they will be priced lower. If one assumes different cost curves in the two markets (e.g. because firms producing for market *Y* are too small to fully exploit economies of scale), the competitive price in market *Y* (defined by the meeting of the supply and demand curves in that market) may well be300. But then, who suffers more from a power relationship, the purchaser of shoes in market *X*, victim of a monopolist seller who imposes a price of 200 (higher than the price that would prevail in those given circumstances if the market were perfectly competitive) or the purchaser in market *Y*, perfectly competitive, who pays 300 for the shoes (and who therefore has to work longer hours to be able to buy them)?

Just as it is not possible to define a distribution of property rights that is neutral in terms of power relations (by definition, private property confers rights on one subject while depriving others of them), neither does it make sense to define a price system that is neutral in terms of power (as the dominant theory pretends by constructing the model of perfect competition). If, for some reason, market prices coincide with the theoretical prices of the perfect competition model, then a particular system of budget constraints between market actors is determined; if, on the other hand, actual prices are different from theoretical prices, the system of budget constraints will be different. In any case, however, these budgetary constraints *exist* and owe their existence to the very existence of private property and the market, not to the existence of a *particular* distribution of property rights and a *particular* price system. Therefore, the fact that the prices actually realized in the market are equal to or different from those established by a given theoretical model in no way changes the coercive role of private property and the market as general forms of social interaction.

The point that escapes the bourgeois economic theory, all centred on the myth of perfect competition, is that power relations (economic and otherwise) find their basis in social relations, not in relations between isolated agents. Two isolated agents exchanging in the market (competitive or otherwise) still exchange property rights, and property is a social relation. The structure of property rights itself defines a network of power relations between agents, as it confers rights and duties and, hence, *power*. In addition to property, the existence of a market in which exchanges take place presupposes a whole series of institutions (from legislative norms to social conventions) without which exchange would not take place, and these institutions, according to the form they take, modify existing power relations. Today, for instance, at the legal level there is a tendency to assign the worker the status of self-entrepreneur, from riders who deliver pizzas to call centre employees and more. It is clear that these legal measures shift the balance of power in favour of the boss and to the detriment of the employee. And it is equally clear that if in some countries, riders, through struggle, are granted the status of employees, the balance of power shifts in the opposite direction, to the benefit of the working class. But to speak of a shift in the balance of power in one direction or the other one must at least recognize the existence of power relations. And if property and the market are sufficient to bring power relations into being, they characterize all spheres of social interaction, including the market, irrespective of the particular legislation in force and the competitive or monopolistic form of the market itself. The exit from perfect competition modifies power relations but is not the cause of their existence: you cannot modify something that does not exist. Therefore, the attempt of bourgeois economics to relegate the question of power out of the scheme of perfect competition does not work.

Nor is the elaboration of a theory – according to which a perfectly competitive market is a context devoid of market power – sufficient to eliminate power relations from the market, since market power is only one particular form of economic power. Bourgeois economics therefore also needs to exclude other forms of economic power from scientific investigation. This is done with different arguments based on the difficulty of measurement or the analytical precision of the concept of economic power itself (Williamson, 1995). In this regard, it would suffice to observe that, firstly, there are in fact various measures of economic power, each with its own purposes and limitations and, secondly, it is by no means certain that all entities that produce real effects are susceptible to measurement (in many cases, in social sciences as in hard sciences, it is only the effects of the existence of certain relationships that can be quantified). But the point is that, regardless of the validity of Williamson's arguments and those of economists who deny the existence of a causal relationship running from society to the individual, the fact remains that property and the power relations it gives rise to are nonetheless the very premise of market interaction. Therefore, if only for this reason, power relations exist. By excluding the analysis of power relations from scientific enquiry, bourgeois economics paints a picture in which power vanishes (leaving one to believe that the agents are all on an equal footing). But neglecting a problem or concealing it does not erase its existence.

It is obvious, however, that even bourgeois economics, always so attentive to the market and competition, cannot ignore the social assumptions on which the market and competition are based, first and foremost private property and the institutions that guarantee it. Private property, in fact, is a fundamental assumption of the theory and cannot be explained as the result of purely voluntary interactions even by returning to the mythical time zero. What were individuals exchanging at time zero if property was not already there? Somehow, then, bourgeois economics itself, although it rejects the social foundations of interpersonal relations, is still based on them. The fact is that, once property is accepted as the implicit foundation of the whole theory, neoliberal economics would like to maximize the degrees of freedom of property right holders. Thus, market regulation itself is presented as a violation of freedom. And indeed, it is, if one recognizes that the freedom of the one is the constraint of the other: the regulation of firing is certainly a constraint on the master's freedom to do what he wants with his employees.

In the legal sphere, moreover, the existence of asymmetrical relations between the parties, even when the contractual relationship arises on a purely consensual basis, is a widely recognized fact and constitutes the very presupposition of the principle of the protection of the weaker party. It would make no sense to protect the tenant vis-à-vis the landlord if one did not recognize the asymmetry in their positions of power, nor would it make sense to defend the consumer in disputes with companies, or to safeguard the rights of the worker vis-à-vis the master, even though, in recent times, these general principles are increasingly denied in facts (a comrade has informed me that she has been sentenced for participating in a strike, which the court has equated with extortion against the master!).

In the economic field, instead, by ignoring all existing asymmetries, mainstream economists reason as if we all had the same opportunities and, on the basis of this completely false assumption, they then portray rules, norms and all sorts of protection of the interests of the weaker as violations of freedom (of the stronger), as external obstacles to individual free expression.

If the great boxing champion Mike Tyson and I find ourselves sitting at the same poker table, the rule against punching each other during the game, for Tyson is a restriction of freedom, for me is a guarantee of physical integrity. Obviously, Tyson can win the game without throwing any punches, simply because he is better at cards than me or perhaps because he is luckier. What is certain is that I will not be the one calling for the 'deregulation' of the game. Nor would I feel safer if instead of sitting at the poker table we were to face each other in the ring, even with all the guarantees that Tyson will respect the rules of the game (and if someone tries to reassure me arguing that the fight will still be 'on equal footing' because 'the rules of the World Boxing Association are the same for everyone' I would more likely think it is Tyson's manager than a real friend of mine).

The presence of rules necessarily alters power relations and individual freedoms. In the absence of rules, however, the law of the strongest asserts itself in its pure form. The market, with its rules equal for all (applied to subjects that are not equal at all), can by no means be considered a context in which people interact on an equal footing. On the contrary, uniformity of rules in the market is only the tool that allows the giants to crush the smaller ones. That is why, in the presence of asymmetrical powers, the rules must not be symmetrical, but must protect the weakest: to put it bluntly, just by imposing a series of strong restrictions on Tyson and allowing me every blow, I might have a chance of walking out of the ring on my own feet; whereas Tyson's interests would be much better protected in a world where every social and economic relationship could be regulated by punches. No matter how much bourgeois economics tries to ignore it, market relations are power relations: the deregulation of markets only means the integral assertion of the law of the strongest in the economic sphere, and the expansion of markets only means the defence of the interests of the richest in ever larger spheres.

## The myth of the market of equal opportunities (the market without social classes)

According to dominant economic thinking, social classes have now disappeared. In the market we are all equal, there are no slaves or masters, there are only individuals. To speak today of opposing interests between capitalists and workers is at the limits of permissibility in economic discourse. It is in the name of the common good that economic policy is made, not in the interest of a social class. After all, today we are all workers and capitalists at the same time. Many of us have some savings invested in the stock market or in the old government bonds, and it is therefore for our good that economic policy intervenes (even though, to tell the truth, many others do not have a single dollar to spare). And even Elon Musk, Jeff Bezos and Bill Gates are workers after all. And if we are all workers and capitalists at the same time, why persist with these old, historically outdated, economic categories?

Perhaps because, one might reply, the economic categories of capital and labour are not at all outdated, given that it is precisely on the capital-labour relationship that the entire capitalist system rests. And also, because, beyond American self-made-man fairy tales, a worker in the car industry, on 1,000 dollars a month, will never save enough to be able to buy one of the cars he/she produces, while Musk will never work enough to equalize the labour contained in his car fleet.

On a theoretical level, neoliberal theory nevertheless insists that the worker is granted the possibility of becoming a capitalist himself/herself. It is true, some concede, that in the capitalist system it is possible to define social classes in more or less precise terms on the basis of the ownership of economic resources other than one's own labour power (in Marxian terminology, 'labour power' is the capacity of the worker to work, which is distinguished from the 'labour' actually provided in the production process). But it is equally true, they say, that this concerns society as a whole, not the individual. At the individual level, nothing prevents a person with only labour power and willpower from accumulating capital with which to start his/her own business.

Certainly, on a theoretical level, this is an existing possibility. The problem, however, is that if social mobility is limited, it is not because everyone is comfortable where he/she is, but because the worker does not, in fact, accumulate anything. And, if he/she does not accumulate, it is not because he/she prefers the egg today to the chicken tomorrow (like the sober capitalist), but because he/she needs the egg today to get to tomorrow. As Maurice Dobb noted, the story of the capitalist who enjoys a profit by virtue of his abstinence, his renunciation of consumption, is a historical falsehood: this is not how capitalism was created (Dobb, 1958). But, above all, to describe Musk, Bezos or Gates as people who abstain from consumption is simply ridiculous.

That social classes still exist, although they have undergone different evolutions over time and in different countries, is first and foremost a question of historical analysis. But it is also the very premise of the capitalist system. Capitalist production is based on the wage-labour relationship, which presupposes that labour power is a commodity that can be sold and bought on the market like any other commodity. Capitalism, therefore, to function and stay alive needs, firstly, an army of workers who sell their labour power to someone who can buy it and, secondly, mechanisms that reproduce this social division into classes. Despite the fact that the labour contract, like any contract, is the product of free and voluntary agreements, it is realized on the basis of heterogeneous economic constraints (if we could freely choose, without economic constraints, whether to work for a living or to live without having to work, we would all choose to be capitalists) and on the basis of market conditions that in fact prevent the worker from accumulating sufficient wealth to disengage from the wage-labour relationship. The reproduction of the heterogeneity of constraints is itself the product of the market mechanism and is made possible by the existence of wage-labour, that is, the labour market (and its economic laws regulating the level of wages). Of course, once the distribution of endowments and the existence of the labour market are taken for granted, the worker's pursuit of a wage-labour relationship can be interpreted as the optimal choice of a rational individual. Indeed, for those who possess nothing but their labour power, a job, even if exploited, is always better than unemployment. However much the conditions of workers and those of capitalists are constantly changing, the fact remains that the entire system rests on the relationship between these two social figures: workers and capitalists, sellers and buyers of labour power. No wage-labour, no capitalism.

Today, then, following the political risks of an explicit class clash, we have thought of sweetening the story by also changing the name of one of these two social figures. Thus, albeit with some theoretical imprecision, we prefer to call the capitalists, the bosses, as entrepreneurs, to emphasize their leadership qualities in undertaking economic activities; or, also, as employers, to emphasize their character as gentlemen who offer opportunities to needy workers (this is why we sometimes even make them knights of labour) . . . as if it were really them giving work to the workers and not the other way around.

The thesis of the disappearance of social classes is just the umpteenth mystification of bourgeois economics that has found fertile ground in the theoretical disorientation of a left-wing that, in the economic sphere, has fully espoused the neoliberal ideology of the right (forgetting the important scientific successes achieved precisely in criticizing the neoliberal model) and has renounced class struggle in the name of the common good.

## The myth of the wealth-producing market (the market as a discipline mechanism)

One of the vaunted virtues of the market and competition would be the capacity to bring out the best in everyone. In striving to outdo one another, each of us would give his/her best and thus contribute to increasing the mass of goods available to society and to finding ever better solutions to existing economic problems. How else can we explain the impressive leap forward in the production of goods and services achieved with the advent of capitalism? And is it not precisely the defeat in the race for the production of goods and services that led the main systems of real socialism to collapse?

The greatest experts in competition, the competitive sportspeople, know well that the direct challenge between two athletes improves the performance of both. The desire to always do better, in sports as in business, would therefore be the key to the success of the competitive mechanism and this is because competition is human nature itself. And if sport is the field in which ludic competition is best expressed, the market is the institution in which economic competition is best developed.

Leaving aside the fact that this conception of sport is very restrictive, given that sport was born as an activity of leisure, entertainment, and education of one's body (the word 'sport' comes from the old French 'desport', in English 'recreation') and the affirmation of its competitive dimension is, if anything, a consequence of the progressive extension of market relations, as, more generally, is the affirmation of an individualistic and competitive human nature; the point is that the economic sphere has its own specificities concerning the relations between the performance and the distribution of the benefits that performance produces. In particular, the abundance of products found in the market system is by no means independent of the mechanisms for distributing production among the population, so that the criteria for distributing this abundance should be discussed before defining abundance in production as a social success.

In capitalism, production and distribution are two interdependent processes. The owner of the economic means (the capitalist) buys the means of production on the market: the machinery, raw materials, labour power and everything else needed for production. Under the pressure of competition, the capitalist tries to pay as little as possible for these resources and seeks to exploit them in the best possible way, both quantitatively (avoiding waste) and qualitatively (using them intensively and combining them in the best possible way). At the end of the production process, a product is obtained. This product is the capitalist's, not society's, since it is he/she, the capitalist, not society, who has advanced the capital. The action of competition, then, leads the capitalist to sell his/her product at a relatively low price and this increases the need to produce at minimum cost, remunerating the means of production at the minimum and squeezing them as much as possible. Among the means of production, as we have seen, is labour power, which the capitalist buys from the worker. As with the other means of production, market competition leads the capitalist to exploit it optimally: in a quantitative sense, by trying to make the employee work as long as possible for the same pay, in a qualitative sense, by trying to make him/her work as hard as possible during the same working hours. The story of course does not end there: competition also operates on the workers' side. For the worker, the stronger the competition and the greater his/her and his/her family's needs, the greater the necessity to make do with the minimum possible, giving the maximum in return.

Here, then, lies the secret of the abundance of commodities in the market system: abundance is the result of the competitive drive that leads the worker to work hard (qualitative aspect) and to work a lot (quantitative aspect) and that leads the capitalist to economize on working conditions and to remunerate labour at the lowest possible wage. And here is also revealed the class, and not societal, interest in national abundance and wealth: the abundant production obtained through the market process does not belong to society, but to the capitalist, who is fully entitled to do with his/her product what he/she wants, consume it, reinvest it, sell it, throw it away. For the worker, on the other hand, the possibility of enjoying the benefits of the wealth (produced by him/her) remains subordinate to his/her capacity to purchase the goods produced, which, however, is compressed precisely by the game of competition.

The opulence of the market is therefore not a common good, but the good of one part of society: not of the part that by working produces wealth, but of the other, which by making people work appropriates that wealth. Measuring the economic success of a society on the basis of the wealth produced, without reference to the final distribution of that wealth (how much of the goods produced can ultimately be bought by the workers with the real wages in force) is meaningless from a logical point of view, but this is precisely the teaching of bourgeois theory and this is what the (bourgeois) economic institutions that call themselves *super partes* do: central banks, economic observatories, international bodies. One only has to take the monthly bulletin of any central bank or consider the same economic criteria on which the European economic and monetary union (the so-called eurozone) is established to realize that what counts is the growth of wealth, not its distribution, as if the two phenomena were truly independent and as if growth were truly a common good (even when it is achieved by squeezing the incomes of a part of the population). However, mystifications aside, wealth produced does not measure the success of society, but the success of capitalists.

Marx and Engels (1848, ch. 2) responded in this way to the argument that competition, based on the market and private property, is necessary for the economy and society:

> It has been objected that upon the abolition of private property, all work will cease, and universal laziness will overtake us. According to this, bourgeois society ought long ago to have gone to the dogs through sheer idleness; for those of its members who work, acquire nothing, and those who acquire anything do not work.

And it is certain that a society where ten-year-olds work for 12 hours a day (the economic *miracle* of many new developing countries) is more productive and competitive than a society that would like to provide people with the tools for their emancipation. What is more, the continual replication of such miracles even in the North of the world is not so difficult: it is simply a matter of having workers with water at their throats. The worse the labour market conditions are, the more labour can be extracted from workers for the same wage and the greater the growth in output (and profits).

Once the origin of abundance in capitalism has been discovered, one would like to place the responsibility for the distribution problem on specific personal figures: who better than the capitalist should be held responsible for the exploitative relations through which (his/her) wealth is created? But in fact, market discipline operates as much on the worker, forcing him/her to accept ever harsher conditions as a necessary premise to make himself/herself more attractive than his/her unemployed colleagues, as it does on the capitalist, who does not exploit the worker because he/she is greedy and covetous (although undeniably sometimes he/she is), but simply because the competitive market imposes discipline on him/her as well, the discipline of minimizing costs. And there is nothing to do about it: workers, from the point of view of production, are costs to be cut down.

There is no morality to be invoked in the market. Its discipline, Marx teaches, operates as an external impersonal mechanism. Capitalists may be the most morally exquisite people, but if they do not lower their costs, they are priced out of the market. They must, therefore, exploit the workers because it is the market that forces them to do so. Of course, in many cases, one might observe, they could exploit them a little less. But it is sufficient that another capitalist exploits them a little more, making his/her own product cheaper, and everyone is forced to turn the screw on working conditions and wages. With the globalization of markets, then, the game becomes even tougher since it suffices for the turn of the screw to take place anywhere in the world (where workers are in a position to have to accept any conditions), that it imposes itself, as an objective condition of survival on the market, in every part of the planet.

The parallel with sport also becomes clearer at this point. The competitive mechanism, as it operates in the economic sphere, does not correspond at all to that which in the sporting sphere leads athletes to improve one another. Instead, it corresponds to the mechanism that leads sports team managers to feed anabolic bombs to their athletes, which, on the one hand, helps the latter to overcome their limits (sometimes even hurting themselves) and beat their rivals, and on the other hand, helps the former to line their pockets with the proceeds of sporting victories. Of course, in mediatized sport practised at high levels, the game is also attractive to bombastic athletes who earn enough to compensate for the side effects of anabolics and injuries (although it is hard to believe that footballers who progressively lose all motor functions due to Gehrig's disease, or amyotrophic lateral sclerosis, most likely caused by anabolics, really consider themselves compensated by their successes during periods of glory).[3] But this simply amounts to the fact that there are also huge differences between workers, and that skilled workers, who are sufficiently important to the production process, can demand respectable working conditions and remuneration, just as top footballers earn a thousand times more than second-rate footballers. The point remains, however, that in the sporting economy, the transformation of a ball game into a multi-billion-dollar business is not the result of a process of subjective pursuit inspired by self-improvement, but the result of a process of exploitation of others' abilities aimed at appropriating the results achieved. And this is also what happens in the economy in general.

The imperative for the Olympic hundred-metre runner to go under ten seconds is a fact imposed by sporting competition. Of course, it is possible to try to set rules to safeguard healthy competition. But the goal imposed by the competitive mechanism is to go fast, not to be healthy. And the problem is that rules that would like to defend health actually slow down the race. And so it is in economics. The goal is the capitalist's profit, certainly not the emancipation of the worker, and defending the worker's health (and his rights in general) necessarily slows down the process of accumulation. That competitive sport at certain levels is in many cases harmful is a fact on which many doctors agree. But that economic competition is bad for the worker is sadly borne out by statistics on accidents and deaths at work (without, however, affecting the economist's certainties): the World Health Organization and the International Labour Organization (2021) jointly estimate that globally 1.9 million workers die for accidents in the workplace and for work-related diseases each year, adding that this number may be vastly underestimated due to poor reporting and coverage systems in many countries. In the first economy of the world, the United States, on average 100,000 workers die every year. In 2019, 5,333 workers died on the workplace (15 per day, including public holidays and Sundays) and 95,000 died for occupational diseases (260 per day) (American Federation of Labor – Congress of Industrial Organizations, 2021).

The sportsman, then, chooses to practise sport and also chooses whether to practise it at competitive levels (assuming he/she has the ability) or merely as an amateur. The worker, instead, does not choose anything: he/she must work and must work under competitive pressure, whether he/she likes it or not. Lastly, the discipline of the athlete imposed by sporting competition is a great achievement of the individual's psycho-physical education (which, however, could be achieved even without the stimulus of competition, as eastern martial arts, e.g. demonstrate). The discipline of the worker imposed by economic competition, by contrast, is the annihilation of the individual. In this, in the annihilation of the person, consists ofthe subordination of the individual to the impersonal law of the market and competition.

## The myth of the market as a discovery procedure (the market as signal system)

According to an old but, in the opinion of many, still relevant criticism, the market constitutes the only institutional form capable of managing the complex information problems that inevitably arise as the social division of labour proceeds. This thesis constitutes the mainstay of the Austrian economic school's critique of socialism developed during the planning debate (Mises, 1920; Hayek, 1935). This debate developed mainly in the 1920s and 1930s but, still today, according to many economists, it is more relevant than ever.[4]

According to Ludwig von Mises, the problem of rational resource allocation cannot be solved, even in principle, in the absence of private property and market prices. In the absence of synthetic indicators of the relative scarcity of various resources (market prices) it is impossible for economic agents to correctly assess the consequences of their choices. Thus, Mises concludes, socialism in its attempt to dispense with the market is the very abolition of economic rationality.

The importance of market prices as an instrument of efficient resource allocation is developed by Hayek. Hayek's thesis is that a centrally planned system cannot function because it cannot handle the large mass of data that economic agents use in productive activities, a problem that the market instead solves automatically through the information signals provided by the price system.

Although the thesis of the necessity of prices for the efficient allocation of resources was mainly developed in the 1930s, that is, before the advent of the computer, it remains one of the strong points of the neoliberal thesis. In fact, in 1967,

Oskar Lange (1967, ch. 1), one of the leading figures in the planning debate on the pro-planning side, challenged the claim by Hayek and his colleagues of the Austrian school that no planner could replicate the allocative solution that the market automatically finds, with the following consideration:

> Were I to rewrite my essay [in defence of central planning] today my task would be much simpler. My answer to Hayek and Robbins would be: so what's the trouble? Let us put the simultaneous equations on an electronic computer and we shall obtain the solution in less than a second.

From a Marxist point of view, the problem with Lange's retort (which as a tradition of thought is inscribed in so-called 'market socialism') to the Austrians is that, in both criticism and reply, the principle of market rationality is accepted, and the only question addressed is whether it is possible or impossible for a centralized system to replicate the allocative logic of the market. This approach is problematic because the Marxist conception of socialism is that of a mode of production capable of doing better than capitalism (not simply imitating it), that is, capable of overcoming the contradictions of capitalism, resolving its allocative irrationality defined by the market, preventing its recurring crises, and eliminating the conditions of alienation and exploitation that characterize capitalist production. Instead, in Lange's proposal there is no reference to the problems of alienation and exploitation, and the only question addressed is that of the efficient allocation of resources, on the assumption that the market is in any case capable of resolving it.

From the point of view of the academic debate, however, Lange's answer is valid because it rejects Hayek's criticism by accepting his own assumptions (those of market rationality): the so-called Lange-Lerner procedure in fact demonstrates that planning can replicate the allocative solution of the market and that it can also produce different allocations if the market one is not agreeable. In fact, let us recall that the Pareto efficiency of the market is compatible with even very unequal distributional arrangements (the important thing is that, with respect to the starting situation, in the final position no one worsens his/her condition), which means that, by letting the market mechanism operate freely, there is no guarantee that the final distribution of goods among the agents of the system can be considered socially acceptable. By contrast, this problem can be obviated through the Lange-Lerner procedure, which not only allows Pareto efficiency to be obtained, but also makes it possible to choose, among the various Pareto-efficient configurations, the one with the most socially appropriate distributional characteristics. This is equivalent to saying that, precisely according to the allocative rationality of the market, planning is a superior allocative mechanism to the market (at least on paper). A second advantage of the Lange-Lerner procedure is that, through price control, the planning centre has a way of combining its own preferences with those of consumers, incentivizing the consumption of those goods it considers deserving and discouraging the consumption of those it considers socially harmful, something that cannot be done if prices are determined entirely by the market (the main theoretical references of the Lange-Lerner procedure are collected in Lange and Taylor (1938)).

Compared to the Lange-Lerner procedure, planning theory took a leap forward with the discovery, in 1939, of 'linear programming' by the Soviet mathematician and economist Leonid Vitalevic Kantorovic who won the Lenin Prize in 1965 (the highest scientific award in the socialist bloc) and the Nobel Prize for economics in 1975 (the only Soviet economist to have received this recognition) together with the American economist Tjalling Charles Koopmans, who, in an independent path, had discovered (about ten years later) the same mathematical technique in the United States (Kantorovich, 1939; Koopmans, 1951).[5] With the discovery of linear programming, the question of the necessity of market prices as indices of scarcity of economic resources is definitively resolved. Planning, from a formal point of view, is a constrained optimization (maximization or minimization) problem in which the objective function is set by the planning centre and the constraints are given by the existing technology and available resources. The solution of the constrained maximum problem leads to the determination of the 'optimal plan', that is, the best strategy for achieving the goals defined in the plan. This solution provides an assessment of the relative importance of each resource used in the plan with respect to the established goals. This assessment is called the 'shadow price' (or 'solution multiplier' in the Soviet terminology). From the point of view of the efficient allocation of resources, mathematical programming shows that shadow prices play the same role in the planned system as market prices do in the capitalist system: like market prices, they provide an assessment of the relative scarcity of each resource, the only difference being that this scarcity is not measured in relation to the objectives of the market agents (weighted according to the principle 'one dollar, one vote'), but in relation to the objectives set by the planner. This means that economic planning is not at all irrational: simply, whereas the market values different resources according to the preferences of those who have the means to buy, planning values different resources according to the preferences of the planner (which, at least on paper, can be as much the result of a democratic process as a pure dictatorial imposition from above).

From the point of view of Western academic debate, however, the Soviet mathematical school remained substantially on the margins of the planning controversy, as the Soviet Union's priority was to improve the practice of planning and not to engage in an academic debate about the theoretical possibility of the optimal plan or the necessity of market prices.

Returning to the market socialists' reply to the Austrians, it was not considered convincing by the latter, who increasingly appealed to the tacit nature of knowledge. Much of the information that economic agents use on a daily basis is in fact, according to Hayek, impossible to codify and cannot therefore be communicated to the central planner in charge of drawing up the plan. The advantage of the market would instead consist in the possibility of managing the information necessary for the system to function in an automatic and tacit manner, without any need to make the existing and commonly used mass of information explicit. To convince us of this, Hayek (1945, pp. 526–527) develops the following example:

> Assume that somewhere in the world a new opportunity for the use of some raw material, say tin, has arisen, or that one of the sources of supply of tin has

> been eliminated. . . . All that the users of tin need to know is that some of the tin they used to consume is now more profitably employed elsewhere, and that in consequence they must economize tin. There is no need for the great majority of them even to know where the more urgent need has arisen, or in favour of what other needs they ought to husband the supply. . . . The whole acts as one market, not because any of its members survey the whole field, but because their limited individual fields of vision sufficiently overlap so that through many intermediaries the relevant information is communicated to all. . . . The marvel is that in a case like that of a scarcity of one raw material, without an order being issued, without more than perhaps a handful of people knowing the cause, tens of thousands of people . . . are made to use the material or its products more sparingly; *i.e.*, they move in the right direction.

A first serious problem in the Austrian economist's argument is that (as we shall see better in Chapter four) the thesis that market prices provide the appropriate signals to move in the 'right direction' is a thesis that proves indefensible when analysed in less discursive and logically more rigorous terms: in the presence of so-called market failures, market prices do not in fact provide the appropriate signals to realize the efficiency conditions; on the contrary, economic agents responding to the price signals provided by the market do not bring the system closer to Pareto efficiency but instead bring it to a sub-optimal position. This means that, even accepting the bourgeois mystification that identifies social desirability with efficiency, the 'marvel' of which Hayek speaks cannot, in fact, come about.

But the more serious problem is perhaps that, in reasoning in purely intuitive but not sufficiently rigorous terms, Hayek touches on a very delicate theoretical issue that later turned out to be a very bitter note in research on the market's ability to coordinate the decisions of independent agents. In fact, Hayek's argument insists on a problem of stability of the equilibrium between the supply and demand of goods, that is, the ability of the equilibrium position to attract the system to itself from disequilibrium positions. The marvel of the market would then consist in the possibility of moving the system in the 'right direction' (towards the new equilibrium) when a change in the data that defined the old equilibrium (a shift in tin supply or demand curves, in Hayek's example) has occurred. However, the point is that all of the more rigorous theoretical developments of the equilibrium stability problem, in a context of interdependent markets (i.e. in which disequilibrium in the tin market produces effects on the tin pot market), have failed in their attempt to demonstrate the actual ability to converge to equilibrium from disequilibrium positions. In particular, in the 1950s some of the best-known mathematical economists attempted to formalize the process of convergence to equilibrium through a system of equations that explicitly take into account the time factor to determine under which conditions the system actually approaches equilibrium. In the course of this study, several examples emerged in which the process is unstable, that is, does not converge to equilibrium. As the research progressed, it became apparent that cases of instability are by no means the exception, but rather constitute the norm. Finally, in 1973, the mathematical economist Hugo Sonnenschein proved an important theorem (later generalized by Rolf Mantel and Gérard Debreu) that gives a negative answer to the search for equilibrium stability. This theorem states that, given a model of interdependent markets, in which all commonly assumed assumptions regarding the behaviour of agents, the shape of markets etc. are fulfilled, it is impossible to rule out cases of equilibrium instability (Sonnenschein, 1972, 1973; Debreu, 1974; Mantel, 1974). This, of course, does not mean that the equilibrium is always unstable. It does mean, however, that assuming the economic system is adequately represented by the equations of the perfect competition model, it is in no way possible to count on automatic convergence to equilibrium if the system is in disequilibrium. Theoretical research, at this point, has attempted to determine particular conditions in which stability can be guaranteed. However, these conditions require the introduction of ad hoc hypotheses that have no theoretical justification. All this means that the 'marvel' of which Hayek speaks is by no means certain to occur. Incidentally, the failure of economic theory to solve the problem of equilibrium stability is a fact recognized by several leading exponents of neoclassical theory, which is more attentive to questions of logical-deductive rigour than the Austrian school (Hahn, 1982).

But let us leave aside for a moment the mathematical problems, which are certainly not the strong point of Austrian economists and return to their conception of the market. The conception of the market that is outlined in Austrian theory is that of a powerful sensor system capable of capturing the dynamics that take place in the conditions of production and in people's needs, wherever they manifest themselves, and moreover capable of satisfying these needs automatically. Through the market, in fact, an individual who prefers a yellow shirt to a green one has only to express his/her preference by buying the yellow shirt instead of the green one. In this way, according to the Austrians, not only does the market allow for the manifestation of individual preferences but, at the very moment this happens, it simultaneously satisfies them (a feat considered impossible by a planner, who would be required to know in detail the preferences of each individual citizen for the yellow and green shirts). The mechanism may be imperfect, but it remains, in their view, the most powerful mechanism for coordinating agents in a system in which the amount of information required for the system to function reaches thresholds that cannot be managed at the centralized level, nor can it be properly communicated by decentralized agents since this would require the codification of knowledge that exists only at the tacit level. This, according to the ultra-liberals of the Austrian school, is the true limitation of central planning and the strength of the market.

The fact that information problems are a point in favour of the market and against planning is, however, far from obvious. Not so much because the codification of information has by now reached extremely advanced stages (sounds, images, missile trajectories, individuals' tastes and behaviours, viruses, DNA, everything is codified); but above all because the centralization of information and planning are the tools of the capitalist system's main actors: the corporations. Since the time of Lange and his commentary on the revolution in information management brought about by the advent of the computer, new mathematical, statistical and informatics techniques, which were simply unimaginable at the time, have developed, making it possible to intersect databases of all kinds and sizes. The *Aladdin* electronic system developed by *BlackRock* manages 21.6 trillion dollars in diverse financial assets through a network of 5,000computers that instantly analyse all sorts of economic, financial, political, military, behavioural, psychological, geological, meteorological data in order to optimize the portfolio strategies of its clients.

Only in bourgeois mystification does capitalism coincide with a network of markets, where there are alert and awake entrepreneurs, ready to respond to the signals that the market sends them through the price system and to seize the profit opportunities left unexplored, thus helping to disseminate the relevant information to the various agents of the system (in this is summed up, in particular, the scientific contribution of Israel Kirzner (1973, 1992, 2000), the new leader of the modern Austrian school, after the death of Hayek). The capitalism of the 21st century (but also that of the 20th and 19th centuries), however, is not made up of alert entrepreneurs but of enterprises that plan. And enterprises, the bigger they are, the more they plan. Large multinationals plan everything: production, sales, marketing, transport, financial variables, customer service, internal careers, relations with other companies, relations with politics, relations with states. Nor can this be made a question of size, since today's multinationals have budgets comparable to and, in many cases, larger than those of entire countries, and often range in the production of quite different goods. A look at the data may be useful.

In a provoking article in 1996, Sarah Anderson and John Cavanagh cross-reference *Forbes* magazine's data on the sales of the largest multinationals and the World Bank's data on the gross domestic product of the world's different countries. Since then, we know that the trends have only accelerated. These are the results they get.

Of the world's top 100 'economies' (whereby an 'economy' is meant either a state or an enterprise), only 49 are states, the other 51 are multinational corporations (1995 data). *Mitsubishi*, the world's largest corporation, was bigger than Indonesia, the fourth most populous country in the world. *General Motors* was bigger than Denmark, *Ford* was bigger than South Africa, *Toyota* was bigger than Norway. *Fiat*, 82nd in this ranking, was bigger than Egypt, Algeria and Hungary. *Walmart*, the 12th largest corporation in the world, was larger than 161 of the 191 countries on the planet. The total sales of the top 200 corporations were equivalent to more than a quarter of the world's gross product. If we subtract the gross domestic product of the nine largest countries (the United States, Japan, Germany, France, United Kingdom, Italy, Brazil, Canada and China) from the gross domestic product of the world's 191 countries, the total gross domestic product of the remaining 182 countries is less than the sales of the top 200 corporations (Anderson and Cavanagh, 1996, 2000).

Today things are even better for corporations: some have merged to become even bigger; others have simply been displaced by the rise of new giants developed precisely in the information sector. The top ten largest companies by market capitalization in 2023 are *Apple*, *Microsoft*, *Saudi Aramco*, *Alphabet*, *Amazon*, *Nvidia*, *Meta Platforms*, *Tesla* and *Louis Vuitton*, eight of which from the United States and all strongly dependent on high technology and information management

(Statista, 2023). The development of new information technologies, however, has not really followed the invisible hand of the market but the invisible hand of the US secret services. The 2013 revelations of Edward Snowden, former CIA contractor, showed in fact the existence of a planetary surveillance system by the NSA called *Prism*, in which all the biggest telecommunications and internet giants, such as *Google*, *Facebook*, *Microsoft*, *Skype*, *Apple*, *AOL* and many others, participate.

The increase in the size of corporations naturally also increased the concentration of personal wealth. By now, there are people on the planet who count their wealth in hundreds of billions of dollars (Forbes, 2024). State budgets, by contrast, have been progressively reduced, through privatizations and the containment of public spending, extended to practically all sectors, including those of greatest social urgency, except of course the expenditure for interests on public debt: that one, everyone agrees, must be paid and that's it, there is no way to reduce or rediscuss it.

This being the case, it is difficult to understand why Larry Fink (*BlackRock*) Elon Musk (*Tesla*, *SpaceX*), Jeff Bezos (*Amazon*), Larry Ellison (*Oracle*), Bill Gates (*Microsoft*), Larry Page (*Google*) and Mark Zuckerberg (*Meta Platforms*), or the chiefs of the CIA and the NSA, William J. Burns and General Timothy D. Haugh, are so good in managing information, while for the minister of the economy of a socialist state this should be an insurmountable problem; nor, more generally, can it be explained why, when planning is capitalist, it is synonymous with profits and efficiency and when it becomes socialist, it is synonymous with theoretical and practical impossibility.

But evidently even questions of realism are not the main concern of Austrian theorists. And so, since neither theoretical criticism nor that of realism is sufficient to undermine the ideological convictions of this school of thought, let us take one last step in the critique of Austrian neoliberalism, by focusing precisely on its strictly ideological dimension, which, after all, is the real reason for the renewed interest that this school of thought arouses. Let us therefore take a closer look at what the 'marvel' of the market mechanism that fascinates Hayek so much consists of. Along the lines of the example of the tin developed by the Austrian author, let us consider the following example.

Assume that somewhere in the world, in the middle of a desert, a new opportunity for the use of some raw material, say water, has arisen, as a rich sheikh has discovered the pleasures of water games and is willing to pay a large sum of money to dive down a long slide into a huge pool. All that the users of water need to know is that some of the water they used to drink is now more profitably employed in the water park and that in consequence they must economize water. There is no need for the great majority of them even to know where the most urgent need has arisen, or in favour of what other needs they ought to suffer dehydration. The whole act as one market, not because the sheikh or his worshippers survey the whole field (forcibly imposing the sheikh's wishes on the heads of the population), but because their limited individual fields of vision sufficiently overlap so that through many intermediaries the water ban is communicated to all (through an increase in the price of water, which has now become scarcer). The marvel is that in a case like that of water scarcity, without an order, without more than perhaps a handful of people knowing the cause, tens of thousands of people are led to die of thirst so that the sheikh can splash around in the pool. This is the 'right' direction in which the market leads.

*Voilà* then the 'marvel' of which Hayek speaks: a mechanism that transfers resources, not according to the urgency of needs, as the author mistakenly suggests, but according to economic willingness to pay (which obviously has more to do with wealth than needs). Had the sheikh been a dictator in full control of the economy, it would have been easy to see the perversity and inhumanity of an allocative system that subordinates the needs of the population to the wishes of their ruler. Precisely because of its inhumanity, the construction of the sheikh's pool in the middle of the desert would have inevitably brought with it the risk of protests and insurrections. Hayek himself would have spoken in such a case of 'tragedy' and 'the road to serfdom' ('the road to serfdom' is the title of a famous book by the Austrian author against all forms of state intervention (Hayek, 1944)). When, by contrast, it is through the market that resources go from those who need them most to those who have the most economic means to enjoy them, the 'tragedy' becomes a 'marvel', the 'road to serfdom' becomes the 'right direction' and the satisfaction of the sovereign becomes the highest end around which to organize the economic system. These are the principles of justice that inspire Austrian neoliberal ideology. At this point, all that remains is to raise the market to the status of a natural and neutral mechanism, and the risks of insurrection are also reduced: it is one thing when the despot takes it away from you by an act of force, it is another thing when an impersonal mechanism takes it away from you by a simple price movement. In this sense Hayek is right: the market is truly a 'marvel'.

Before closing this discussion of the theoretical positions developed during the planning debate, it is worth recalling what remains of this great controversy in modern economics teaching: in general, nothing. Indeed, according to a widespread opinion, the end of Soviet-style real socialism would render the whole debate obsolete. The fall of the Soviet Union and the disintegration of much of the socialist bloc would provide proof of the validity of the Austrian criticism of planning.

This kind of *ex post* demonstration obviously baffles historians, who focus, if anything, on the concrete problems encountered in the different planning systems and on factors such as the internal forces of disintegration in Eastern European countries and the bipolar international context characterized by the Cold War (and its high economic and political costs).

In the field of economics, instead, this view finds fertile ground, since the historical dimension (both of the history of economic thought and of economic history) is certainly not prevalent. According to the new concise version of the planning debate proposed by many economics textbooks, the thesis of the unsustainability of a planned system is simply based on the twofold observation 1) that there was central planning in Soviet Union and 2) that the Soviet Union collapsed economically and politically. It is obvious that such a way of reasoning should not even be taken seriously: in the Soviet Union there was also my grandmother; then, perhaps, the real cause of the collapse of Soviet socialism is not planning, . . . is Grandma Iole!

Understandably, given the epochal scale of the phenomenon, there is no unanimous consensus among historians on the various causes of the Soviet crisis and their relative weight. What is certain is that, from a historical point of view, planning cannot be identified as the cause of the Soviet crisis. Not least because, in doing so, one forgets that the Soviet Union of planning was nevertheless capable of transforming a semi-feudal country into an economically, socially and militarily advanced one, the only one able to repel the Nazi advance in the Second World War (until then victorious across the board) and, subsequently, the only one able to rival the main capitalist superpower, the United States, which entered the war late and emerged practically unscathed, from the first moment more worried about communism than Nazism.

Without wishing to go into the merits of these complex historical issues here, nor on the different political evaluations of the Soviet model's correspondence to the socialist ideals it was inspired by, one point is nevertheless clear: the rise and fall of Soviet socialism are problems to be analysed from a historical perspective and cannot be trivialized in the abstract comparison between the centralized and decentralized model, as the new economic vulgate would have it.

## Notes

1 Unlike the other Nobel Prizes, the Nobel Prize in Economics is not awarded by the Nobel Foundation, but by the Swedish Central Bank. Technically it is called the 'Bank of Sweden Prize in Economic Sciences'.

2 The issue of power in economic relations and in economic theory is one of my main lines of research. For an organic presentation of my critique and the Marxist conception I develop, see Palermo (2016).

3 According to a journalistic investigation conducted by Alessandra Anzolin and Paolo Mondani for *Report*, which aired in Italy on *Raitre* on 30 September 2003, all interviewed footballers suffering from Gehrig's disease were taking 'something' even though they did not know what it was. With the imposition of anti-covid 'vaccines', the number of people who have had experimental serums injected without knowing the real content has grown to some billions, but in this case, for many of them, it was not the mirage of better sports performance but only the blackmail of being barred from working and having a social life.

4 In the history of economic thought, important reconstructions of this debate from an Austrian perspective are developed by Vaughn (1980), Lavoie (1985), Kirzner (1987) and Gloria-Palermo (1999). A modern text that instead defends the theses of market socialism, the rival school of thought to the Austrian one in this theoretical dispute, is that of Jossa and Cuomo (1997). Although certainly not a classic reference, my views on this are expressed in Palermo (1998).

5 The studies that led to the discovery of linear programming in the United States, in which the mathematician George B. Dantzig also played a decisive role (in fact, it was the latter who made the most important contributions), were largely financed by the American Air Force and the *Rand corporation*, an institution linking the military apparatus, industry and universities, which started out as a research and development organization of the American Air Force and later became a non-profit institution. In fact, although the theorists of the socialist planning debate have never dwelt on this fact, centralized planning, as an alternative allocative instrument to the market, is by no means an exclusive concern of socialist systems but concerns any system that attempts to rationalize the allocation of resources according to pre-established objectives.

## References

American Federation of Labor – Congress of Industrial Organizations (2021) *Death on the job: the toll of neglect*. Available at: https://aflcio.org/reports/death-job-toll-neglect-2021

Anderson, S. and Cavanagh, J. (1996) 'Corporate empires', *Multinational Monitor*, 17(12).

Anderson, S. and Cavanagh, J. (2000) *The rise of corporate global power*. The Institute for Policy Studies, pp. 1–14. Available at: www.iatp.org/sites/default/files/Top_200_The_Rise_of_Corporate_Global_Power.pdf

Debreu, G. (1974) 'Excess demand functions', *Journal of Mathematical Economics*, (1), pp. 15–21.

Dobb, M. (1955) 'A review of the discussion concerning economic calculation in a socialist economy', in Dobb, M. (ed.) *On economic theory and socialism. Collected papers*. London: Routledge and Kegan Paul.

Dobb, M. (1958) *Capitalism yesterday and today*. London: Lawrence and Wishart.

Forbes (2024) *World's richest people*. Available at: www.forbes.com

Gloria-Palermo, S. (1999) *The evolution of Austrian economics: from menger to Lachmann*. London: Routledge.

Hahn, F. (1982) 'Stability', in Arrow, K. J. and Intriligator, M. D. (eds.) *Handbook of mathematical economics*. Amsterdam: North Holland.

Hayek, F. A. von (1935) *Collectivist economic planning*. London: Routledge.

Hayek, F. A. von (1944) *The road to serfdom*. London: Routledge.

Hayek, F. A. von (1945) 'The use of knowledge in society', *American Economic Review*, 35(4), pp. 519–530.

Hayek, F. A. von (1978) 'Competition as a discovery procedure', in von Hayek, F. A. (ed.) *New Studies in philosophy, politics, economics and the history of ideas*. London: Routledge and Kegan Paul.

Jossa, B. and Cuomo, G. (1997) *The economic theory of socialism and the labour-managed firm. Market, socialism and labour management*. Cheltenham: Edward Elgar Publishing Limited.

Kantorovich, L. (1939) *Matematicheskie Metody Organizatsii i Planirovaniia Proizvodastva*, Leningrad: Leningrad University Press. English translation (1960). 'Mathematical methods of organizing and planning production', *Management Science*, 6(4), pp. 363–505.

Kirzner, I. M. (1973) *Competition and entrepreneurship*. Chicago: Chicago University Press.

Kirzner, I. M. (1987) 'The economic calculation debate: lessons for Austrians', *Review of Austrian Economics*, 2, pp. 1–18.

Kirzner, I. M. (1992) *The meaning of market*. London: Routledge.

Kirzner, I. M. (2000) *The driving force of the market*. London: Routledge.

Koopmans, T. C. (1951) *Activity analysis of production and allocation*. New York: John Wiley and Sons.

Lange, O. (1967) 'The computer and the market', in Feinstein, C. (ed.) *Capitalism, socialism and economic growth, essays presented to M. Dobb*. Cambridge: Cambridge University Press.

Lange, O. and Taylor, F. M. (1938) *On the economic theory of socialism*. Minneapolis: University of Minnesota Press.

Lavoie, D. (1985) *Rivalry and central planning: the socialist calculation debate reconsidered*. Cambridge: Cambridge University Press.

Mantel, R. (1974) 'On the characterization of aggregate excess demand', *Journal of Economic Theory*, (7), pp. 348–353.

Marx, K. and Engels, F. (1848) *Manifesto of the communist party*. Available at: www.marxists.org/admin/books/manifesto/Manifesto.pdf

Mises, L. von (1920) 'Die Wirtschaftsrechnung im Sozialistischen Gemeinwesen', *Archiv fur Sozialwissenschaft und Sozialpolitik*, 47, pp. 86–121. English translation (1935). 'Economic calculation in the socialist commonwealth', in Hayek, F. A. (ed.) *Collectivist economic planing*. London: Routledge.

Palermo, G. (1998) 'The socialist planning debate: a historical and analytical reconsideration', *History of Economic Ideas*, 6(3), pp. 115–150.
Palermo, G. (2016) *Economics and power: a Marxist critique*. London: Routledge.
Sonnenschein, H. (1972) 'Market excess demand functions', *Econometrica*, 40, pp. 549–563.
Sonnenschein, H. (1973) 'Do Walras identity and continuity characterize the class of community excess demand?', *Journal of Economic Theory*, 6, 345–354.
Statista (2023) *The 100 largest companies in the world by market capitalization in 2023.* Available at: www.statista.com/statistics/263264/top-companies-in-the-world-by-market-capitalization/
Vaughn, K. I. (1980, October) 'Economic calculation under socialism: the Austrian contribution', *Economic Inquiry*, 18, pp. 535–554.
Williamson, O. E. (1995) 'Hierarchies, markets and power in the economy: an economic perspective', *Industrial and Corporate Change*, 1(1), pp. 21–49.
World Health Organization and International Labour Organization (2021) *WHO/ILO joint estimates of the work-related burden of disease and injury, 2000–2016.* Available at: www.who.int/publications/i/item/9789240034945

# 4 Theoretical and real markets

The market critique I have developed so far concerns, first of all, those schemes that entrench themselves behind the construction of ideal markets. These schemes, precisely by idealizing the market, believe in fact that they can provide a representation that justifies the virtues of the market. However, in addition to failing in this objective, such an approach exposes itself to another type of criticism that concerns the relationship between theory and reality.

All the supposed benefits of the market refer only to idealized markets that never existed in reality; but when we entrust a certain allocative space to the market, we must necessarily call-in real markets. Therefore, if one wants to defend a market-based society (or even simply a society that entrusts a certain space to the market), one should first of all explain why real markets are desirable and not just why ideal markets are desirable. Instead, the (alleged) desirability of the market is always about theoretical models that have little to do with real market systems.

This is not simply a problem of realism, but a theoretical own goal of bourgeois economics. Indeed, one only has to reflect on the unbridgeable distance between the assumptions of the theoretical model and the characteristics of the real world to realize that, precisely to the extent that the theoretical market can be considered rational, efficient or desirable, real markets are necessarily irrational, inefficient and undesirable.

In this chapter we therefore accept, if only as a theoretical challenge, the bourgeois approach based on the allocative rationality of the market and study more closely the conditions required for markets to actually realize Pareto efficiency. Given the high development of theoretical research in mainstream economics, a critical examination of its assumptions necessarily requires some effort. Let us begin with the results that neoclassical theory obtains from the perfect competition model and then analyse the assumptions introduced to obtain these results.

## General economic equilibrium and welfare economics

The neoclassical general economic equilibrium model constitutes the most ambitious and advanced research project on the normative properties of the market to date. From the perspective of the history of economic thought, the theory of general economic equilibrium is founded by the French economist Léon Walras in 1874

DOI: 10.4324/9781032726168-5

and developed by the Italian economist and sociologist Vilfredo Pareto in 1896, both professors at the University of Lausanne (this is why the general economic equilibrium school of thought is also called the 'Lausanne school'). The fundamental problem tackled by the two economists was to demonstrate the existence of a set of prices capable of ensuring equality between demand and supply in all markets (the problem of the existence of a general economic equilibrium). However, in the treatises by Walras and Pareto, this problem is inadequately addressed, in the belief (later revealed to be wrong) that the existence of equilibrium is guaranteed by the equality between the number of unknowns and the number of equations in the model. The first rigorous demonstration of the existence of equilibrium did not occur until the 1930s, thanks to the contributions of Abraham Wald and John Von Neumann. Then, in the 1950s, Wald's contribution was generalized by Arrow, Debreu and Lionel W. McKenzie, whose contributions earned the first two economists the Nobel Prize and the ownership of the model itself, now commonly referred to as the 'Arrow-Debreu model'.[1]

The Arrow-Debreu model describes a world in which all agents optimize particular objective functions (utility for consumers, profits for firms) within a set of economic and technological constraints. Specifically, the model is based on three sets of assumptions concerning *technology*, individual *preferences* and individuals' *endowments*. These three sets of assumptions are represented in mathematical terms through appropriate expressions and functions, which makes it possible to formalize, for each agent, the particular constrained optimal problem it is called upon to solve. With this formal representation, the first problem that arises is whether a situation exists in which all agents succeed in optimizing their objective function, given the constraints of their decision problem. Such a situation, if it exists, is said to be of equilibrium since, under such circumstances, no agent will have an interest in unilaterally changing its behaviour (since it is already achieving the maximum possible), which means that if the system is in an equilibrium position, it will remain there, unless exogenous shocks to the fundamental data of the model occur.

This definition of equilibrium, as a situation in which nothing moves, is only apparently different from the more usual definition of equilibrium as the equality of supply and demand. In fact, in neoclassical theory, the demand and supply curves are constructed precisely as a synthesis of the solutions of the constrained optimal problems of the individual agents so, as we immediately verify, the two definitions coincide. The demand curve for a good, in the Arrow-Debreu model, expresses the total quantity of the good that the agents decide to demand, after having solved their optimization problems. Similarly, the supply curve expresses the total quantity that agents decide to offer, as a solution to their optimization problems. Along each point of the demand and supply curves, therefore, all agents willing to buy or sell respectively are solving their own constrained optimization problems. The intersection between the two curves thus expresses an equilibrium configuration, in the sense that all agents in the system (both those buying and those selling) realize their optimal exchange plans and, as we said, have no reason to change their behaviour.

The existence of an equilibrium is of decisive importance for the entire theory. To understand why, let us assume for a moment that, with the assumptions made about the three exogenous variables in the model (technology, preferences and endowments), no equilibrium exists. Let us also assume that the assumptions made in the model are actually fulfilled in reality (otherwise the model must be considered useless, in the sense that it does not help to explain the existing economic configuration at all). It must then be deduced that, in reality, the various agents do not manage to maximize their objective functions at all simply because their plans are incompatible with each other. The result is that the model is unable to determine what the outcome of the economic interaction will be.

The next step after demonstrating the existence of an equilibrium is to examine the normative properties of the equilibrium itself. In this respect, general economic equilibrium theorists demonstrate two important theorems: the first states that any equilibrium of perfect competition in the market is Pareto-efficient; the second states that any Pareto-efficient equilibrium can be achieved through the competitive interplay of markets, starting with an appropriate initial distribution of resources among agents. These two theorems, called 'fundamental theorems of welfare economics', are particularly important as they rigorously show the conditions and meaning of the thesis of competitive market efficiency.[2]

The meaning of the first theorem is simple: the market is Pareto-efficient provided it is characterized by perfect competition. In regulatory terms, then, all one has to do (if one aims at Pareto efficiency) is to ensure the maximum degree of competition. To understand the meaning of the second theorem, one must first remember that, in general, there is a multiplicity of Pareto-efficient allocations. The message of the second theorem is then that whatever Pareto-efficient allocation is considered socially desirable, the competitive mechanism is capable of realizing it. Thus, if, for example, the competitive mechanism were to lead to a particularly unequal Pareto-efficient allocation, it is possible to modify the distribution of initial endowments among agents and let the competitive mechanism lead the system to a new, more socially desirable Pareto-efficient allocation (obviously, however, redistributive intervention on individual endowments cannot be achieved in a Pareto-compatible way, since, in a context of given resources, to give to someone one must necessarily take away from someone else). In short, the beauty of competition would lie not only in its ability to lead to Pareto efficiency (first theorem) but also in its ability to realize any Pareto-efficient allocation existing on paper (second theorem).

This line of defence of the market of perfect competition through the two welfare theorems needs some clarification. First, it should be noted that, while remaining within neoclassical logic and welfare economics, these two theorems do not demonstrate the superiority of the market's allocative mechanism over alternative allocative mechanisms, such as central planning. On the contrary, if the assumptions underlying the two welfare theorems hold, central planning enjoys exactly the same Pareto efficiency properties as the market of perfect competition. What the two theorems instead affirm only concerns the internal comparison within the capitalist mode of production between different forms of market: according to the two welfare theorems, perfect competition produces superior results from the Pareto efficiency point of view compared to monopolistic forms of the market or in any case forms characterized by a certain concentration of market power in the hands of a few.

Moreover, the very logic of the two welfare theorems has provoked strong criticism in the theoretical field. In fact, with regard to the second welfare theorem, the real problem is that, if one knows exactly the Pareto-efficient allocation one wants to realize, it is not clear why one does not realize it directly through appropriate redistributions and instead puts in place different redistributions that will then lead to the socially desired allocation only through the mediation of the market. In other words, in order to argue that the market is desirable (because it always succeeds in realizing the socially desired Pareto-efficient allocation), it must be assumed that an authority outside the market (e.g. the state) is able to determine and impose the appropriate redistributions, from which the market process will then lead to the socially desired allocation. But, with these assumptions, the passage to the market is only unnecessary and redundant. In fact, if one accepts these assumptions of omniscience and omnipotence of the state (without which the second welfare theorem is inoperative), what makes the socially desired allocation possible is not the market but state planning.

Finally, a further theoretical problem emerges as soon as one places alongside the two welfare theorems the important result achieved by Arrow, known as the voting impossibility theorem. This theorem, as we have already seen in Chapter two, states that all attempts to derive a social preference scale from individual preferences, through a democratic voting procedure, either run into internal consistency problems or are incompatible with Pareto efficiency. This is a theoretical contribution that does not stem directly from research on market properties, nor does it fit into the logic of general economic equilibrium analysis. However, due to its importance in the context of welfare economics, it is also sometimes referred to as the 'third fundamental theorem of welfare economics'. Let us then see what the joint message of the three welfare theorems is. If the first two welfare theorems are generally interpreted as theoretical results in favour of markets of perfect competition (albeit with the reservations just advanced), the third theorem (Arrow's theorem) specifies the conditions under which these results can be obtained: the attainment of Pareto efficiency through recourse to the competitive market (sanctioned by the first two theorems) is made possible by the removal of the hypothesis 'one head, one vote' (on which the third theorem is based), and is instead conditional on the acceptance of the principle 'one dollar, one vote'. The third theorem then demonstrates that it is only by falling within this logic alien to the basic principles of democracy that the first two welfare theorems appear as results in favour of the market of perfect competition, in the sense that it is precisely by renouncing the principle of 'one head, one vote' that the competitive market can achieve Pareto efficiency.

Leaving aside these general problems about the very meaning of the defence of the market of perfect competition through welfare economics, the issue we must now deal with concerns the difficulties that the theory encounters in attempting to prove the two fundamental theorems of welfare and the assumptions it must introduce for this purpose. The problem arises at two distinct theoretical levels.

First, it is possible to question the validity of the underlying *methodological assumptions* of the competitive model and the worldview implicit in them. In particular, as mentioned earlier, the dominant theory's method consists of starting from three fundamental data – technology, individual preferences and the endowments of individuals – which are treated as external to the model and are therefore not themselves explained as products of the competitive interaction. Such a methodological choice, as we shall see, is far less innocent than it would appear at first sight.

Second, we must consider the specific *analytical assumptions* that have to be introduced to mathematically develop the model. The exogeneity of technology, preferences and endowments is in fact only a general methodological assumption. In order to obtain specific results (propositions, theorems, corollaries) these assumptions must be specified analytically and mathematically. Thus, the field is further circumscribed, not obviously with an eye to the conditions of realism, but with respect solely to analytical convenience, formal elegance and the analyst's mathematical abilities. Of these analytical restrictions, the first ones we must discuss concern the conditions of *existence* of the equilibrium and its Pareto efficiency. A second type of restriction then concerns the further restrictive assumptions that must be introduced for the equilibrium to also be *unique* and *stable*. Indeed, as we shall see, from the point of view of the general coherence of the theory, it is only when the equilibrium exists and is unique and stable that it makes sense to discuss its normative implications in terms of Pareto efficiency. Finally, as a third set of restrictions, for the purpose of proving the two welfare theorems, a number of specific assumptions must be introduced to prevent the occurrence of so-called *market failures*.

## Methodological assumptions

The dominant economic theory is based on three sets of assumptions concerning technology, preferences and endowments of individuals. They are common not only to orthodox neoclassical theory but also to the various heterodox versions of the market model that, with the new liberal wind, have regained respect at the academic level (classical Smithian approach, Austrian school, the theory of contestable markets) and to those critical theories that question market efficiency from within, that is, accept the methodology of neoclassical theory, but not the additional analytical assumptions necessary to demonstrate Pareto efficiency (neo-institutionalism, neo-Keynesian theory and parts of the radical school). It is from these general methodological hypotheses that the neoliberal theory constructs the schema that serves to discuss the rationality, efficiency and desirability of the market. Let us therefore look at them in detail.

### *Technology*

According to the dominant economic theory, technology is given. The analysis of the technological structure and its changes is the task of the engineer, not of the economist. The economist, in his various mathematical formulations, is able to consider different types of technology. The crucial point, however, is that whatever assumptions he/she makes about the technological structure, these are part of a methodological approach according to which technology is an exogenous variable to the model and must therefore be taken as given in economic theory. Moreover, according to the assumptions of the competitive model, technology is in the public domain, which excludes information asymmetries and implies that any technological innovation that comes out of the engineer's drawer becomes immediately available to all.

### *Preferences*

According to the dominant economic theory, preferences are given. The analysis of individual preferences, their origin and changes, is the task of the psychologist, not of the economist. As with technology, the economist can of course formalize different structures of individual preferences. These, however, must be taken as a fact in the economic problem, not as a phenomenon to be explained. Thus, here too, thanks to the compartmentalization of sciences, the economist unloads the problem.

### *Endowments*

According to the dominant economic theory, endowments are given. Here, however, economic theory does not quite know who to entrust with the thankless task of their study. Who if not the economist should explain how economic resources are distributed among agents and how this allocation is the result of a market-centred process of social interaction? The fact remains that even in this case, without much justification, the economist prefers to take the problem as given.

Let us analyse the limits of realism of these methodological assumptions. Let us begin with *technology*. Neoclassical theory states that technology is exogenous to the economic model and is publicly accessible. In reality, however, technological development is one of the main keys to economic success. US world leadership, both militarily and economically, is heavily dependent on high-tech supremacy. This primacy allows for geopolitical and economic hegemonic policies in which several countries would like to participate, but which, after the fall of Soviet Union and before the rise of China, no other country would dream of undertaking as a leader. Space missions, telecommunication advancements, systems for intercepting and managing information, genetic manipulation, biotechnology and climate control not only demonstrate the state of technological advancement of the United States but are in turn the weapons of US economic power. According to some analysts, moreover, the importance of the military apparatus, with the leading role of the American Air Force and the American Navy, and an articulated series of organizations that channel private investment and scientific research according to military needs, is one of the keys to US technological supremacy (see, e.g. Bernstein, 2001). In 2023, global military spending was 2.4 trillion dollars, 37% of which came from the United States. The runner-up, China, spent less than a third of that (12% of global spending), followed at some distance by Russia (4.5%), India (3.4%), Saudi Arabia (3.1%) and the United Kingdom (3.1%). No other country in the world exceeds three per cent of global spending (Statista, 2024).

Historically, one of the most powerful organizations linking academia and military interests is undoubtedly the *Rand Corporation*. The *Rand Corporation* is a think tank (research institute with a major scientific and cultural impact) located in Santa Monica, California. The original project that led to its establishment developed during World War II when the US Department of Defence began recruiting leading physicists, mathematicians, economists, political scientists, engineers, psychologists, and communications experts from the academic and scientific worlds to work on projects of national defence interest, from international espionage techniques to the development of the atomic bomb. In 1945, commissioned by the *Douglas Aircraft Company*, the US Air Force initiated the *Rand Project* (*Rand* stands for 'Research and Development'). As the war came to an end, the American military authorities (especially the Air Force generals) insisted on turning the *Rand Project* into an enduring peacetime research centre. In 1948, the *Rand Project* separated from the *Douglas Aircraft Company* and became a non-profit agency, the *Rand Corporation*, with the aim of creating an effective and lasting link between military strategy, scientific research and the political apparatus. Many leading figures from the major American universities passed through the *Rand*, and it was at *Rand* that important milestones in theoretical and applied research were marked, rewarded by a large number of Nobel prizes. The technological contributions of *Rand*'s researchers go far beyond the development of new weapons and strategies for their 'efficient' use and include practically all fields of strategic interest in the post-war geopolitical context: it is at *Rand* that important results are obtained in space research, in the development of computers and artificial intelligence systems, in information transmission technology (which will later become the basis for the development of the internet) and in the optimal solution of logistical and strategic problems. Given the strategic importance of the research conducted, the work within *Rand* during the Cold War years remained largely top secret, so much so that the journal *Magazine* describes *Rand*'s site in Santa Monica as one of the most difficult American buildings to gain access to. Today, the research objectives of the *Rand Corporation* have greatly expanded on the economic and social fronts and include subjects such as poverty, crime, urban decay, the environment, health and education system problems, obesity, drug use, and of course anything that has to do even indirectly with American national security.[3]

The 'virtuous' circle between investment in technological innovation, economic gains from technological supremacy, and new investments produces cumulative processes that tend to increase, not decrease, the gap with other countries. This does not mean, of course, that there are no countervailing trends that could undermine American supremacy in the medium and long term. Nor does it imply that the United States has an absolute monopoly in high technology and, in particular, the military industry. On the contrary, alongside them a handful of countries claim their exclusive right to nuclear weapons and, on the basis of this, claim to prevent others from joining the club of the powerful. But from the more limited point of view, we are dealing with – the realism of the hypotheses of the theoretical model – what is of interest is that this is not only not contemplated in the theory of perfect markets but even incompatible with it.

To grasp the unrealism of the exogenous technology hypothesis, however, one need not look that far. The choice of one technological trajectory rather than another has important social, political and economic repercussions even in events at home. In fact, technology has a significant impact on industrial relations systems and on social relations in general: think of the assembly line that concentrates a large mass of workers in the same area, causing changes at a social, trade union and political level (and the feedback effects of these on economic variables) and compare it with the new technologies based on telework (which is nothing more than the new form of the old institution of piecework) in which the opportunities for socialization and solidarity between workers are reduced to a minimum, or with the impetuous spread of informatics platforms and algorithms that impose work rhythms, shifts, rewards and punishments without workers ever coming into contact with the architect of their exploitation.

There is no need to multiply examples, let us rather see what the general implications of the technological hypothesis are. The hypothesis that technology is provided from outside the economic system ('by the engineer') is not only naïve but also misleading because it makes us lose sight of the economic actors who finance, direct, coordinate and apply technological innovations: companies (and, in certain cases, the state and its organizations, as well as often international organizations). By erasing the problem at its source, the economist gives the erroneous impression that there is no problem with the choice of technological trajectories and that it is therefore not even worth discussing. Yet, the upstream control of technological development trajectories affects international relations, defines patterns of social relations and conditions the entire structure of economic, trade union and political relations.

Let us turn to *preferences*. According to methodological individualism, to which all neoliberal currents belong, all economic and social phenomena must be explained starting from individuals and their interactions. The individual is therefore a starting point for the analysis and must not be explained as a product of society and the economy. The individual, according to the general economic equilibrium model, is represented 1) by a system of exogenously defined preferences and 2) by the behavioural assumption that he/she will try to maximize the realization of these preferences with the instruments at his/her disposal.

These hypotheses are introduced without any attempt by the proponents of the model to prove their validity. They are proposed as hypotheses but in fact become dogmas to be accepted as acts of faith. In fact, any behaviour, even the most absurd, can always be interpreted from the point of view of methodological individualism, as the result of an optimal choice based on certain (given, but unknown) preferences. This undermines those who wish to challenge these hypotheses by claiming, for example, that in reality individuals often cannot even do elementary arithmetic, and it would therefore seem strange to assume that they inspire their economic behaviour to sophisticated optimization criteria. In fact, such an objection cannot be proved, just as the supporters of methodological individualism cannot prove the contrary, since any choice can be very good or very bad depending on the preferences of each individual and these are known only to the person concerned. This constitutes a problem from a methodological point of view because, in the field of science, if there is not even the theoretical possibility of falsifying a theory, any possibility of comparison between alternative approaches falls away (and the boundaries between science and religion fall away as well).[4]

While on the technological discourse, partly out of ignorance, partly out of humility, the hypothesis of technology's exogenousness, however debatable, might have seemed worthy of respect, here, by contrast, one might want to dismiss the problem as simply nonsense. How is it possible that the most rigorous of social scientists (at least that is how economists consider themselves) do not realize that a large part of the economic problem of those who produce and sell consists in creating a preference, if not a need, a necessity, for their product? What, then, do the overpaid marketing departments do? What is the purpose of the advertising bombardment we are constantly subjected to? To inform us about the properties of a new product that might respond to our innate preferences? I doubt that anyone really believes this. Advertising, the control of information, and the active production of consumption models are real instruments of domination that not only affect the individual's preferences and behavioural patterns but also impede the very functioning of the competitive mechanism, given the very high costs of advertising campaigns. From the point of view of resource allocation, then, how is it possible to argue that two companies investing in advertising in an attempt to take market share from each other produces Pareto-efficient results? If the mad race for advertising would slow down a bit, would this not be a Pareto improvement? The two companies would save resources (that could be used in ways that really improve the quality of their product) and we would be able to watch a film on the TV in two hours instead of four.

In the academic field, then, the work of heterodox schools critical of the neoclassical model has highlighted the limits of the individualistic approach in the analysis of consumption. Thorstein Veblen's contribution is, in this respect, a classic. Veblen argues that it is not possible for individuals to evaluate a good outside the context in which it is presented and that the very ends that are pursued through consumption are essentially social in nature. Consumption patterns serve primarily to assert one's position in the social hierarchy, one's status, not to maximize an exogenous utility function based on innate preferences (Veblen, 1899).

Not to mention how political preferences are also influenced by the market. How is it possible to form a political opinion when information itself is in the hands of interested parties? How can one think that political competition is won by the best or the luckiest when economic and information means constitute an insurmountable barrier to entry into politics? As soon as Berlusconi announced his entry into politics, the question of his political leadership immediately arose; I have been in politics for decades and no one has yet noticed. Since I am lucky, it will undoubtedly be because of my incapacity. . . . But what about the United States, the heart of the capitalist system, where skill and luck only seem to attend the Bush and Clinton houses (George and George W. on one side, William, aka Bill, and Hillary on the other) or other very rich and powerful men struggling to get richer and more powerful? Are all Americans also incompetent and unlucky?

But then, why does the theory so naively expose itself to such an obvious criticism of realism? The truth is that the assumption that preferences are given and thus not influenced in the slightest degree by the market process is crucial to the entire normative theory of the market. What would be the point of proving that the market satisfies the sovereign-consumer if it were found that the consumer is not even sovereign of what he/she wants because it is the market society itself that makes him/her want it? But there is no need to go so far as to argue that the individual is a mere product of society. The theory also breaks down if one merely admits that the individual is just influenced by society.

Methodology is not independent of worldview. Claiming that the individual is a given, that it is not influenced by any external factor, is not a simple choice of method. It reflects a conception of economic reality in which society itself does not exist other than as a collection of isolated individuals. In such a conception, there is no place for causal links from society to the individual simply because society does not exist. The hypothesis that the individual can be influenced by society can have no place in such a methodology of scientific investigation.

Finally, *endowments*. Endowments, which the economist takes as a given in the problem, are clearly the product of the market process. At time $t$, endowments may well be taken as given, if one wants to focus on how they will affect the distribution of resources at time $t+1$. But it goes without saying that, if this is the logic, it is foolish not to ask the question of how endowments at time $t$ themselves are the product of the interactions that took place at time $t-1$. From this point of view, it might seem that this is an initial hypothesis introduced for the sole purpose of having a point of attack to the problem (which otherwise would have neither head nor tail), to be questioned at a later date, through a more general theory that finally explains the historical processes of wealth (and poverty) accumulation. Instead, the point of attack remains the only point of analysis, and time $t-1$ is never investigated (except through the usual speculative method of *ex post* rationalization, in an attempt to explain how even at times $t-1$, $t-2$, . . . and back as far as time $0$, all interactions have always resulted in Pareto improvements that are unanimously desired).

Students of economics who expect to understand a little better the mechanisms that have led to the fortune or misfortune of particular families, alliances, industrial and financial groups, states and economic areas will find themselves faced with nothing but great disappointment (unless they decide to study economic history in its true sense, that which explains the reality of time $t$ as the product of interactions at time $t-1$, taking time $t-1$ for what it is and not for what it should have been, so that time $t$ can be interpreted as its Pareto improvement).

The theoretical importance of the hypothesis that endowments are a datum of the problem that need not be investigated is closely linked to the definition of the Pareto principle as a criterion of efficiency. The problem to be explained is not why at time $t$ individual $A$ has 100 and individual $B$ has one. The problem is instead to show that, this being the case, it would be better if at time $t+1$ at least one of the two subjects had a little more, without the other having a little less (Pareto criterion). Thus, first case, if at time $t+1$, $A$ ends up with 1000 and $B$ keeps his one, this means that the market works. If, on the other hand, in the second case, $A$ ends up with 99 and $B$ for example with 70, then the market is not efficient. Taking the endowments at time $t$ as given and assuming the Pareto efficiency criterion, all the general economic equilibrium theorist can hope to prove is that, under certain conditions, the first case is realized. What an economics scholar should ask instead is why we should care about Pareto efficiency.

With the introduction of these bizarre hypotheses, a peculiar division of labour begins to emerge between the theoretical economist, the methodological economist and the political apologist. The theorist introduces the hypotheses that are most comfortable to him, with the sole condition that, from them, the thesis be rigorously demonstrated. This general way of doing theory is defended by the methodological economist, who argues that it is only in the application phase that the problem of the realism of hypotheses arises, but that, in an abstract sense, the validity of a theory depends only on its internal consistency. The politician, backed by his/her right to technical incompetence, takes the theorist's result (the thesis) and draws the appropriate applied conclusions from it.

Faced with this situation, one first goes to the theorist to ask for an explanation of the hypothesis introduced. But his/her answer admits no reply: 'I am only a theorist, and it is not my job to empirically verify the validity of the hypotheses'. Then one attacks the methodological economist, who is responsible for the protective shield created for the theorist. But the methodological expert correctly points out that a theory that is based on unrealistic hypotheses is not to be rejected because even negative results can be extremely useful. The problem is, if anything, in the possible misuse of the theory. At this point, one seems to have spotted the weak link in the chain and goes to the politician and asks him/her how it is that the thesis (that the market works) is stated so clearly by him/her while in his/her speeches there is no trace of the hypotheses necessary for the demonstration. And the politician then sends you back to the theorist: 'wouldn't you expect a politician to discuss the hypotheses introduced by eminent scientists?!'

## Existence and Pareto efficiency of the competitive equilibrium

Let us now analyse the analytical restrictions necessary for the demonstration of the existence of a general economic equilibrium. These are hypotheses introduced for the sole purpose of making the mathematical problem tractable and guaranteeing a solution to the model, not hypotheses derived from the observation of empirical reality. According to the axiomatic method, in fact, the restrictions necessary and/or sufficient for the existence of equilibrium are not introduced by deriving them from the analysis of the actual behaviour of consumers and producers. The question of the realism of the assumptions is deliberately left out of the general economic equilibrium theory, deferring its assessment to empirical studies.

Thus, for example, in the case of *technology*, the methodological assumption that it is externally given is further restricted on the analytical level by excluding a whole series of technological possibilities, which, of course, continue to exist in reality even if they disappear from the model and are incompatible with Pareto efficiency of the market. (On the technological restrictions that must be imposed for the purposes of the Pareto efficiency of the market thesis I will return shortly, as this is an issue that has been developed extensively in the field of market failure theory.)

In the case of *preferences*, one must instead specify particular preference structures compatible with Pareto efficiency, which means that our preferences, even if innate, must nevertheless respect certain restrictions (which, translated into mathematical terms, allow for Pareto efficiency). In fact, the theory of consumer behaviour is constructed from a series of axioms about preferences (in philosophy, an axiom is an a priori true hypothesis, a self-evident truth that does not need demonstration). Of these axioms, two are fundamental to the entire neoclassical construction, in the sense that without them the neoclassical modelling of human behaviour would not even be possible; others are introduced as additional restrictions in order to obtain particular theoretical results, such as existence, stability, uniqueness and Pareto efficiency of equilibrium.

The first two axioms, those that are vital to neoclassical theory, state that preferences are 1) complete and 2) transitive. In formal terms, the axiom of completeness states that, taken any two baskets of goods $X$ and $Y$ (or, more simply, taken given quantities of any two goods $X$ and $Y$), a consumer is always able to determine whether he prefers $X$ to $Y$, $Y$ to $X$ or is indifferent between the two. In other words, the consumer should have no dilemma in choosing between two baskets: either he/she unequivocally prefers the former, or he/she unequivocally prefers the latter, or it means that the two baskets are equivalent for him/her; what is excluded is that the consumer may have doubts as to which basket best suits his/her tastes. The axiom of transitivity states instead that given three baskets $X$, $Y$ and $Z$, if a consumer prefers $X$ to $Y$, and $Y$ to $Z$, then he/she also prefers $X$ to $Z$. This axiom constitutes a kind of internal consistency condition in the consumer's choice criteria.

Alongside these two axioms are then introduced the axioms of 3) monotonicity, 4) continuity and 5) convexity. Without going into the details of these additional axioms, which require some familiarity with formal analysis in order to be discussed in depth, I will limit myself here to discussing some of their economic implications. Take convexity: in non-formal terms, it implies that when faced with two goods with respect to which the consumer is indifferent, the consumer always prefers a mix of the two goods. For example, I find one plate of pasta and one plate of rice equally good, so, according to axiomatic preference theory, it is true a priori that I prefer two half-portions of pasta and rice instead of one good plate of one or the other. And yet I detest 'tastings' and there is no restaurateur who has ever managed to convince me to opt for two half-portions instead of a whole one. So, it only takes me, with my non-convex preferences, to blow the Pareto efficiency of the market of perfect competition.

Obviously, the neoclassical economist does not allow himself/herself to be so naively defeated, and immediately hastens to relax the axiom of convexity and introduce others, with the usual aim of proving theorems on general economic equilibrium and its normative properties. Of course, there is nothing that prevents me from empirically contesting the validity of the newly introduced axioms, but, even though I am an economist, I have by now realized that this is just a game of formal logic in which nobody cares about the true preferences of individuals. At the empirical level, it is in fact well known that the axioms on preferences, both the first two (those strictly necessary for the construction of economic models according to neoclassical methodology) and the others (those necessary for the demonstration of particular properties of the market of perfect competition) are generally not verified. Many experiments in social psychology have shown that real people, unlike those in the model, choose according to criteria that are completely different from those of constrained optimization, giving rise to results that are often incompatible with the neoclassical axioms: apart from the easy examples of violations of monotonicity, continuity and convexity, empirical research has shown that in numerous circumstances consumers are not even able to order the different available alternatives among themselves (incompleteness of preferences), nor, when faced with problems of a certain complexity, do they comply with the conditions of internal consistency required by the axiom of transitivity.

This, however, is not enough to prevent neoclassical economists from continuing to play with their models, introducing and removing axioms and assumptions with the greatest of ease, as if the real goal was the model itself and not its ability to explain reality. But the truth is that a game should at least be fun. Instead, the only ones having fun are those who believe that to become a good economist one must prove oneself capable of playing with the most absurd models, leaving aside the problems of the world. Universities have in fact long since stopped teaching economics as a critical science of society (if they ever did), and instead devote themselves to selecting aspiring economists on the basis of their skills as players with formal models – skills that ensure that good economists, instead of asking questions, and perhaps developing criticisms, only try to answer the questions that are put to them time after time.

Let us now turn to *endowments*. Here a decidedly strong hypothesis is introduced, according to which all individuals in the model have an initial endowment of goods that allows them to survive even without the need to engage in market exchanges (the so-called 'consumer survival' hypothesis). From a mathematical point of view, this hypothesis is extremely important for what we might call 'technical' reasons (in the sense that, without it, it would not even be possible to prove the existence of equilibrium).[5] However, from an economic point of view, this hypothesis has no foundation: it implies that no one is obliged to sell his/her labour power in order to obtain in exchange a wage that allows himself/herself and his/her family to live (a hypothesis that is evidently false for the great majority of the population of any real existing market economy).

This assumption, often 'forgotten' even in many high-quality expositions of the Arrow-Debreu model, has important implications for the general image the model provides of capitalist interaction. Thanks to it, market exchange can be represented as a purely voluntary fact, based solely on mutual benefit. On the normative level, then, it allows for the a priori exclusion of the entire discourse of the objective needs of individuals (the need for water and nutrition, the need for physical and mental health, needs of a social and cultural nature etc.), assuming by hypothesis that each person could satisfy his/her own needs even without having to go through the market. This, moreover, is the only theoretical factor that justifies the adoption of a normative criterion (the Pareto criterion) entirely centred on subjective preferences and completely unrelated to objective needs: the problem of the welfare economy is in fact not to determine whether, with the existing endowments, market interaction allows for the satisfaction of needs, but, let us repeat it once again, to demonstrate that, as a result of the interaction, someone is a little better off than before.

## Uniqueness and stability of the competitive equilibrium

As we said, the analytical hypotheses of the Arrow-Debreu model are introduced for the sole purpose of verifying its implications in terms of the existence or non-existence of equilibrium. The introduction of a particular mathematical hypothesis is thus reduced to a purely logical-deductive exercise. Following this logic of economic analysis, regardless of the degree of realism of the hypotheses, the internal consistency of the model then becomes extremely important. For the purposes of the general internal consistency of the model, however, in addition to the problem we have just dealt with of the existence of an equilibrium configuration, two further problems arise concerning the uniqueness and stability of the equilibrium. Indeed, for the model to be considered a coherent tool from an interpretative and/or normative point of view, the analytical restrictions introduced must allow all three problems of the existence, uniqueness and stability of equilibrium to be resolved. Let us try to understand why.

The demonstration of the existence of an equilibrium is equivalent to stating that if the system, for some reason, is in such a position, there would be no forces tending to move it. Since each agent is already achieving the maximum possible within its decision-making constraints, no one will change its behaviour unless the data on the basis of which each agent determines its optimal behaviour change. In this case, if the equilibrium turns out to be Pareto-efficient, it would seem fair to assume that Pareto efficiency is a lasting characteristic of the system.

However, if perfect competition were compatible with different equilibrium situations (non-uniqueness of the competitive equilibrium), the problem of determining which of the equilibrium configurations would actually tend to materialize would remain open. The most serious implication of this problem probably concerns so-called comparative statics. With multiple equilibria it is in fact impossible to carry out those comparative exercises, much used by economists when providing their recipes, consisting in analysing the system's displacements in the face of a change in the model data. Suppose, in fact, that in examining his/her model, the economist determines that it is appropriate to move the system from position *A* to position *B*. He might then be tempted to intervene in the data on which the equilibrium position depends, changing it so that the new solution at the aggregate level is *B* and no longer *A*. However, if with the new data in the model, the equilibrium is not unique, that is, there is a second equilibrium *C* in addition to equilibrium *B*, it will still be impossible to determine which of the new equilibrium positions the system will actually move towards as a result of the change in data. In such circumstances, not only does the model not help to understand the real shifts in the economic system over time, but it is also useless from a regulatory point of view.

Moreover, assuming that the competitive equilibrium exists, be Pareto-efficient and unique, if it were not also stable, that is, if there were no forces capable of leading the system towards equilibrium from positions of disequilibrium, the slightest perturbation of the equilibrium position would suffice to progressively move the system away from conditions of equilibrium and, hence, Pareto efficiency.

This means that, in order for the general economic equilibrium model to be interpreted as theoretical support for the market mechanism, in addition to the restrictions necessary to prove the existence of the equilibrium and its Pareto efficiency, additional restrictive assumptions must be introduced that also guarantee the uniqueness and stability of the equilibrium.

We have already seen, with regard to the dynamic conception of competition developed by Hayek, how the problem of equilibrium stability is one of the least fruitful chapters of the entire research on the capacity of the market system to self-regulate. Indeed, let us recall that Sonnenschein's theorem demonstrates the impossibility of excluding cases of equilibrium instability in the Arrow-Debreu model. The same theorem also has equally strong implications for the problem of uniqueness of the general economic equilibrium. Indeed, the mathematical conditions required for stability are very similar to those required for uniqueness of equilibrium. Sonnenschein's theorem, by demonstrating that the assumptions of neoclassical theory are insufficient to guarantee these mathematical conditions, therefore also nullifies all attempts to solve the problem of uniqueness of equilibrium.[6]

Both in the case of stability and uniqueness, in the face of this heavy negative result, neoclassical theory has attempted to reduce the damage by introducing a series of additional mathematical hypotheses that allow to exclude the cases of multiplicity and instability of equilibria on which Sonnenschein's result is based. This evidently amounts to abandoning the initial project aimed at explaining, under general conditions, the functioning of markets and proving their Pareto efficiency. Even in this less ambitious view, however, the problem is that the additional hypotheses that are to be introduced are of little significance from an economic point of view and above all have no empirical confirmation. Furthermore, they impose a series of completely arbitrary restrictions on the overall structure of the economic system that violate the fundamental methodological assumption of neoclassical theory that all economic phenomena must be traced back solely to the assumptions about individuals' behaviour.[7]

Faced with Sonnenschein's theorem, which demonstrates the impossibility of obtaining satisfactory general results on the functioning of markets within the framework of the general economic equilibrium model, neoclassical theory has therefore not reconsidered its scientific project. On the contrary, it has chosen to continue along its path in a stubborn attempt to obtain a predefined result, even at the cost of introducing hypotheses of pure convenience. This probably helps to keep the main research of the most established school of economic thought on its feet, but it certainly distances the theoretical model more and more from the reality it would like to explain and prevents (or, at least, should prevent) the normative results obtained from being applied to the real world.

In view of the joint importance of the three problems of existence, uniqueness and stability of equilibrium, some commentators have concluded that the results achieved with regard to stability and uniqueness (in addition to other problems concerning the conditions of existence, on which I cannot dwell here) are sufficient to demolish the entire general economic equilibrium research programme (for a critical, precise and articulate review of the research on the general economic equilibrium model, see Guerrien (1985)).[8] From this point of view, the very way in which this model is academically taught should be reassessed, as it has been superseded by the theoretical results obtained from neoclassical theory itself.

The need for a general reconsideration of the academic teaching of neoclassical theory is one of the claims of the 'post-autistic' movement, which was born in France in 2000 from the initiative of a group of students, and rapidly developed internationally, with the participation also of economists with important academic and institutional positions (the website of this movement is www.paecon.net). According to some of the spokesmen of this movement, the study of general economic equilibrium, which today constitutes the hard core of all 'microeconomics' teaching, should be completely revised, placing it within a course on the history of economic thought, as an example of one of the least fruitful research chapters in the entire discipline.

## Market failures

Let us now consider the problem of market failures. There are three broad categories of market failures, that is, situations in which the market of perfect competition is inefficient according to Pareto: *increasing returns to scale*, *externalities* and *public goods*.

We speak of *constant*, *increasing* or *decreasing returns to scale* when, by doubling the inputs, the output increases by twice as much, by more than twice as much or by less than twice as much. Linked to these concepts are those of *economies* and *diseconomies of scale*. The former allow unit costs to be economized as the size of the production plant increases; the latter occur when costs per unit of output increase as the scale of production increases. While the concept of returns to scale refers strictly to the technological structure, the concept of economies of scale also involves input costs, which may also vary as the quantity produced varies. For example, a large firm may be able to source at a lower cost than a small firm and this may be sufficient to reduce the cost per unit of output even in the presence of a technology with constant returns to scale (simply because it pays less for the inputs).

Examples of technologies with increasing returns to scale abound empirically. A typical example is containers: with six square metres of material one can build a container with a volume of one cubic metre (six square surfaces with a side of one metre); with 24 square metres of material one can build a container with a volume of eight cubic metres (six square surfaces with a side of two metres). The material used is increased by four times, the volume obtained by eight. Economies of scale are then even more widespread: the supermarket cuts costs better than the small shop, industrial production costs less than handicraft production.

Technologies with constant returns to scale are also relatively widespread. They characterize all those productions in which inputs must be combined according to fixed proportions. For example, to build a car you always need four wheels (and thus a certain proportion of rubber), a tractor cannot be driven by two individuals at the same time, and, more generally, most machinery only works with a specific number of workers (which means that if you want to increase production, you have to increase both the machinery and the number of workers in the same proportion).

On the contrary, the difficulty of encountering technologies with diminishing returns to scale in reality stems from the conceptual problem that, if the output increases by less than twice as much when the inputs double, it is always possible to divide the production plant in two and use the same quantities of the inputs in each of the two new plants, thus obtaining twice as much product. Let us imagine, for example, that with a certain production plant, it takes five cubic metres of wood to produce one table and 11 cubic metres of wood to produce two tables. But then, having to produce two tables, it would be better to split the plant into two separate plants and use five cubic metres of wood in each of them, thus obtaining the two tables with ten cubic metres of wood, instead of 11. In technical terms, this means that when faced with a technology with diminishing returns of scale, it is always possible to achieve production with at least constant returns of scale (by decreasing the size of the plant and increasing the number of plants). The assumption of diminishing returns to scale is thus incompatible with the assumption that the production techniques used are chosen from within a technologically efficient set.

Curiously, however, the Arrow-Debreu model discards the hypothesis of increasing returns to scale, not that of decreasing returns to scale (constant returns to scale pose some theoretical problems but are nevertheless contemplated in the model). The reason for this singular assumption about technology has, in fact, nothing to do with questions of realism, but is rather dictated by questions of 'theoretical convenience': with increasing returns to scale, monopolistic markets characterized by large production facilities are more efficient in a technical sense (they produce at lower unit costs) than markets characterized by the presence of many small producers in competition with each other and this impedes Pareto efficiency in the competitive market. So why not remove such a hypothesis from the model altogether and consider only those technological hypotheses that are compatible with the Pareto efficiency of the market of perfect competition? The mathematical game is simple. But it is clear that this may resolve the issue in the model, but certainly not in reality, where increasing returns to scale abound and technologies compatible with the Pareto efficiency of perfect competition are scarce.[9]

As for the conceptual problems posed by diminishing returns to scale, these are solved (even if only at a formal level) through the assumption that, in the model, the number of production plants is fixed. This prevents the process of subdividing the production plants into smaller and smaller units, which would eventually lead to an infinity of plants of infinitesimal size, from being set in motion. Even this expedient, however, only serves to solve the problem in the model, certainly not in reality. In reality, in fact, the number of plants is not fixed, and if a technology with diminishing returns really were to arise, companies, which hypothetically optimize everything, would not hesitate to subdivide their plants into smaller and smaller units.

*Externalities* are effects of a subject's economic activity on other subjects that do not pass through the market. We speak of negative or positive externalities depending on whether other actors suffer harm or benefit from such economic activity.

A case of negative externality is that of the enterprise that discharges waste products of the industrial process into the environment, increasing pollution. A famous example of a positive externality is that of the beekeeper's activity that has positive effects on the adjacent orchard as the bees help the fertilization of the flowers. Beyond the textbook examples of economics, the phenomenon of externalities is general in social interactions since, despite the spread of markets, every action produces a series of consequences for which there is no economic compensation: if you fertilize your field on which my dining room overlooks, I cannot claim for compensation for the inconvenience you cause me, nor can you get a reparation for the noise I produce when I practise punk-hardcore drumming in your meditation hour; when McDonald's spreads the smell of its products in the air, it is not obliged to compensate me for the disgust I feel, nor can it demand a reward from cheeseburger lovers just for the mouth-watering it makes them feel.

From the point of view of economic theory, this creates a difference between the private cost (the cost borne by the company) and the social cost (the cost borne by society as a whole) of economic activity. In the case of the polluting company, it will act on the basis of minimizing its own 'private costs', which, however, are lower than the 'social costs', that is, those it brings to society as a whole (which also include the damage suffered by others). Indeed, the company does not have to compensate anyone for the pollution it produces, nor can consumers with sufficient willingness to pay against pollution offer a reward to the polluting company to entice it to use fewer polluting techniques. The result is a production of more pollution than that compatible with Pareto efficiency.

As in the case of technology, in order to avoid the occurrence of inefficiency, appropriate assumptions must be introduced into the Arrow-Debreu model. The assumption that is introduced here is that a complete system of markets exists (i.e. that there is a special market where any effect of social interaction, such as 'pollution rights', can be bought and sold). This basically removes the problem of externalities from the theoretical model, since any effect of social interaction becomes, by definition, internal to the logic of the market.

The definition of a *public good* is purely theoretical and does not refer to the fact that the good is produced by the public sector. (Pure) public goods have two fundamental properties: 1) 'non-excludability' (the exclusion of an additional consumer from the enjoyment of the good is impossible); 2) 'non-rivalry' (the enjoyment of the good by an additional consumer costs nothing, which means that exclusion is not even desirable, according to individualistic logic). Next to pure public goods, mixed public goods are defined as those goods that enjoy one or the other property according to different degrees.

A textbook example of a pure public good are light buoys as an aid to navigation: once installed, it is neither technically possible nor economically viable to prevent ships of competing companies or foreign countries from also using them. Examples of mixed public goods are numerous and range from national defence to public hygiene, from transport services to fire brigades.

From a regulatory point of view, the existence of mixed public goods is sufficient to prevent the Pareto efficiency of the market of perfect competition. In the presence of public goods, pure or mixed, in fact, no one has an interest in financing the production of the good since they realize that the benefits produced will also be enjoyed by others and will therefore wait for other subjects to subsidize it (in literature this problem is called 'free-riding', an expression that refers to the case of people who use public transport without paying the ticket, counting on the fact that the service is in any case financed by the tickets paid by other travellers). Symmetrically, no private enterprise will have an interest in producing the good since, once it has been produced, it will then be impossible for it to exclude others from its enjoyment, and it will therefore be impossible to make a profit from its sale.

In the case of pure public goods, the result is that no one will take action to produce the good and the community will be left without a good that would benefit so many different people (although the cost of installing a light buoy is modest and the social benefit it produces is considerable, no one will want to contribute to the installation costs). In the case of mixed public goods, on the other hand, the level of production will be positive but still insufficient with respect to the Pareto-efficient level (the Pareto-efficient level of production, for public goods, was determined by Paul Samuelson (1954) and depends on the different willingness to pay of different individuals; attempting to put Samuelson's solution into practice, however, raises the problem of correctly identifying each individual's willingness to pay).

Consider, for example, rail transport. It obviously makes no sense for trains to run with lots of empty seats (or with overcrowded second-class cars and half-empty first-class cars) and it would be more efficient from a Pareto point of view to allow free-rider passengers to travel by train without having paid for a ticket by occupying the empty seats (or to allow second-class travellers to sit in first class): the total benefits would increase without any increase in total costs. This, however, as we said, is not feasible because if the principle applied that one could occupy empty seats without paying a ticket, everyone would want to be a free-rider, and no one would pay a ticket with the result that no railway company would find it profitable to offer the transport service.

If, under these circumstances, one leaves it to the market, one must first set a price at which to sell the rail transport service. At that price, travellers with a sufficiently high willingness to pay (i.e. those rich enough and willing to travel) will be able to enjoy rail transport, while the others will be excluded (this solution is feasible because we are considering a mixed public good in which exclusion of consumers is technically possible). The result is far from Pareto-efficient (since other users would be able to enjoy the service without cost increases) but at least allows for positive output. In the case of pure public goods, instead, in which exclusion is not technically possible (the light buoy in the middle of the sea), the output of the good will tend to be even lower, or at most nil, since consumers know that they will still be able to enjoy the good even without any monetary outlay.

To avoid these problems, the general economic equilibrium model simply assumes that there are no public goods, neither pure nor mixed.

With these clarifications on the logic of the general economic equilibrium model and its developments in the field of market failures we are now in a better position to understand the neoclassical approach to the study of state-market relations. In a nutshell, the general economic equilibrium model determines the theoretical conditions for Pareto efficiency in the competitive market; the theory of market failures, on the other hand, studies the situations in which these conditions are not met. This general approach dictates that in the presence of increasing returns to scale, externalities and public goods, the state must intervene to re-establish the Pareto efficiency conditions that the market of perfect competition fails to achieve.

Such a justification of state intervention as a substitute for imperfect markets raises, however, a theoretical problem. For, if the assumptions of neoclassical theory of perfect information and unlimited mathematical capabilities in solving optimization problems apply, then centralized state planning can still achieve Pareto efficiency even in cases where the market of perfect competition does not give rise to 'failures'. In other words, in cases where the market works 'well', planning works equally well; in cases where the market 'fails', planning still works well. Therefore, in the neoclassical view, the problem of the relationship between the state and the market could be solved simply by eliminating markets, in all their forms, and leaving the state to manage the economy entirely. After all, the state may well install a light buoy in the sea and a railway network on land, offering these services free of charge to all, and subsidizing itself through the general fiscality and, by the same logic, may produce the goods and services currently produced by private enterprises.

However, this conclusion should not be misinterpreted. From the point of view of the critique of the neoclassical conception of state-market relations, the critique just developed takes on significance above all as an internal critique. Indeed, the problem lies in the inconsistency between the model's assumptions and the normative prescriptions it attempts to derive from them. However, as we have seen, neoclassical theory is also unconvincing from numerous other points of view, including the validity of its methodological choices and the realism of its assumptions. In this sense, it is extremely dangerous from a scientific point of view to attempt to derive the superiority of central planning solely from this theoretical result since, in so doing, one exposes oneself to exactly the same criticisms of method and realism to which neoclassical theory is exposed. As I shall argue later, the advantages of planning do not lie so much in its potential for efficiency (which, however, should not be underestimated when considering the prevalence of market failures in reality) as in the possibility of combining efficiency and social objectives in a context of real economic democracy. For the time being, however, one thing is certain: for all those who believed they could defend the market through the construction of a theoretical framework highlighting its virtues (the general economic equilibrium model), it must not have been a great blow to discover that, in that same theoretical framework, centralized planning is even more virtuous.

## Neoclassical economics' responses to market failures

Given the generality of the problems associated with market failures, one would expect a general rethinking on the part of neoclassical theory about the actual efficiency and desirability of a world entirely regulated by the market. Instead, in a kind of general paradox, neoclassical economics' solutions to market failures all pass through the prescription of further market expansion or, when this is not possible, the introduction of centralized mechanisms that emulate the market mechanism. In short, neoclassical theory admits that in reality the market fails to achieve Pareto efficiency, but this does not lead it to revise regulatory prescriptions based on the assumption that the market is the instrument par excellence that leads to Pareto efficiency (an assumption that is moreover unfounded since, as we have just noted, Pareto efficiency is also compatible with centralized planning), but rather leads it to conclude that, if Pareto efficiency is not achieved in reality, it is only because markets are still too little widespread. Let us take a closer look at how this further logical leap is made by distinguishing the three problems of increasing returns to scale, externalities and public goods.

In the case of *increasing returns to scale*, faced with the undeniable observation of the increasing diffusion of monopolies in all real markets (made convenient precisely by the advantages linked to economies of scale), neoclassical economics refined its theory by relying on brilliant theoretical exercises capable of making even monopolistic markets appear as competitive. This is the case with the theory of 'contestable markets' by William Baumol, John C. Panzar and Robert D. Willig (1982). According to this theory, it is not actual competition that counts, but potential competition (for a concise but technically advanced presentation of the theory see Willig (1987)).

Whereas standard neoclassical theory defines the degree of competition in a market from the empirical analysis of its structure (a high degree of industrial concentration, with a small number of firms operating in the market, denotes a low degree of competition), the theory of Baumol, Panzar and Willig argues that even monopolistic markets can be competitive, provided there is freedom of entry and exit at zero cost in the market. Indeed, under such circumstances, even if a market were dominated by a single monopolist, the monopolist would not be able to take advantage of his market power (by setting the price at an excessively high level, which would harm the consumer), since other potential producers could enter the market by offering the same good at a somewhat lower price thereby bringing monopoly extra-profits to zero. From a regulatory perspective, the prescription is therefore to create a potential market where monopoly prevents the real market mechanism from functioning.

In itself, the theoretical contribution of Baumol, Panzar and Willig does not enrich the standard theory of competition to any great extent: for just as there are no markets that satisfy the assumptions of perfect competition, there are also no markets in which it is possible to enter and leave overnight without incurring any costs. The contribution becomes interesting, however, as soon as one reflects on its practical repercussions, particularly with regard to the regulation of monopolistic markets.

According to the old regulatory principles, based on the desirability of the competitive model, anti-trust agencies had to intervene in the face of any situation that was outside the competitive model. The intuitive principle was that, when faced with markets dominated by a few players (or a single monopolist), the state had to intervene in defence of the consumer and competition, preventing positions of excessive market power. With the theory of contestable markets, by contrast, monopolistic markets need not be placed under surveillance since, if 'contestability' exists, they retain the Pareto efficiency properties of competitive markets.

Obviously then, since perfect contestability is impossible in exactly the same way as perfect competition is, it becomes a matter of necessity to accept the desirability of imperfect competition and imperfect contestability, with the result that what appear to us as obvious examples of high industrial concentration or even monopoly (banking sector, insurance, automobile, information, transport, telecommunications etc.) are considered as perfectly efficient according to the criteria of the various control and regulatory authorities, all based on the neoclassical theory and its refinements.

Faced with the problem of *externalities* (the second major case of market failure), the solution proposed by market failure theorists is to create new markets for 'external effects' (in the case of pollution, the solution involves creating a market in which to buy and sell pollution rights). In this way, the external effects would cease to be 'external' to the logic of the market, as they too could be traded on a specific market. Externalities would then themselves become commodities and, like all other commodities, receive a market price that would allow them to be allocated in a Pareto-compatible manner (provided the new markets for external effects are characterized by perfect competition). This is, for example, the neoliberal solution to the pollution problem put forward in the Kyoto Protocol on Climate Change, which led to the creation of a special international market for pollution rights in which the right to produce environmental damage can be traded (United Nations, 1997).

With the creation of these new markets, the one true objective of neoclassical economics – Pareto efficiency – can thus be re-established, allowing the holders of purchasing power to enforce their privileges even in the new markets thus created and effectively preventing all those with sufficiently tight budgetary constraints from enforcing their rights. In the case of pollution, it is the richer countries and companies (those with a greater willingness to pay) that can buy pollution rights from poorer countries (which cannot afford to pay to pollute). This at least allows countries that pollute less to at least get compensated for the damage caused by countries that pollute more. In fact, the reason why the United States withdrew its signature from the Kyoto treaty is precisely that, despite being one of the countries most responsible for global environmental degradation, it does not even want to pay compensation for the damage it does (with a population of 4 per cent of the world's population, the United States emits 20 per cent of the total carbon dioxide).[10] However, regardless of the strength with which individual countries defend their national priorities over the interests of the world as a whole, it is clear that the market solution to the pollution problem distributes costs and benefits in a necessarily asymmetrical manner: the reduction of the total level of pollution will in fact be increasingly at the expense of the weakest, that is, those who have nothing else to sell but their pollution rights, or there will simply be a shift of polluting production towards countries with greater pollution rights (or towards countries that have not ratified the agreement).

But to make the solution of enlarging markets truly operational in a Pareto-compatible manner, a market for pollution rights would also have to be created at the level of individuals and not only at the level of countries and large corporations. Each actor would then be free to buy and sell pollution rights from other actors. Thus, the big industries that pollute and destroy will only have to buy more and more pollution rights on a special market and their harmful effects on us and on the environment will become perfectly lawful and efficient, while we, with our four cents in our pockets just enough to make ends meet, will not be able to afford to buy pollution rights and will end up having to give up even the use of our car.

Instead of attempting to rationalize the production of polluting effects according to general principles that prohibit or hinder the production of harmful substances, the sole concern of economic theory is to bring global pollution to its Pareto efficiency level (which is determined by the sum of the levels of pollution that each individual can afford to produce, given his/her spending constraints, which has nothing to do with ecological sustainability or other environmental parameters, with the consequence that the much coveted Pareto efficiency could very well lead to the complete destruction of the planet). Instead of placing limits on the market, prohibiting, regulating, enforcing general principles that prevent the manifestation of its perverse and discriminatory effects, the solution of economic theory is to extend markets further, allowing those effects to occur unhindered, re-establishing Pareto efficiency (and increasing discriminations).

Note, finally, that the solution of enlarging markets suggests the erroneous idea that the system can function on a purely decentralized basis, without the intervention of any external authority. In other words, when faced with a concrete coordination problem, which leads decentralized agents to behave in a Pareto inefficient manner, the idea put forward is that individual agents can still cope on their own (by interacting in a special market), realizing the economic goal of Pareto efficiency, without intrusion of politics. This, however, raises several questions: who creates these markets for external effects? How should these markets be organized? What must be done to ensure that they operate on a competitive basis? What are their operating costs? That these are extremely concrete questions is demonstrated by the controversy that accompanied the signing of the Kyoto Protocol, concerning the initial distribution of pollution rights and the level of pollution to be considered socially desirable.

Despite the efforts of economic theory to present the market as apolitical and aimed only at the pursuit of the common good, the answers to these questions are necessarily political. There is no advancement of technology or science that can determine a measure of pollution that can be considered both economically efficient and socially desirable, and it is certainly not a committee of experts that can recompose the different evaluations of the parties involved on the right to ruin the world we live in more or less quickly. Regarding the initial distribution of pollution rights, according to the Kyoto Protocol, each country's allowed levels of pollution have been set on a historical basis, taking as a reference the level of carbon dioxide emissions of different countries in 1990. This introduces an asymmetry of treatment between the different industrial powers since the countries most responsible for global pollution in 1990 retain their right to pollute more than the others. It is then easy to see that the decision to create a market for pollution rights is entirely political. In what sense can the allocation criterion chosen be considered fair? And then, once the Protocol has come into force, how is it possible to imagine that such a market is truly competitive given that it is dominated by a few major powers? But above all, how is it possible to hope that the willingness of polluters to pay be compatible with the sustainability of the ecosystem, considering that in one case it is the result of a purely economic calculation and in the other of a purely ecological one?

On a less superficial examination, one realizes that the solution to enlarging markets cannot do without a political authority outside the market to establish, organize and operate the market itself. The very fact that there is talk of creating new markets shows that markets are complex institutions, which in no way coincide with the neoclassical portrayal of them as coordination mechanisms that emerge spontaneously whenever they are needed. The neoclassical image of capitalism as an efficient system capable of self-regulation (already difficult to defend in itself, given the role played in reality by the state in the establishment, organization and control of real markets) is simply indefensible in the presence of externalities: as shown by the hard efforts and lengthy negotiations between the parties in the attempt to reduce pollutant emissions worldwide, the existence of externalities opens up a conflict between private and collective interest (which manifests itself as a conflict between the interests of different countries, as a conflict between the interests of different companies, as a conflict between the interests of companies and those of citizens), whose possible solutions are in any case political in nature (even when they are based on the establishment of new markets) and need central authorities capable of making them operational.

Finally, in the case of *public goods*, in order to realize the Pareto-efficient level of production (as identified by Samuelson), one must first estimate the different willingness to pay of all individuals interested in the good. Once these willingness to pay are known, customized prices must then be imposed on individual consumers based on their respective willingness to pay in order to finance the production of the public good (this condition is called 'Lindahl equilibrium' (Lindahl, 1958), named after the Swedish economist who first determined it). Because of the free-riding problem, however, consumers will have no interest in declaring their true willingness to pay.

Imagine, in fact, that an enterprise producing a public good attempts to determine the willingness to pay of different consumers, in order to charge customized prices, proportional to their respective willingness to pay (so to achieve the Lindahl-Samuelson equilibrium). The individual consumer, with the sole aim of paying little for the good, would simply respond by declaring a lower willingness to pay than the true one, thus attempting to pass on the costs of financing the public good to others. However, the same reasoning will be developed by the other consumers as well, with the result that the total funds collected will be less than those needed to produce the Pareto-efficient level of the public good.

Faced with this problem, economic theory has developed a number of mechanisms that incentivize individual consumers to reveal their true willingness to pay for the good and thus not to behave as free-riders. These schemes are based on the hypothesis that a central authority is able to organize a sophisticated auction mechanism through which individual consumers are induced to reveal their true willingness to pay for the public good, so that customized prices can then be effectively calculated (Vickrey, 1961; Clarke, 1971; Groves and Ledyard, 1977).

As in the case of externalities, the Pareto-efficient solution involves passing through a central authority that is highly informed (able to determine the level of Pareto-efficient production), powerful (able also to operationalise the individual willingness to pay mechanism) and efficient (able to perform these functions at zero cost). Again, therefore, whatever solution is adopted to re-establish Pareto efficiency, the state must still play a decisive role.

To summarize, whether faced with the problems of increasing returns to scale, or with the problems of externalities and public goods, the responses of neoclassical theory are all paradoxical: in the first case, the theory responds to market failure by interpreting monopoly itself as a form of competition; in the second case, it responds instead by proposing to create yet more markets (or, in the case of public goods, to create centralized auction mechanisms that emulate the market mechanism). These theoretical responses obviously do not solve the problem of market failures in reality at all but reinforce the economist's (unfounded) dream of a society entirely based on market relations in which the only thing that matters is Pareto efficiency.

## The inefficiency of real markets

The considerations of the realism of the fundamental and boundary assumptions necessary for the Pareto efficiency of the competitive model allow to appreciate the limitations of those approaches that interpret this model as a scientific foundation of market desirability. In fact, at this point it should be clear that the general economic equilibrium model does demonstrate not only the efficiency of theoretical markets, but also the inefficiency of real markets, given the impossibility in practice of finding real markets 1) populated by agents with particular preferences that respect the axioms of neoclassical theory and with endowments that allow life in autarky (the so-called 'consumer survival' hypothesis) 2) in which, for some accidental reason, the problems of multiplicity and instability of equilibrium (which neoclassical theory itself is not able to exclude even at the theoretical level) do not occur and 3) in which the phenomena of increasing returns to scale, externalities and goods that are at least partly public (the so-called 'market failures') do not arise.

Repeating the model's assumptions every time one refers to its theses is not a waste of time, but the only guarantee of a correct use of the logical-deductive method. The main quest in the history of bourgeois economics to prove the desirability of the market, culminating in the paradigm of research of the general economic equilibrium, has not exactly yielded pro-market results, and this is not so much because in the abstract conditions in which the market is efficient, so is central planning (whereas the opposite is not valid in the presence of increasing returns of scale, public goods and externalities), but because of the concrete impossibility of realizing the necessary conditions for market efficiency: one only has to recall all the theoretical assumptions that have to be introduced to ensure market efficiency to understand the shortcomings of real markets. And, instead, all that remains in the mystified culture of market societies (and, alas, in the scientific culture of economists, who, at least, should know the hypotheses of their models!) is the message that 'the market works', without specification and without reference to the hypotheses introduced.

Economists know that their method is abstract, and they strongly claim (on methodologically questionable grounds) their right to introduce the most abstruse hypotheses as long as the mathematical developments are rigorous. They know they are stepping into a world that is not our own when they build their models. Yet, once a certain result is reached, the whole analytical apparatus, made up of hypotheses introduced at different levels of abstraction, ceases to act as a counterweight to the thesis reached and instead becomes the guarantee of the scientificity of the thesis itself. And, if a proposition is scientific, it is also true. At least that is how scientists themselves have let the world believe (ignoring the most elementary principles of science itself). Thus, the fact that they have filled entire pages and books with formulae and words designed to specify the particular context in which certain assertions have validity, instead of downplaying the magnitude of the result achieved, is presented as an element of strength of the entire argument, forgetting that all those words and formulae only served to move the model further and further away from reality. On the other hand, however, this is the price to be paid for arriving at the thesis of market rationality and efficiency (even while accepting the mystified meanings of these terms).

## Notes

1 The main bibliographical references are Walras (1874), Pareto (1906), Wald (1934, 1935), Von Neumann (1938), Arrow and Debreu (1954), McKenzie (1954), Debreu (1959). A 'classic' reference in the developments of general economic equilibrium theory is Arrow and Hahn (1971). For a historical reconstruction of general economic equilibrium research, rich in bibliographical references, see Ingrao and Israel (1990). For a

general, technically advanced presentation of general economic equilibrium theory, see the entries 'General equilibrium' and 'Arrow-Debreu model of general equilibrium' in the New Palgrave Dictionary of Economics written by McKenzie (1987) and Genakoplos (1987) respectively. Also in the same dictionary, see Debreu (1987) for a review of the main works on the subject of equilibrium existence.

2 Welfare economics is the branch of neoclassical theory that deals with normative issues. In the history of economic thought a distinction is made between the 'old' and the 'new welfare economics': the former is linked to the name of Arthur C. Pigou and is based on the idea that, in analysing possible state interventions, it is possible to compare the level of utility of different individuals (Pigou, 1920); the latter stems instead from the contribution of Vilfredo Pareto, according to whom interpersonal utility comparisons are scientifically inadmissible and leads to considering as scientifically valid only those interventions that benefit someone without harming anyone. Today, given the absolute predominance of the latter over the former, when we speak of 'welfare economics' we refer to the Pareto approach.

3 As Bernstein (2001) notes, the decisive intervention of the military apparatus in the quest for technological and scientific supremacy in turn had a major impact on economic theory, profoundly changing the academic landscape itself. While in the first decades following the marginalist revolution of 1870, the economic research of the nascent neoclassical and Austrian schools was still characterized by extremely polemical tones towards the Marxist tradition, from the 1950s onwards, the development of mathematical economics, with its claimed objectivity, independence from politics and formal elegance, allowed neoclassical theory to establish itself as a hegemonic school of thought independent of any ideology, leaving even the confrontation with Marxism in the background. Among the major economic researches directly financed by the US Department of Defence and the *Rand corporation* are Arrow and Debreu's general economic equilibrium model and Arrow's impossibility theorem (considered fundamental by the military in the study of problems of conflict and coordination between decentralized agents), the linear programming of Dantzig and Koopmans (central from the point of view of the efficient use of resources according to given objectives) and the game theory of John von Neumann and Oskar Morgenstern (suitable for the study of decision-making problems in a context of strategic interaction). The latter two lines of research were the most financially supported due to their direct military implications both in wartime and in the context of the Cold War (game theory actually only reached its full maturity in the context of the nuclear duopoly between the United States and the Soviet Union).

4 Falsificationism is a demarcation criterion between scientific and non-scientific propositions introduced by Karl Popper (1972).

5 All general economic equilibrium theorems are derived from particular properties of the demand and supply functions of different goods. The theoretical problem therefore consists in proving that the assumptions on the three model data are able to guarantee these properties of the demand and supply functions. In particular, for the existence of an equilibrium it is important that the demand and supply curves do not present discontinuity traits (otherwise, they might not intersect and, therefore, an equilibrium point might not exist). In the case of initial endowments that do not meet the consumer survival hypothesis, the problem that emerges is precisely that the demand and supply curves in general turn out to be discontinuous. This is therefore a strictly mathematical problem, to which neoclassical theory responds by imposing conditions that make the model 'run' mathematically, without any regard for their empirical validity.

6 For a review of the mathematical problems related to the uniqueness of general economic equilibrium, see Allingham (1987); mathematical problems related to stability are discussed by Hahn (1982) and Gandolfo (1987).

7 The problem that arises at this point is no longer simply one of realism, but also one of methodological consistency, and deserves a little technical elaboration. The hypotheses

that must be introduced in order to obtain a unique and stable equilibrium do not derive from particular hypotheses on the three data of the problem (preferences, endowments and technology), but rather directly concern the form of the demand and supply functions (or, more precisely, the form of the excess demand function, which is obtained as the difference between the demand and supply functions). In the absence of an analysis that establishes a relationship between the shape of the excess demand function and the assumptions about the three fundamental data of the problem, the model is made up of a mix of assumptions concerning individual behaviour as well as the aggregate structure of the system, which contradicts methodological individualism and makes the model itself difficult to interpret economically.

8 Of the three problems of equilibrium existence, uniqueness and stability, the second two are undoubtedly more complicated mathematically. This perhaps helps to explain why in many popular presentations the analysis of the existence of an equilibrium (and its Pareto efficiency) is favoured, leaving the other two problems in the background. What is certain is that the results achieved on the latter two fronts raise serious doubts about the very internal coherence of the entire general economic equilibrium research programme.

9 In market failure theory, the emphasis is on increasing returns to scale, rather than on economies of scale. This is because the theory develops from a criticism of the realism of the general economic equilibrium model (questioning, in particular, its assumptions about technology). In general, however, the presence of economies of scale (even in the absence of increasing returns to scale) is sufficient to make monopoly technically more efficient than competition.

10 A *Times* poll on 11 December 1995 revealed that 65 per cent of United States citizens believed that their country should decrease its pollutant emissions regardless of what other countries do; only 17 per cent of respondents believed that reducing pollutant emissions would excessively increase production costs and harm the United States economy. Unfortunately, this 17 per cent included the largest companies responsible for polluting emissions. Thus, in 2001, under pressure from the oil lobby, Bush withdrew United States' signature from the Kyoto treaty. Even today, after several presidents have succeeded each other in the White House and the United States has launched the so-called green new deal (a massive plan of public investment and incentives for United States companies engaged, at least formally, in the green sector), the United States refuses to ratify the Kyoto Protocol and fulfil its international commitments on pollution.

## References

Allingham, M. (1987) 'Uniqueness of equilibrium', in Eatwell, J., Milgate, M. and Newman, P. (eds.) *The new Palgrave dictionary of economics*. London: MacMillan Press.

Arrow, J. K. and Debreu, G. (1954) 'Existence of an equilibrium for a competitive economy', *Econometrica*, 22, pp. 265–290.

Arrow, J. K. and Hahn, F. H. (1971) *General competitive analysis*. San Francisco: Oliver and Boyd.

Baumol, W. J., Panzar, J. C. and Willig, R. D. (1982) *Contestable markets and the theory of industry structure*. New York: Harcourt Brace Jovanovich.

Bernstein, M. A. (2001) 'Rethinking economics in twentieth century America: a political-economic approach to the history of thought', *Post-Autistic Economics Newsletter*, (8). Available at: www.paecon.net

Clarke, E. (1971) 'Multipart pricing of public goods', *Public Choice*, 11, pp. 17–33.

Debreu, G. (1959) *Theory of value. An axiomatic analysis of economic equilibrium*. New York: Wiley.

Debreu, G. (1987) 'Existence of general equilibrium', in Eatwell, J., Milgate, M. and Newman, P. (eds.) *The new Palgrave dictionary of economics*. London: MacMillan Press.

Gandolfo, G. (1987) 'Stability', in Eatwell, J., Milgate, M. and Newman, P. (eds.) *The new Palgrave dictionary of economics*. London: MacMillan Press.
Genakoplos, J. (1987) 'Arrow-debreu model of general equilibrium', in Eatwell, J., Milgate, M. and Newman, P. (eds.) *The new Palgrave dictionary of economics*. London: MacMillan Press.
Groves, T. and Ledyard, J. (1977) 'Optimal allocation of public goods: a solution to the free-rider problem', *Econometrica*, 45.
Guerrien, B. (1985) *La Théorie néo-classique: Bilan et perspectives du modèle d'équilibre général*. Paris: Economica.
Hahn, F. (1982) 'Stability', in Arrow, K. J. and Intriligator, M. D. (eds.) *Handbook of mathematical economics*. Amsterdam: North Holland.
Ingrao, B. and Israel, G. (1990) *The invisible hand: economic equilibrium in the history of science*. Cambridge, MA: MIT Press.
Lindahl, E. R. (1958) 'Just taxation: a positive solution', in Musgrave, R. A. and Peacock, A. (eds.) *Classics in the theory of public finance*. London: Macmillan.
McKenzie, L. W. (1954) 'On equilibrium in Graham's model of world trade and other competitive systems', *Econometrica*, 22, pp. 147–161.
McKenzie, L. W. (1987) 'General equilibrium', in Eatwell, J., Milgate, M. and Newman, P. (eds.) *The new Palgrave dictionary of economics*. London: MacMillan Press.
Neumann, J. von (1938) 'Über ein Ökonomisches Gleichungssystem and eine Verallgemeinerung des Brouwerschen Fixpunktsatzes', in Menger, K. (ed.) *Ergebnisse eines Mathematischen Koplloquiums*. Vienna: Springer-Verlag. English translation (1971). 'A model of general economic equilibrium', in Hahn, F. (ed.) *Readings in the theory of growth*. London: Palgrave Macmillan.
Pareto, V. (1906) *Manuale di Economia Politica con una Introduzione alla Ricerca Sociale*. Torino: Einaudi. English translation (1971). *Manual of political economy*. New York: Augustus Kelley.
Pigou, A. C. (1920) *The economics of welfare*. London: Macmillan.
Popper, K. (1972) *Conjectures and refutations: the growth of scientific knowledge*. London: Routledge and Kegan Paul.
Samuelson, P. (1954) 'The pure theory of public expenditure', *Review of Economics and Statistics*, 36(4), pp. 387–396.
Statista (2024) *Distribution of military spending worldwide in 2023, by country*. Available at: www.statista.com/statistics/272481/shares-of-selected-countries-in-world-military-spending/#statisticContainer
United Nations (1997) *Kyoto protocol*. Secretary-General of the United Nations.
Veblen, T. B. (1899) *The theory of the leisure class: an economic study in the evolution of institutions*. New York: Macmillan.
Vickrey, W. (1961) 'Counterspeculation and competitive sealed tenders', *Journal of Finance*, 16(1), pp. 8–37.
Wald, A. (1934) 'Über die eindeutige positive Lösbarkeit der neuen Produktions gleichungen I', in Menger, K. (ed.) *Ergebnisse eines mathematischen Kolloquiums, 1933–34*. English translation (1968). 'On the unique non-negative solvability of the new production equations, part I', in Baumol, W. J. and Goldfeld, S. M. (eds.) *Precursors in mathematical economics*. London: London School of Economics.
Wald, A. (1935) 'Über die Produktionsgleichungen der ökonomischen Wertlehre II', in Menger, K. (ed.) *Ergebnisse eines mathematischen Kolloquiums, 1934–35*. English translation (1968).'On the production equations of economic value theory, part II', in Baumol, W. J. and Goldfeld, S. M. (eds.) *Precursors in mathematical economics*. London: London School of Economics.
Walras, L. (1874) *Éléments d'Économie Politique Pure ou Théorie de la Richesse Sociale*. Lausanne: L. Corbaz & cie. English translation (2013). *Elements of pure economics*. London: Routledge.
Willig, R. D. (1987) 'Contestable markets', in Eatwell, J., Milgate, M. and Newman, P. (eds.) *The new Palgrave dictionary of economics*. London: MacMillan Press.

# 5 Post-Walrasian economics

## The post-Walrasian research program

In light of all the restrictive and unrealistic assumptions that need to be introduced into the neoclassical theory in order to achieve the thesis of Pareto efficiency of markets, theoretical research takes two distinct paths.

On the hand, the problem is tackled by simply assuming that reality conforms to the hypotheses of the theoretical model (or, worse, by asserting that there need not be a close relationship between reality and the theoretical model), leaving the analyst free to play with the hypotheses as he/she pleases. In the academic literature, in fact, it has been affirmed the principle that the validity of a model must be judged solely on the basis of its internal consistency and logical-deductive rigour, and, since the ambition of every good academician is to publish in the leading scientific journals, there has been a proliferation of models that assume convenient hypotheses about technology, preferences and endowments, which by assumption exclude market failures and eliminate the problems of multiplicity and instability of equilibria, but which, with sophisticated mathematical techniques, demonstrate the fantastic result of Pareto efficiency of the market: of course, of the virtual market of their model, not of the real market of the capitalist world. This line of research is followed by mathematical economists most faithful to the hard core of the Walrasian general economic equilibrium research paradigm.

A second path consists instead in relaxing some assumptions of the general economic equilibrium model with an eye to the conditions of realism. In some respects, this operation is similar to that already discussed with regard to the attempts to put a patch on the problems of stability and uniqueness of the equilibrium, by appropriately playing with the hypotheses of the model. In other respects, however, the operation is profoundly different, if not quite the opposite. In the case of the problems of stability and uniqueness, the departure from the set of general assumptions that characterize neoclassical theory is made by attempting at all costs to save the thesis of market Pareto efficiency, even at the cost of exasperating the problems of realism and methodological consistency. In this case, instead, it is developed by renouncing the objective of demonstrating the Pareto efficiency of perfectly competitive markets, but trying to bring the model closer to reality, in an attempt to obtain some second-best result, that is, some outcomes that approach Pareto

DOI: 10.4324/9781032726168-6

efficiency as much as possible. Thus, in the various developments of neoclassical theory, some of the more restrictive and less realistic assumptions are questioned for the sake of providing a more articulated version of the normative properties of a system made up of markets that are not necessarily perfect.

Of the absurdity of the first theoretical path, we have already said. In this chapter, we now deal with the second one, which in the specialist literature is referred to as 'post-Walrasian economics'.[1]

Before starting the critique of this new voluminous body of theory, let us note the basic weakness on which it is based. Historically, in fact, post-Walrasian economics develops just as the Walrasian paradigm comes to an end. While serious general equilibrium theorists largely recognize the consequences of the negative results on stability and uniqueness on the general coherence and interpretative power of this research program (cf. Hahn, 1982; Fisher, 2011), post-Walrasian economists start their research program precisely from this cul-de-sac. Be that as it may, let us analyse how they erect this new theoretical construction on this fragile foundation.

In winter 1993, the editors of the *Journal of Economic Perspectives*, one of the main journals through which the *American Economic Association* dictates to the world the principles of scientific rigour in economic research, asked some authoritative economists representing mainstream and heterodox schools of thought to present their approaches and discuss the relationships among them. Exponents of the new Keynesian economics, the new institutional economics, and the radical political economics have thus clarified their indebtedness to John Maynard Keynes, old institutionalists and Marx, the specificity of their 'new' approaches and their positions towards orthodox neoclassical economics. The picture that emerges is that, notwithstanding some theoretical differences, there exists a common methodological ground among these approaches, which makes them largely compatible with each other and with mainstream neoclassical economics (despite the fact that a synthesis between Keynesianism, institutionalism and Marxism has proven to be a much more problematic issue). This explains the friendly relationships that exist today between them.

The acceptance of methodological individualism is the first important aspect of this process of convergence. A second aspect regards the attempt to overcome some of the restrictive assumptions of the general equilibrium model, which implicitly or explicitly is the theoretical benchmark of all these theoretical developments. The logic is the following.

In the Walrasian world, characterized by complete markets, perfect information, full rationality and free contract enforcement, general equilibrium theorists have reached the following results:

1. The state has no economic role to play, since resources allocation can occur entirely through the market.
2. There is no economic room for the firm, since production can be carried out by interpersonal contracts, without managerial coordination.
3. There exists no power relation in market interaction, since perfect competition alone may govern interpersonal relations.

According to new Keynesians, new institutionalists and radicals, the economic role of the state, the nature of the firm and other capitalist institutions, and the existence of power relations must then be explained by modifying the assumptions of the Walrasian world. Methodologically, these new approaches can thus be seen as part of a common research program, aiming at extending the Walrasian framework: the latter assumes that agents interact in what might be called a 'perfect' decision-making context; post-Walrasians deal with 'imperfect' decision-making contexts.

This mode of proceeding immediately raises a fundamental methodological problem, apparently neglected by the entire post-Walrasian school. In fact, as we have seen in Chapter 3, in the perfect decision-making context of the Walrasian world, even centralized planning achieves Pareto-efficient results (without even running into the problems of market failures), as demonstrated by Kantorovich (1939) through the optimal planning model. Thus, there is no reason to step outside the perfect decision-making context to explain the role of the state, the firm and power relations. Simply, on purely ideological grounds, both Walrasians and post-Walrasians assume the market as eternal and natural. Only the state, the firm and power relations, being man-made, must therefore be explained. The market and its supposed freedom, conversely, need no scientific explanation in their eyes. William Dugger's (1992, p. 89) judgement is trenchant:

> The neoclassical market is an act of God, not an act of man. It is natural rather than artificial. . . . The natural market is beyond the will of humans. It is a product of nature existing outside of history. . . . But the spontaneous market, the natural market, is an assumption. It is not a unit of enquiry, something to be investigated. Instead it is something to be assumed, taken for granted. . . . The market is taken as the only real circulation process and the market is simply assumed to exist. It is viewed as a self-generated phenomenon, a product of immaculate conception and virgin birth.

The term 'post-Walrasian economics' is also sometimes used in a narrower sense, as a synonym for the radical approach to power initiated by Samuel Bowles and Herbert Gintis, based on 'contested exchange'.

In order to develop a systematic critique of post-Walrasian economics, I begin with the two main research strands of the broadly defined post-Walrasian paradigm: new institutionalism and new Keynesianism, led by Oliver Williamson and Joseph Stiglitz (both Nobel Prize winners in economics in 2009 and 2001 respectively, the latter also an economic advisor in the Clinton administration and former deputy general director of the World Bank). Then, I show the convergence with the approach developed by the radical school and focus the critique on the latter. My critique is developed on two levels, a methodological one, and an ontological one (i.e. concerning the assumptions about the structure and entities that make up reality which, implicitly or explicitly, are assumed when one adopts a particular method of scientific investigation). This allows me to discuss the main formal similarities between Marx and post-Walrasian radicals and the opposite conceptions in which they are developed. The 'scientific critique' ends at this point. My critical path, however, continues with the discussion of the pre-scientific elements that lead post-Walrasian economics to define its scientific problem. In an academic conception of science, the choice of the scientific problem is not generally an object of critique: researchers are supposed to choose freely their scientific problems and are not called to defend these choices. They see themselves as external observers of the system they describe and do not even conceive of themselves as actors operating within a system of power. Within post-Walrasian economics, however, the acceptance of a common ideology and the definition of an identical scientific problem by all of its members – from ultra-liberals to radical thinkers – are part of the phenomenon to be explained and must then be scrutinized carefully. Given the complexity of the issues addressed in this chapter, in the last section, I recap my arguments and draw some conclusions.

## New institutionalism and new Keynesianism

New institutional economics uses the neoclassical analytical toolkit to explain the evolution of capitalist economic institutions as a succession of Pareto moves in the rules of social interaction.[2] Existing economic institutions – the firm and the state above all, but also every other type of economic community, from small neighbourhood associations to international organizations – according to this theory, would be the result of a process of progressive reduction of transaction costs. The latter, however, has never been rigorously defined in the literature, despite the fact that within new institutionalism a veritable school of thought has emerged called the 'transaction cost economics'. The general idea, anyway, is that, in the impossibility of realizing perfectly competitive markets, transaction costs, understood in a vague sense as costs related to the functioning of the market mechanism, can be reduced through alternative coordination mechanisms (in particular through allocative mechanisms operating through forms of command and planning). These mechanisms and the institutions that incorporate them would thus find their reason to exist in capitalism in their capacity to bring the system closer to Pareto efficiency, where the market alone is not sufficient. In this way, even if the myth of a system entirely regulated by the market falls, the myth of the efficiency of capitalism as a system characterized by a plurality of allocative institutions in which, for the good of all, alongside the market there are also different institutions, remains standing.

Clearly, however, of these different institutions, the market remains the central one, the only one capable of guaranteeing economic freedom, while the others, the hierarchical firm and the authoritarian state, function only through coercive mechanisms. In this sense, it is true that the capitalist system does not coincide with the realm of individual freedom, given that part of social relations is regulated precisely by coercive mechanisms, but this is the price to be paid to come as close as possible to Pareto efficiency and this explains why, in the case of equivalence in terms of Pareto efficiency, the market is still to be preferred to any other allocative mechanisms.

This method of explaining the institutions of capitalism in terms of their supposed efficiency creates more problems than it solves. First, theoretically, there is no reason why a system should evolve towards Pareto efficiency. By following the neoclassical logic, this might be the case if the sequence of Pareto moves that new institutionalists assume is characterized by equilibrium points that are also stable and unique, but, as we have seen, there is no theoretical guarantee that this should actually occur. Second, this method inverts the relation between history and the present, as in the case of the economist's *ex post* rationalization that we have already discussed in Chapter 2. With respect to economic historians, new institutionalists simply go the other way round. They do not start from the past in order to *explain* the present; rather, they start from the present and *assume* that the past was such that the present is economically superior to it. The goal is not to provide a theory that explains reality but to *define* reality in accordance with the theory.

In a similar fashion, new Keynesian economics, develops the problem of nominal wage rigidities and information asymmetries between economic agents as the fundamental cause of the impossibility of achieving Pareto efficiency in market interaction and therefore proposes forms of state intervention that allow the causes of existing inefficiencies to be reduced. Again, the practical impossibility of achieving Pareto efficiency conditions is seen as the ultimate reason for state intervention, whose task, according to this theory, should be to create the conditions that allow the market to function better, improving the existing equilibrium according to Pareto.

As with new institutional economics, the market thus remains at the centre of the normative theory and state intervention becomes meaningful only as an instrument to bring the system closer to Pareto efficiency. From a methodological point of view, then, the attempt to ground all macroeconomic propositions in the analysis of the behaviour of individuals (the so-called microeconomic foundations of macroeconomics, which would constitute the value added of the new Keynesian approach compared to Keynes' theory) falls perfectly within the neoclassical logic, centred on methodological individualism.

Despite formal references respectively to the old American institutionalism of John Commons and Veblen and to the thought of Keynes, new institutionalism and new Keynesian economics do not actually have much in common with these two scientific traditions now on the fringes of academic debate. Indeed, the methodological assumptions of the old institutionalist and Keynesian schools are profoundly different from those of the neoclassical school and its more recent developments. In particular, these two schools of thought reject methodological individualism and the dogma of market efficiency. Instead, they assume that institutions condition human behaviour in an important way and regard economic policy as a necessary instrument to regulate the capitalist system, in the face of the market's evident inability to regulate the economy autonomously.

Of these two traditions of thought, particularly influential in certain phases of the economic debate in the last century, the 'new' schools take up only some purely formal aspects. In particular, they resume the great theme of the relationship between institutions and the economy (on which the old institutionalists insisted) and the ever-present problem of the market's inability to employ all existing productive resources, including labour power (a central problem in Keynes' work). However, these issues are analysed according to the neoclassical methodology and the market view it presupposes, which leads to a complete distortion of the original perspectives of analysis. The theoretical reference, in some cases explicit, in others only implicit, is the general economic equilibrium model, a model that plays absolutely no role in the theoretical constructions of the old institutionalists and Keynes. Simply, once acknowledged the excessive abstractness of this model, new institutionalists and new Keynesians attempt to remedy it by abandoning some of the assumptions they consider excessively restrictive. The theoretical problem that emerges is that, in a world more complex than that of the general economic equilibrium model *tout court*, the same normative results on market efficiency cannot be obtained. Hence, according to the logic of neoclassical theory, it becomes important to analyse the other economic institutions of capitalism and the role of the state and economic policy.

However, in view of the different methodological and ideological assumptions, the same questions posed by the old institutionalists and Keynes are completely overturned and end up taking on totally different meanings. The firm and the state are not studied as organizations necessary to the very functioning of capitalism, as organizations complementary to the market, that is, as parts of an organic system whose functioning depends on the relations established between its various components. Instead, they are conceived solely as alternative instruments to the market in the performance of strictly allocative functions. Fully consistent with the neoclassical approach, the economic problem is conceived as a pure problem of scarcity and all the institutions of capitalism are analysed as a response to this problem. The various institutions of capitalism thus lose their complementary character and become merely alternative allocative mechanisms capable of handling the universal problem of scarcity.

Williamson, for instance, with the utmost nonchalance, imagines that capitalism originated from a system of pure markets, in which neither the state nor the firm existed. In his words: 'I assume, for expositional convenience, that in the beginning there were markets' (Williamson, 1975, p. 21). If productive organizations such as the capitalist firm and institutions that regulate economic activity such as the state, with its administrative, legal and political apparatuses, eventually developed, this is only because the market alone strayed too far from Pareto efficiency.

Similarly, for the new Keynesians, economic policy loses the meaning attributed to it by Keynes, as the main instrument to regulate and govern the economy, make public services possible, support demand and reduce unemployment, and instead takes on significance only as an instrument to improve market equilibrium according to Pareto in a context where entrepreneurs and workers experience asymmetric information.

The problem I wish to discuss here, however, is not so much the extent to which these new theories remain consistent with the scientific project of the masters they claim to refer to. Rather, the question we must deal with concerns the relationship with neoclassical theory and the internal consistency of this attempt to reason about the desirability of capitalism and economic policy within a theoretical framework that is slightly more refined than that of the general economic equilibrium model, but still derived from it, that is, within a framework in which Pareto efficiency is the only thing that matters. The problem, in fact, is that precisely because of the departure (even if only partial) from the general economic equilibrium paradigm, these new theoretical developments are incompatible with the general thesis of the desirability of the market (if by desirability one means Pareto efficiency), since in these models Pareto efficiency is not attainable anyway.

The following question then arises: what sense does it make to use the normative instruments of general economic equilibrium – the Pareto improvements criterion, first of all, – in a context in which Pareto efficiency in the system is precluded by hypothesis? Remember that the apparent robustness of Pareto efficiency as a normative criterion is in fact linked to the minimal benevolence principle that, when there is a change that improves someone's situation without worsening that of others, it would be desirable to implement it. However, when faced with the impossibility of realizing Pareto efficiency, Pareto improvements are by no means unanimously desirable. Consider the following example.

In a situation which, for the sake of argument, we refer to as the 'starting situation', there are two individuals, *Alby* and *Billy*, who have a level of preference satisfaction, or 'utility', of one and ten, respectively. Assume also that Pareto efficiency occurs in the theoretical situation *Z* in which *Alby* and *Billy* would both enjoy a utility of 100. Suppose, however, that due to the imperfections in the real world, this theoretical situation cannot be realized in practice. Let us now imagine that there are two different ways of Pareto improving the starting situation: in situation *X*, *Alby* has a utility of 90 and *Billy* a utility of 10; in situation *Y*, *Alby* has a utility of one and *Billy* a utility of 15. As can be seen, situations *X* and *Y* are both Pareto superior to the starting situation and switching to one of them would pose no problem if one could then continue to make Pareto move up to the Pareto-efficient situation *Z*. However, under the assumptions of our example, situation Z cannot be realized. Therefore, once you arrive in *X* or *Y*, you will not actually be able to continue to *Z* but will have to stop there. In this case, it is not at all neutral to prescribe a Pareto move that takes the system from the starting situation to *X* or *Y*: if you go to situation *X*, of course, then it is no longer possible to go to *Y* by means of another Pareto move; if, on the other hand, from the starting situation you go to *Y* by means of a Pareto move, it then becomes impossible to go to *X*. Thus, *Alby* will insist on improving the starting situation by moving the system to *X* and *Billy* will instead want the system to go to *Y*, and even if both *X* and *Y* are Pareto superior to the starting situation, it is not possible to say that *Alby* and *Billy* will agree to make either move.

In general, therefore, in cases where Pareto efficiency is by hypothesis not feasible, it is not even clear what the point of prescribing Pareto improvements is, since these changes cannot be considered unanimously acceptable at all, even according to the neoclassical logic.

**Power in post-Walrasian economics**

Although the notions of power, coercion and domination have been discussed since the beginning of political economy by authors such as Smith, Marx and Friedrich Wieser, the modern academic debate rarely goes back to these authors. Rather, the role of power in economics has come to the forefront of the academic debate in the 1970s, mainly as a by-product of the debate on the nature of the firm, with the contrasting contributions of ultra-liberals Armen Alchian and Harold Demsetz (1972) on the one hand and Stephen Marglin (1974, 1975), of radical inspiration, on the other.[3]

The former contends that formal authority within the firm is only an appearance that hides a reality of perfect reciprocal freedom; the latter argues that power relations play a decisive role in the organization of the firm. In the background of this debate, however, is the 1937 article by Ronald Coase, one of the founders of new institutionalism and winner of the Nobel Prize in economics in 1991 'for his discovery and clarification of the significance of transaction costs' (Sveriges Riksbank, 1991), which however, after almost a century, still lack a precise definition. In this paper, Coase explicitly sets the mechanisms of authority and command within the firm against the market price mechanism as alternative modes of coordination.

Coase's paper is not about the nature of capitalist power relations, but rather deals with 'the nature of the firm' in capitalism. This problem may appear trivial, for the firm is an integral part of the capitalist system; therefore, one might argue, it is by analysing the historical origin and development of capitalism that one can understand the nature of the firm and of the other institutions of capitalism.

The problem, however, is anything but trivial if placed within the context of neoclassical economics, a context in which economic institutions are seen as universal and everlasting, just as is the economic problem they solve: the allocation of scarce resources. Within neoclassical economics, the firm and the market are just two alternative allocative mechanisms. The theoretical problem is that, in the Walrasian model, coordination among isolated individuals takes place entirely within the market, which makes all other institutions economically redundant: the story told to describe the general equilibrium model sometimes makes reference to the firm and to other institutions (such as the family), but analytically they are superfluous add-ons. This leaves the internal relations of the firm undetermined. As Paul Samuelson (1957, p. 894) put it, 'in a perfectly competitive model, it really doesn't matter who hires whom; so let labour hire capital'.

The general equilibrium model, like any theoretical model, is defined by a 'decision-making context' and an 'organizational structure'. The former defines the features of the world in which agents of the model live and interact; the latter defines the relations among them and the way in which they interact. The decision-making context of the Walrasian model is characterized by perfect information, full rationality, zero transaction costs and contracts that are automatically enforced. This is the 'perfect' decision-making context. The organizational structure is a completely decentralized one, based on market relations among isolated agents.

Starting from the fact that the firm is redundant within the Walrasian model, Coase raises his scientific questions: Why do hierarchies exist in the market system? Where do the principles of authority and command regulating intra-firm relationships come from? These questions can be approached in many ways. Coase's method consisted in exploring the reasons why coordination by explicit direction can be economically superior to the invisible hand of the market in a decision-making context of positive transaction costs. Methodologically, Coase thus rejects the perfect decision-making context and investigates how organizational structures with some degree of centralization and formal authority might perform better than the Walrasian one in this new decision-making context. In one way or another, thus, Coase introduces a form of power into the neoclassical model and uses it to analytically characterize the firm as an institution qualitatively distinct from the market.[4]

Against this picture, some liberal authors have denied the existence of real authority relations within the firm by explaining them as particular forms of competition (Alchian and Demsetz, 1972; Jensen and Meckling, 1976; Cheung, 1983). Theoretically, this approach – often labelled the 'contractual approach' – is characterized by an internal tension between two conflicting objectives: on the one hand, it introduces imperfections in the decision-making context as a way to point out the specificity of the firm with respect to the market; on the other hand, however, it claims that interpersonal relations within the firm involve no power, an assertion that holds true only within the perfect decision-making context. Alchian and Demsetz's (1972, p. 777) provocation is famous:

> It is common to see the firm characterized by the power to settle issues by fiat, by authority, or by disciplinary action superior to that available in the conventional market. This is delusion . . . . [The employer] can fire or sue, just as I can fire my grocer by stopping purchases from him or sue him for delivering faulty products.[5]

This provocation, however, is simply contradictory since it is implicitly based on a perfect decision-making context. However, with positive transaction costs, as the authors assume explicitly, even firing a grocer is generally costly on both sides of the relationship.

In a second line of development of Coase's intuitions, costs and benefits of competition and command have been analysed systematically in an attempt to determine the virtues and vices of markets and hierarchies. 'Transaction costs economics' and the 'property rights theory' are the main outcomes (Coase, 1937; Williamson, 1975, 1985, 1996; Grossman and Hart, 1986; Hart and Moore, 1988, 1990; Hart, 1995; Moore, 1992). With respect to the contractual approach, this line of research provides a more articulated picture in which real world imperfections guide the evolution of the organizational structure of the firm and, more generally, of all capitalist institutions. Here there is no attempt to deny the existence of power relations in capitalism. On the contrary, the goal is to explore different decision-making contexts in the attempt to find the imperfections that explain the main forms of power existing in capitalist organizations. But the assumption is explicit: hierarchies or other forms of power may exist only where the conditions for perfect competition do not hold.

The most explicit attempt to deal with the issue of power within the institutions of capitalism, however, has been developed out of these branches of new institutional economics, by two economists belonging to the radical school, namely Bowles and Gintis (Bowles, 1985; Bowles and Gintis, 1988, 1990, 1993a, 1993b, 2000). Unlike the new institutionalists, they do not assume that eventual power relations should necessarily be sought within hierarchical organizations, such as the firm. They show instead that within imperfect decision-making contexts even market relations generally involve power.

On a path that is largely independent of this debate on institutions and power, new Keynesians have followed the same method, based on the introduction of imperfections into a general equilibrium framework. In the words of Greenwald and Stiglitz (1993, p. 24):

> Modern Keynesians have identified these real world 'imperfections' as the source of the problem: leaving them out of the model is like leaving Hamlet out of the play.

It is thus not surprising that efficiency wage models (Akerlof and Yallen, 1986; Shapiro and Stiglitz, 1984; Greenwald and Stiglitz, 1988) overlap in many ways with the models developed by Bowles and Gintis to analyse power relations. The common idea is that a wage higher than the market clearing one induces the worker to work harder than he/she wishes (by 'market clearing' is meant the equality of supply and demand). The main difference between them is only that, in one case, imperfections are the explanatory causes of allocation inefficiencies and second-best solutions; in the other, they are the cause of power relations.

Although these post-Walrasian approaches have sometimes confronted each other with harsh polemical tones, their common neoclassical methodology engenders the same conception of reality, a conception in which imperfections are the ultimate cause of institutional developments and of the forms of interpersonal relations.

## The radical school

The radical school consists of a heterogeneous set of theories critical of economic orthodoxy, with interests in issues such as power relations, inequalities, gender, race and class relations, which are often addressed with explicitly political objectives and militant participation. The breadth of this school's lines of research and the theoretical differences between its internal streams prevent here a systematic discussion of its main scientific contributions. For sure, the political motivations and the critique of the market society, or some aspects of it, distance this school of thought from the dominant theory (and, in many cases, from the official teachings of university courses).

Without any claim to completeness or representativeness, I focus on the contributions of two leaders of this approach: Bowles and Gintis. The reason is that the main theoretical contributions of these authors are explicitly inscribed in a close relationship with neoclassical theory and act as a bridge between Marxist problematics and neoclassical methodology.

Analytically, Bowles and Gintis remove some of the assumptions of the neoclassical model while remaining faithful to the general approach of the theory. The aim is to regain some of the Marxist theses on the functioning of capitalism from the methodological assumptions of neoclassical theory. In other words, these authors accept the neoclassical challenge and, by acting from within, question the image of capitalism provided by the general economic equilibrium model as a system of harmonious relations detached from any issue of power.

As an internal criticism, this way of proceeding is undoubtedly effective since, without any recourse to assumptions truly external to those of the neoclassical paradigm, it shows that even in neoclassical markets, under rather general assumptions, power relations between different agents exist. The problem, however, is that, from a constructive point of view, these developments are subject to the same criticisms levelled against neoclassical theory and thus constitute rather unstable foundations on which to develop an alternative proposal. Moreover – by accepting the neoclassical methodological approach, problematics and worldview – these new theories distort the very meaning of the conception of power relations with respect to the Marxist approach.

At a very general level, it is possible to distinguish two forms of power, one as 'power to act' (the power to perform this or that action), the other as 'power over somebody' (the power of a subject to condition the behaviour of another subject). The radical theory of Bowles and Gintis, but more generally the whole of bourgeois economics, focuses solely on the second form, according to which power is, by definition, an interpersonal relationship and not, more generally, a social relationship, determined by the heterogeneous distribution of power to act that society imposes on its participants. To put it bluntly, Elon Musk can choose whether to further develop his presence in the automobile sector, to expand into the media and space sectors or to invest everything in Bitcoin, the metalworker can choose whether to work for Musk or for Ford. Well, in the radical approach to power, this asymmetry is regarded as having no consequences in terms of eventual power relations at the interpersonal level.[6]

From a methodological point of view, this is the consequence of the usual assumption of bourgeois theory that endowments are exogenous to the model and that therefore what each person can do (the power to act) should not be studied, but rather taken as given. Analytically, however, Bowles and Gintis (somewhat like Williamson and Stiglitz) depart from the general economic equilibrium model by introducing a number of 'imperfections', which certainly bring the model closer to reality. Assuming a less aseptic context than the one crystallized in the general equilibrium model, Bowles and Gintis show how, in market interaction, power relationships between the agents are inevitable. In particular, the assumption that there are information asymmetries, uncertainty and problems in the execution of contracts, prevents the competitive equilibrium from being Pareto-efficient (giving rise to phenomena of rationing or, in the case of the labour market, unemployment) and puts some agents in a position to condition the behaviour of others (Bowles and Gintis, 1993a).

This has important normative effects because it dispels that image of competitive capitalism as a system of spontaneous interactions between free subjects proposed by the extremist advocates of general economic equilibrium. However, precisely because of the manner in which this result is achieved, we are left with the basic idea of bourgeois theory that capitalism is in itself an essentially neutral system in terms of power relations, and that the real drawback is the complexity of the world (the impossibility for agents to have perfect knowledge, to foresee the future, to be able to rely on automatic contract enforcement etc.), which certainly cannot be eliminated simply by changing the rules of social interaction, that is, by changing the type of economic system. In short, the fault would not lie in capitalism, but in the world: in a world without imperfections, according to this theory, capitalism would be an efficient system without power relations.

The 'demonstration' that even perfectly competitive markets operate through power relations comes through the introduction of the concept of 'contested exchange'. Let us therefore consider in some detail how this concept should constitute, according to the radical leaders, 'the new micro foundations for the political economy of capitalism' (Bowles and Gintis, 1990).

Bowles and Gintis define perfect competition as a situation characterized by free entry and large numbers of buyers and sellers, but not by market clearing. With this definition, they demonstrate that even in competitive equilibrium (with non-clearing markets), a market economy sustains a system of power relations among agents (a competitive equilibrium is a situation in which actors are incapable of improving their position by altering variables over which they have control).[7] This result is obtained by relaxing one of the assumptions of the Walrasian decision-making context that the authors consider the most implausible: the assumption that contract enforcement by a third party is costless and unproblematic. As they put it, standard Walrasian theory 'depicts a charmingly Victorian but utopian world in which conflicts abound but a handshake is a handshake' (Bowles and Gintis, 1993b, p. 83). In the real world, however, after handshakes, opportunistic behaviour abounds.

Bowles and Gintis (1993a, p. 325) define power as 'the capacity of some agents to influence the behaviour of others to their advantage through the threat of imposing sanctions'. The absence of power relations in the Walrasian model is a consequence of the condition that supply equals demand, which implies that each agent loses nothing by abandoning his optimal transaction in favour of his next best alternative: in a Walrasian equilibrium, the cost to agent *B* of foregoing an exchange with agent *A* is zero, so that *A* cannot affect *B*'s wellbeing by terminating the relation. Hence, Bowles and Gintis continue, *A* has no power over *B*. More generally, the fact that in Walrasian equilibria no agent can impose sanctions on other agents implies that the economy works without any underlying power relation among agents.

If contract enforcement is problematic, however, the picture changes radically. Bowles and Gintis (1993a, p. 332) 'call an exchange *contested*, when *B*'s good or service possesses an attribute that is valuable to *A*, is costly for *B* to provide, yet is not fully specified in an enforceable contract'. When exogenous contract enforcement cannot be guaranteed at zero cost by a third party (such as the judicial system), the transacting parties must enforce their agreement by themselves. In this case, the terms of the transaction are determined by the monitoring and sanctioning mechanisms instituted by *A* to induce *B* to provide the desired level of the contested attribute. One such enforcement mechanism is *contingent renewal*: 'contingent renewal obtains when *A* elicits performance from *B* by promising to renew the contract in future periods if satisfied, and to terminate the contract if not' (1993a, p. 333).

A typical example of contested exchange is the employer – worker relationship, in which 'while the employer's promise to pay the wage is legally enforceable, the worker's promise to bestow an adequate level of effort . . . is not' (Bowles and Gintis, 1993a, p. 333).

In simple terms, the information advantage of the worker, on which the leaders of the radical school insist so much, consists in the fact that only he/she knows whether he/she is really working with maximum effort and intensity. The capitalist, conversely, knows nothing about the actual activity of working. His/her problem is therefore to design mechanisms to ensure that the worker does indeed always give his/her utmost, even when it is not possible, or it is too costly to put a controller to constantly supervise his/her work activity. Hence the idea of increasing his/her salary a bit compared to the prevailing market wage. In this way, it is in fact the worker himself/herself who, for fear of losing his/her job and ending up competing for the prevailing market wage, disciplines himself/herself and gives even his/her soul to the company he/she works for.

Other examples studied by Bowles and Gintis are the relationships between owner and manager, lender and borrower, and between parties in international exchanges (Gintis, 1989; Bowles, Gintis and Gustafsson, 1993; Bowles and Gintis, 1994). In all these cases, competitive equilibrium is characterized by non-clearing markets, and agents on the *short side* of the market have power over the agents on the *long side* with whom they transact (where excess supply exists, the demand side is the short one, and vice versa). The cause of this power relation is that the agents on the long side who are lucky enough to enter the relation with agents on the short side enjoy a 'rent' (defined as the difference between the utility they obtain thanks to the transaction and the utility they would have if the transaction terminates), which is costly for them to lose. The fact that, within imperfect decision-making contexts, perfectly competitive markets do not necessarily clear produces thus an asymmetry between the two sides of the market, which, in turn, affects interpersonal relations between single buyers and sellers.

In the case of the work relation, employers are on the short side of the labour market and workers enjoy a so-called 'employment rent'. This rent is the instrument by which the employer places the worker under constant threat (similarly,

Bowles and Gintis show that creditors have power over debtors and owners of enterprises have power over managers). It is thus the fact that the unemployment condition is worse than the working one that confers a power of retaliation to the employer over the worker, and that makes the latter provide an 'adequate' level of effort at work, even when the boss is not constantly monitoring him/her.

With respect to the voluntaristic conception of Alchian and Demsetz, Bowles and Gintis take a step forward. Theoretically, Alchian and Demsetz's position, according to which the worker can leave the capitalist without utility losses, holds true only within the perfect decision-making context. Outside of it, it is generally costly to leave an interpersonal relation and individuals may be willing to accept some form of power, even if just for personal convenience.

Bowles and Gintis' theoretical exercise, however, is not methodologically different from that of their liberal rivals: in their post-Walrasian framework, power relations exist only because of imperfections in the decision-making context. Walras could not see this, because he had eliminated all the imperfections of the world from his model. Alchian and Demsetz cannot see it either, because of their contradictory assumption that perfect Walrasian competition is at work even within imperfect decision-making contexts. Radical post-Walrasians, by contrast, claim to have the proper theoretical framework for grasping the nature of power relations in capitalism: imperfections are the cause of power relations and a battery of models formalizing all different sorts of imperfections existing in the real world is the way to shed light on capitalistic power relations.

Even with this very particular method, however, post-Walrasian economics cannot aspire to develop a general theory of power. Contrary to the claim of radical economists, power can only be an exception in this approach, but cannot be the rule. Consider workers. If all workers were really difficult to monitor and endowed with information advantages because of widespread imperfections in the decision-making context, no competitive wage in the labour market would exist. Therefore, the threat of being fired and losing the employment rent would not be credible, and the capitalist would have no power over them. Remember that in this theory of power, just as in the efficiency wages theory, the worker has an incentive to work hard only if a lower (perfectly competitive) wage prevails in the labour market. In other words, this theory can, at best, explain why some particular workers suffer a power relation from their employer, but it cannot explain why workers in general suffer a power relation from capitalists. On the contrary, the demonstration that some individual workers suffer a power relation rests precisely on the assumption that standard workers suffer none.

## Methodological critique

As a development of Walrasian economics, the methodology of post-Walrasian economics incorporates the same general methodological assumptions as found in the Walrasian model. In order to answer its own scientific questions – which are derived from, but do not coincide with, those of Walras – it adds, however, two new explanatory categories: imperfections and opportunism. These are the essential ingredients for a power relation to exist: opportunist behaviours within imperfect decision-making contexts. Both these categories are defined ahistorically. The outcome is an ahistorical conception of power totally detached from the real forms of coercion that characterize capitalism. Let me begin my critique by considering these explanatory categories more carefully.

***Imperfections***

Bounded rationality, imperfect information, historical time etc. are not historically specific to capitalism; rather, they are features of all human relations in any historical context. Clearly, rationality principles and imperfections change in the history of human societies, but each society has its imperfections, degrees of uncertainty, asymmetric information, irreversible phenomena, and so forth. Therefore, according to the logic of post-Walrasian economics, power relations exist in all social systems, since their cause – imperfections – are ubiquitous.

It is not the time to discuss whether this statement is right or wrong. For instance, in the Marxist tradition, all societies based on a certain division of labour and a degree of specialization of their members are considered to be necessarily based on power relations. The methodological problem regards rather the attempt of post-Walrasians to explain historical processes by means of ahistorical categories.

Such a method implies that power relations have always existed, even before the historical development of market relations and economic competition. However, they were invisible and could not be detected by scientific investigation. They became visible only with the historical development of capitalism and the consequent possibility of conceiving of a model of complete markets and perfect competition (and, by symmetry, models with imperfections). Post-Walrasians must therefore consider themselves to be very lucky to live in the sole epoch in which everlasting power relations have finally become visible, as an exception to the Walrasian model.

The historical truth, however, is different. Market interaction and economic competition are not at all everlasting forms of social coordination. Markets played only minor roles in pre-capitalist societies and economic competition has become the main form of social coordination only in relatively recent times. If pre-capitalist systems, with less developed or completely absent markets, were not regulated by economic competition, it was not because of *market imperfections* – as post-Walrasian economics suggests – but because of *lack of markets*.

***Opportunism***

Opportunism is the rationality principle of post-Walrasian economics. Methodologically, it is a generalization of Walrasian maximizing rationality in a decision-making context characterized by imperfections. The novelty is only that, in this new decision-making context in which contracts can be violated, optimal strategies might consist in promising one thing and doing another.

As a methodological by-product of Walrasian categories, opportunism is introduced without explanations. The rise of opportunistic behaviours is assumed to be a natural fact, a consequence of human nature. For some reasons (which I will discuss later), post-Walrasians are more attracted by workers' opportunism than by capitalists'. Even workers' opportunism, however, is mainly seen as an everlasting problem stemming from the very nature of the worker, not as a historical product of this mode of production.

In his discussion of the working day, Marx (1867, ch. 10) points out that establishment of a 'normal working day' was the product of centuries of class struggle. During this process, it was not possible to conceive of workers' behaviour as 'cheating', since there was as yet no social standard of what a normal worker should do. It is only when institutional disciplinary apparatuses emerged (with all the consequences studied by Michel Foucault) that workers might be divided into 'normal' and 'deviant' and that those more reluctant to accept the discipline of the capitalist mode of production could appear as 'cheaters', to use mainstream economics terminology, or, following Foucault (1977), might even be depicted as 'mad'.

At the same time, Marx describes the growth of opportunism on the capitalists' side: for instance, after the promulgation of the factory acts of the 1840s in Britain, which fixed the length of the working day, a great deal of cheating was done by employers, who simply altered the factory clock in order to get extra labour-time.

Although post-Walrasian economics conceives of opportunism as a natural starting point and a universal explanatory cause, it is in fact a product of complex historical processes that have transformed labour into alienated labour and the owners of the means of production into capitalists. These are the preconditions for a problem of monitoring and disciplining labour to emerge. And these are the reasons why a monitoring problem willy-nilly persists even in the concrete process towards other modes of production.[8] The ahistorical methodology of post-Walrasian economics, however, does not allow grasping the historical nature of the problem it tries to rationalize. Rather, it suggests that disciplining labour is a universal problem and that its explanatory causes must be ahistorical categories. Historically, however, both the problem and its causes are products of the capitalist mode of production.

### *Power and competition*

A methodological apparatus based on ahistorical categories leads inevitably to other ahistorical categories. Power in this conception exists only as a violation of perfect competition. It coexists with competition because, in imperfect decision-making contexts, it is more efficient to have two coordinating mechanisms rather than one. But both power and competition exist out of history, as abstract forms of interpersonal relationships.

Post-Walrasian economics does not even try to explain the real processes through which authority and coercive mechanisms have developed in capitalism and have transformed competition into a coercive force. On the contrary, it defines power in such a way that it is incompatible with competition. Competition is thus emptied of its coercive nature, and the forms of coercion existing in capitalism are removed from it. The power-free nature of competition is not a result of the analysis, but a definition. If Walras provided an apparent scientific support to the myth of competition as a natural and socially beneficial mechanism, post-Walrasians willy-nilly support a new myth: the idea that competition is the reign of freedom, in which there is no room for power and coercion.

Here, however, we have another ideological intrusion hidden behind apparently purely methodological choices. Methodologically, the problem of this conception of power and competition as abstract, mutually incompatible, categories implies that this framework cannot explain both of them. It must assume one in order to characterize the other as its violation. Competition and power are therefore perfectly symmetrical in this methodology. So why do post-Walrasians treat them asymmetrically?

Without exceptions, post-Walrasians take power as the phenomenon to be explained, and competition as a natural and everlasting category, deserving no scientific explanation. Remember Williamson's expositional convenience: 'In the beginning there were markets'. Not of course real markets, but neoclassical markets, with atomistic agents and perfect competition. By contrast, power is seen as an unnatural phenomenon, simply because it does not exist in Walras' world. This is the origin of the problem.

The idea that competition is a natural mode of interaction between isolated individuals is nothing but the result of a mix of an ahistorical method and bourgeois ideology. Well before Walras formalized his model, Marx had already criticized the assumption that originally there were isolated individuals, who lived and produced autonomously, and who then came into contact with each other through the market and competition:

> Production by an isolated individual outside society . . . is as much of an absurdity as is the development of language without individuals living *together* and talking to each other. There is no point in dwelling on this any longer. The point could go entirely unmentioned if this twaddle, which had sense and reason for the eighteenth-century characters, had not been earnestly pulled back into the centre of the most modern economics. . . . Nothing is more dry and boring than the fantasies of a *locus communis*.
>
> (Marx, 1857, Notebook M, Introduction)

Marx also points out that human interests, with a highly developed division of labour, are necessarily social interests. Competition, therefore, is not merely a mechanism whereby isolated individuals pursue their goals, according to their innate preferences, but a mode of coordination of social individuals, with convergent and divergent social interests, influenced largely by class relations. Its historical development is a consequence of the development of property relations, another process that bourgeois economists assume rather than explain, since without private property it is not clear what the isolated individuals could exchange in the market. As Engels' (1844) explains:

> We have seen that in the end everything comes down to competition, so long as private property exists . . . because private property isolates everyone in his own crude solitariness, and because, nevertheless, everyone has the same interest as his neighbour, one landowner stands antagonistically confronted by another, one capitalist by another, one worker by another. In this discord of identical interests resulting precisely from this identity is consummated the immorality of mankind's condition hitherto; and this consummation is competition.

Before explaining power as a violation of perfect competition, post-Walrasians should explain why they choose precisely competition as their starting point. If they do not even raise the question, it is only because the starting point is itself a product of bourgeois ideology: in capitalism, competition appears as natural, and Walras' model only formalizes this appearance.

## Ontological critique

Before capitalism, in this conception, there was not feudalism, or other modes of production, but Léon Walras. The nature of power relations is not studied as a transformation of the power relations that regulated the modes of production that preceded capitalism. Rather, power is explained as a deviation of real capitalism from the abstract Walrasian model.

The post-Walrasian ontology is not built as an attempt to discover the essential categories of capitalism. The conditions of reproducibility of the system are not even investigated. Rather, ontology is assumed as an indirect and implicit consequence of methodological choices and 'expositional convenience'. Without much philosophical discussion, ontological individualism is assumed as an implicit premise of methodological individualism.

The starting point of the analysis is an abstract model (the Walrasian model) in which abstract individuals interact, not a historical reality made up of real people. The problem is not to understand how capitalism works and reproduces itself and the social nature of the different individuals that interact in this system, but to explain how power relations can be introduced in the general equilibrium framework. Hence, the debate on power is basically an exercise in pure logic. The consequence is that all these theories can at best solve the problems of the Walrasian model, by means of new assumptions, but cannot explain the nature of power relations in the real history of capitalism.

In the post-Walrasian ontology, the nature of power relations can only be found within the interpersonal relation itself. By construction, the latter can have a power content only by introducing imperfections. In this ontology, there is no room for social coercion and power relations can exist only as violations of perfectly competitive interactions. The notion of power incorporates thus the theory of perfect competition as its essential premise and its study becomes little more than an appendix of the perfectly competitive model.

Although post-Walrasian economics does not develop any explicit ontological reasoning, its specific methodology based on imperfections imposes new conditions on the original Walrasian ontology. This exacerbates the problems already inherent in Walrasian ontology. The problem is twofold: first, this ontology assumes that capitalism coincides with free contracting; second, it conflates the spheres of production and circulation.

### *Free contracting*

According to Walras and post-Walrasian economics, a world of perfect information and free contracting is, by definition, a world free from power relations or, to use Marx's (1867, ch. 6) provocative expression, 'a very Eden of the innate rights of man'. This is why, theoretically, post-Walrasian economics needs imperfections to deal with power-related phenomena. The fact that contracting agents might face completely different material constraints when they 'freely' sign the contract is not seen as a potential cause of their power relation. Their different role in production as members of opposing social classes plays no role in the explanation of their power relationship. On the contrary, the implicit assumption is that contracts are signed in a vacuum in which only subjective choice matters.

As Marx has shown, however, free contracting is only one of the historical conditions of the emergence of proper capitalistic relations. Because, for a capitalist – worker relation to emerge, the labourer must be free in a double sense: 'That as a free man, he can dispose of his labour power as his own commodity, and that on the other hand he has no other commodity for sale, is short of everything necessary for the realization of his labour power' (Marx, 1867, ch. 6).

Free contracting and the lack of the means of production are the two ingredients of capitalistic exploitation. There is no abuse, no asymmetric information or bounded rationality, in the power relation of the capitalist over the worker. The fact that the latter obeys the former is not even the essence of the problem in Marx's ontology. Their interpersonal power relation depends on the relation of exploitation existing between their social classes (and the concrete proof of this is provided to us today by the new methods of disciplining labour based on computer platforms, in which the worker does not obey directly to an individual boss but to an algorithm designed to maximize his/her exploitation). Therefore, the coercive nature of capitalism is not sought in the single interpersonal relation between a capitalist and a worker in isolation, but in the social mechanisms that separate the population into social classes and that reproduce this social structure.

In this ontology – built explicitly on the conditions of reproduction of the capitalist mode of production – the worker is not obliged to exchange his/her labour power with the wage of a *particular* capitalist but is obliged to exchange his/her labour power with the wage of *a* (any) capitalist. Alchian and Demsetz are then right when they affirm that the worker is a free individual, who can leave the capitalist whenever he/she wants. But this is only one side of the coin. Capitalism would not reproduce itself just by means of exchanges between grocers and customers. Only in the abstract reign of free contracts, is this relation formally equivalent to that between capitalist and worker. In real capitalism, however, the coin has a second side. The worker is still free to interrupt the relation with the capitalist, but his/her freedom of choice is very peculiar: he/she *must* obey a capitalist or *choose* another capitalist to obey (or more realistically, hope *to be chosen* by a capitalist). And the worst thing that can happen to a worker, in a society based on capital, is not to enter into a relation with any capitalist wishing to command and exploit him/her.

It is not a problem of uncertainty, bounded rationality or asymmetric information: the worker may know or ignore the fact that, within capitalistic firms, he/she must obey the capitalist and give him part of the value he/she produces; but these are the rules of the game and if he/she does not accept them, he/she will not get the means of subsistence. This is not to say that imperfections are useless categories. On the contrary, if one introduces them explicitly in this more accurate ontology, it is evident that asymmetric information, bounded rationality and other 'imperfections' modify the existing power relations, but do not create them: if a worker is not well-informed or is rationally bounded, he/she might accept worse conditions than his/her colleagues (after all, therein lies the secret of *Walmart*'s economic success, which signs customized contracts with each individual worker and forbids them to tell their colleagues the terms of the contract). Yet, even the most rational and well-informed worker will never get a job if he/she is not ready to obey and to be exploited.

By contrast, post-Walrasian economics introduces imperfections in a contradictory ontology, in which capitalism is reduced to free contracting and nothing else. In Walras' model, this assumption is coupled with the perfect decision-making context. The result is a conception in which, by assumption, the only coordinating mechanism is competition. In the ontology of post-Walrasian economics, free contracting is analysed instead within an imperfect decision-making context. The result is a conception in which power relations exist, beside competition, but, by construction, only as a consequence of imperfections. This suggests a picture of a society in which contracts are the highest expression of individual freedom and power relations emerge only when their enforcement is problematic – the best way to dismiss Marx's critique, without even considering it: in the search of the forms of coercion of this mode of production, Marx's theoretical concern is not that contracts are sometimes violated, but that they are generally respected.

### *Production and circulation*

In Marx's (1867, 1885, 1894) characterization of capitalism as a system of commodity production, there is a clear-cut separation between the spheres of production and circulation of commodities. This separation allows him to discuss how capital may appear to be productive (in circulation), notwithstanding its unproductive nature (in production) and to criticize economic conceptions based solely on circulation.

In the sphere of circulation, capitalists and workers do not appear in the first instance as social entities, but simply as individuals, who exchange commodities. As such, they seem to be on the same ground and their relation seems to be based purely on free will: 'There alone rule Freedom, Equality, Property and Bentham', says Marx (1867, ch. 6) provocatively. But before being exchanged, commodities must be produced. Before discussing the forms of power originating directly in the sphere of circulation, Marx (1867, ch. 6) explains the forms of coercion emanating from production:[9]

> On leaving this sphere of simple circulation or of exchange of commodities, which furnishes the 'Free-trader Vulgaris' with his views and ideas, and with the standard by which he judges a society based on capital and wages, we think we can perceive a change in the physiognomy of our dramatis personae. He, who before was the money-owner, now strides in front as capitalist; the possessor of labour power follows as his labourer. The one with an air of importance, smirking, intent on business; the other, timid and holding back, like one who is bringing his own hide to market and has nothing to expect but – a hiding.

By investigating the sphere of production, Marx argued that the working class is exploited and that the capitalist class appropriates a value it has not produced. This form of social exploitation is also the main cause of the asymmetry between capitalists and workers in the workplace. Historically, the need to supervise the production process is a consequence of the problematic process of extracting living labour from workers' labour power. Marx discusses this process in different parts of *Capital* and explains how the internal organization of the firm and the way workers are disciplined in the workplace evolve according to the needs of capital accumulation. He points out for instance that the development of stock companies and cooperative factories are very different processes, but are also responses to the same problem: in one case, the extraction of living labour from workers' labour power is delegated to a manager, in the other to workers themselves (Marx, 1894, ch. 27).

Modern Marxists, such as Harry Braverman (1974) and Richard Edwards (1979), have developed this conception by discussing the evolution of class relationships and the development of different forms of power, authority and hierarchy within capitalist firms in the 20th century. Social exploitation and interpersonal power relations, in the work of these authors, are dialectically linked: on the one hand, exploitative class relations in society are the cause of the interpersonal power relation in the workplace; on the other hand, the evolution of the forms of power prevailing within capitalist firms transforms class relations and modifies the rate of exploitation.

In this ontology, the forms of power that prevail in the sphere of production are linked to the exchanges that must occur in circulation for the system to reproduce itself. Capitalist production starts with the sale of workers' labour power. By buying this commodity, the capitalist acquires the right to dispose of it. It is not a question of price. The worker might sell it dear or cheap, but the very act of selling his/her labour power gives the capitalist an interpersonal power over him/her during the production process.

Post-Walrasian economics, by contrast, does not start from the real development of capitalism and its reproducing mechanisms, but from an abstract model, based on a flat ontology in which production is, *de facto*, a subset of circulation, an exchange between input owners. The result is a more sophisticated ontology than the Walrasian one, still based on pure circulation, in which however circulation incorporates imperfections. Even the central relation that characterizes production – the capitalist – worker relationship – is considered as a form of exchange, an exchange that occurs in a complex decision-making context, but still a phenomenon of circulation.

Within the sphere of circulation, there can be no production of value but only an exchange of equivalents. Therefore, if, in an equilibrium position, the individual capitalist has power over the individual worker, it is only because he pays for it. Before the exchange, the information advantage belonged to the worker, like the labour power that he/she sells to the capitalist. After the exchange, power is in the hands of the capitalist, and its monetary equivalent in the pockets of the worker.

In this ontology, the price that the capitalist pays to have power over the worker is not simply the wage, as Marx argued, but a part of it. In post-Walrasian economics, by definition, competitive wages involve no power relations. The latter arises only when the capitalist pays additional money to induce worker's self-discipline. Power is thus a sort of commodity, which the capitalist buys from the worker – besides his/her labour power – in order to increase his/her productivity, exactly as he buys machines, work instruments and innovative technologies. Like all commodities, power has its equilibrium price, defined as the amount of money that compensates the worker for not using his/her informative advantages opportunistically.

As Marx explained, in the eyes of the capitalist, the value of production is produced by the total capital he has invested, independent of the real origin of value. By formally including power in the reign of commodities, post-Walrasian economics preserves this appearance. If the capitalist buys a machine or a power relation, it is only because the increase in expected revenues is greater than the cost of the investment. For him/her, power relations are production factors, no less than any other work instrument he/she buys in order to increase workers' productivity. Therefore, the increase in the value of production following the purchase of a power relation over the worker appears to him/her as an effect of the capital spent in this investment, not as a consequence of the increase in the worker's effort (which, in Marxist terms, corresponds to an increase in the amount of living labour extracted from his/her labour power).

Without any ontological separation between production and circulation, the appearances that capital is productive and that individuals are equal becomes in post-Walrasian economics the true essence of capitalism. In this mystified conception, the asymmetry responsible for eventual power relations must be introduced directly in circulation, even when dealing with capitalists and workers. Formal equality in the market becomes synonymous with 'freedom', and power relations are detected only when they manifest themselves formally in asymmetric market relations. All other forms of coercion within capitalism become invisible.

## Formal similarities within opposite conceptions

We have now the elements to discuss how post-Walrasian economics can substantiate the Marxist claim that the capitalist has power over the worker.

### *Marx*

The main theoretical problem faced by Marx in his attempt to explain the working of capitalism and its forms of coercion is that this mode of production is a mystified system. Indeed, one of the specificities of capitalism is that its exploitative nature is hidden behind the appearance of free market exchange. His critique of political economy, therefore, is not a simple reply to his theoretical and political rivals. It is rather a way to demystify the appearances of capitalist reality – which bourgeois economists rationalize – and to explain scientifically what at first glance cannot be seen. The complexity of Marx's analysis stems from this twofold scientific goal: discovering the coercive mechanisms of capitalist accumulation and explaining how social coercion and exploitation might appear as expressions of individual freedom and equality. Both these problems lead him to deepen the role of competition and its relation with capital.[10]

In his work, methodological and ontological issues are strictly related and developed explicitly. The choice of the categories to start with and the method to develop their analysis are consequences of an ontological reasoning: capitalism, like all modes of production, must first of all reproduce itself. Like other modes of production, it is presumably not everlasting. But the fact that it has lasted for centuries suggests that some reproducing mechanisms do in fact exist. The scientific problem is then to discover them and understand how they work. Given the historical nature of the whole mode of production, these reproducing mechanisms have necessarily a historical nature as well.

For ontological reasons, Marx starts from the commodity as the elementary category of this mode of production. The production of commodities, he soon notices, depends on the existence of a class of persons in constant need of selling their labour power. Social classes, in this perspective, are not merely theoretical constructs, but essential ontological entities of the capitalist mode of production: no sellers and buyers of labour power, no capitalism. The necessity to consider them explicitly is not much of a problem related to their concrete empirical configuration, but is first of all one of internal consistency: an economic model must contain mechanisms that allow the economy to reproduce itself.

Competition, in Marx's critique, is precisely the mechanism that regulates this process. More generally, competition regulates the relations among individual capital in the overall process of capital valorization. In the analysis of these processes, Marx shows that competition produces a number of contradictory tendencies that make the reproduction of the system increasingly problematic and that create the conditions for superseding the capitalist mode of production.

Marx's discussion of competition starts with its historical origins, before the rise of the capitalist mode of production, as a consequence of two institutions: private property and the market. Capitalism, however, as we have said, is characterized also by the commodification of labour power, that is, by the extension of private property and the market to labour power as well. This is why, in this mode of production, competition also takes on a class dimension. With the development of capitalism, capital tends to subsume all human activities and put living labour under its command. In this process, competition imposes its logic over an expanding sphere of social relations and tends to become the coordinating principle of the whole society, the 'external coercive law' of this mode of production, in Marx's terms.

Only at this point can a proper discussion of capitalistic power relations begin. Interpersonal power relations do not develop in a social vacuum but are embedded in the capitalist system of power. Their essential, necessary, role can be grasped only after having explained the social asymmetries that shape interpersonal relations and the coercive mechanisms that reproduce them. Otherwise, they may appear as mere theoretical possibilities in a power-free context.

At an interpersonal level, the coercive nature of competition depends on the pressure it puts on market participants. No worker is obliged to sell his/her labour power at the lowest price, and no capitalist is obliged to seek the most profitable productions and the least expensive techniques. But if they do not do it, the former does not get the means of subsistence and the latter is put out of the market. It is only at a social level, however, that the coercive nature of competition can be fully grasped, as the main economic mechanism that regulates the reproduction of class relations. Marx's study of a world regulated by competition, therefore, is not an attempt to see how interpersonal relations would be in a system without power and coercion, but a methodological choice intended to isolate the role of this coercive mechanism in the working and reproduction of capitalism.

Bourgeois economists have made any effort to develop a conception of competition as the driving force of capitalism towards the common good: Smith, Austrian economists, Walras and post-Walrasians have developed different scientific variants of this conception. But they forgot to criticize capital. The result is the celebration of the invisible hand, as a natural mechanism at the service of economic and social progress and a conception of power as its violation. By developing an organic critique of capital, Marx has shown instead that, in fact, this invisible hand only serves the needs of capital. In the capitalist mode of production, the common good is the good of capital and competition simply imposes capital needs over single individuals, social classes and the whole society. In a Marxist conception, the *invisible hand* of competition is nothing but the *armed wing* of capital.

In the process of commodification of society, competition tends to impose its logic at a subjective level as well: as the spectrum of social relations governed by competition develops, competition tends to appear as a natural force, a form of interaction that has always existed, a consequence of human nature. Only at this stage does it become possible to conceive of a world entirely regulated by market relations and competition. Historically, however, the appearance of a competitive 'human nature' – which the bourgeois economist takes as the theoretical starting point of all explanations – is in fact a product of capitalist development.

### *Post-Walrasian economics*

Marx's radical successors within post-Walrasian economics do not develop this conception and do not even consider Marx's critique of bourgeois economics. Rather, without understanding that the latter applies largely to them as well, they uncritically adopt a neoclassical methodology and then try to obtain conclusions with a Marxist sound.

The idea is that Marx's method is weak and fuzzy, and that only a strict neoclassical method can overcome its internal limitations. The historical rise of neoclassical economics – an academic reaction against Marxism and its revolutionary implications – is taken as the birth of the universal economic method, to which even Marx should be converted. As a scientist, Marx is worthless. Only some of his non-scientific intuitions might perhaps be saved (for reasons that Marx himself could not understand). This is the way in which post-Walrasian economists view the founder of scientific socialism. This is the logic of this new 'heterodox' academic fashion, which includes 'Rational choice Marxism' and 'Market socialism' as well: either Marxism becomes a small chapter of neoclassical economics, or it remains scientific bullshit ('non-bullshit Marxism' is the self-assigned label of 'Analytical Marxists').

Unfortunately, neoclassical economics cannot be bought *à la carte*. When you buy its method, you buy its implicit ontology and its ideological premises as well. The result is that the same statement – that the capitalist has power over the worker – takes here a completely different meaning with respect to Marx's conception of this relation and of its role in class struggle.

Methodologically, the starting point is the Walrasian model, in which all economic relations are compressed within the sphere of circulation and analysed according to methodological individualism. With these premises, the only way to demonstrate that economic relations might involve power is to play with assumptions. 'Imperfections' and 'individuals with heterogeneous innate qualities' are the methodological tools of the game chosen by post-Walrasian economics, within an implicit ontology based on free contracting and pure circulation.

In playing this game, Bowles, Gintis and their neoclassical colleagues have not found anything better than assuming an asymmetry in favour of the individual worker against the individual capitalist, before the exchange, in order to explain why, after the exchange, the latter has power over the former. Their story begins with the advantage of the individual worker (remember that this advantage is very special: it is the advantage of knowing how hard it is to work) and finishes with the capitalist having power over him/her. But only because, in the middle, there is the monetization of the worker's advantage. The power relation suffered by the worker is thus caused by his/her supposedly favourable position with respect to the capitalist, not the other way round. Reality is thus turned upside-down, as in the old, mystified conception of bourgeois economics. Although neoclassical economics does not like the notion of exploitation, in post-Walrasian economics, the exploited one might eventually be the capitalist, who pays the rent, but surely not the worker who collects it.

But to fully grasp this mystified conception, we must follow the worker on the day in which he/she finally gets rid of his/her power relation with the capitalist, the day in which the latter introduces a new machine, which regulates workers' effort, their pace of work and their mode of coordination with each other. This same day, the worker loses the information advantage, the rent and perhaps the job. For post-Walrasian economics, however, this is the day of his/her liberation from the capitalist's power. Now, finally, the worker can leave the capitalist without losing anything (having already lost everything, except his/her labour power). This is freedom in post-Walrasian economics.

To show that the capitalist has power over the worker, post-Walrasian economics assumes that the individual worker is not a member of the class of persons who have nothing to sell except their labour power, but, on the contrary, that he/she is a privileged person within this class, having also something else to sell (his/her informational advantages stemming from the fact that he/she does a job that is difficult to monitor). Workers at the perfectly competitive (subsistence) wage, instead, suffer no power relations in this conception. In a complete overturning of Marx's idea, here the interpersonal power relation suffered by the individual worker is not caused by his/her membership in an exploited class, but by his/her privileged position within this class. In a nutshell, in post-Walrasian economics, the worker suffers a power relation not because of his/her social weakness, but because of his/her individual strength.

Even collective action becomes a matter of personal convenience in this approach. To quote again the leaders of radical post-Walrasian economics, employment rents 'are not only enforcement instruments, they are also prizes to be won or enhanced through collective action. Collusion by one group of workers to exclude others on the basis of racial, gender, or ethnic differences, for example, can increase the employment rents of this group' (Bowles and Gintis, 1990, p. 197).

In this framework, workers' union is not in the first instance a tool to resist capital, but a strategy to beat other workers in the struggle for the capitalist's 'prize'. Collective action is not an emancipatory practice, but a cause of discriminations. Faced with the many overlapping sources of power and coercion flowing from class, racial, gender and ethnic relations, radical post-Walrasians do not even try to disentangle this complex set of social relations and, eventually, suggest how to struggle against this multiform oppression. Instead, they provide a rationalization of the battle of the have-nots, in which socially discriminated groups find their enemy in other oppressed groups, not in the general cause of their oppression, namely capital.

According to post-Walrasian economics, collective bargaining, strikes, occupations and all the practices historically developed in class struggle are irrational behaviours and violations of the common good. It would be clearly exaggerated to blame an academic approach for the real transformations of society. But this is precisely how the direct attacks on wages, centralized bargaining and workers' rights – including the right to struggle – have been imposed in the last decades in most of the globe: not as forms of class struggle against the proletariat, but as technical solutions for the good of everybody.

Some post-Walrasians might be satisfied with the formal similarities between their results and Marx's theory. Their conception of science and their role in society, however, resemble closely those of 'the vulgar economist [who] does practically no more than translate the singular concepts of the capitalists . . . into a seemingly more theoretical and generalized language, and attempt to substantiate the justice of those conceptions' (Marx, 1894, ch. 13).

## The scientific problem

Before moving to some conclusions, let me discuss the ideological nature of the scientific problem of post-Walrasian economics. As we have seen, post-Walrasian economics assumes self-interested individuals. Self-interested behaviour, however, is described as 'profit maximization' regarding the capitalist and as 'opportunism', 'shirking' or 'cheating' with regard to the worker. The problem is not only terminological. It reflects rather a precise, although implicit, ideological position.

### *Bourgeois ideology and scientific questions*

Contemporary capitalism offers a wide range of examples of contracts that are not enforced correctly: workers that are not paid for months by their employers, banks that do not pay back depositors' money, states that do not honour their international commitments, women who are molested in the workplace. These are not distortions of capitalism, but normal effects of self-interested behaviours in a society characterized by asymmetrical power relations.

With asymmetric power relations, it is clear that the powerful, not the powerless, can more easily behave opportunistically. For some reason, however, when the capitalist – worker relationship is at stake, post-Walrasians are all preoccupied mainly by the possibility that the worker takes a break, slows down the pace of work or does not maximize effort during the working day – problems that perhaps should concern more the capitalist than the economist. This is the origin of the literature on monitoring, shirking, incentive schemes, principal – agent problems and the rest.

As we have seen, the post-Walrasian framework has been applied to very different situations in which contract enforcement is problematic. Curiously, however, no post-Walrasian focuses on the millions of workers that suffer daily abuse by their boss but have no means to bring him to the tribunal (and perhaps no interest in doing so). Nor do they focus on those who just accept the contract because they have no alternative, no matter the terms of the contract. Not to mention the army of undeclared workers who do not even know how a labour contract looks like.

By assumption, as Bowles and Gintis say explicitly, the employer's promises are legally enforceable, and the problem is only on the worker's side.

Formally, there is no asymmetry between capitalists and workers in this theoretical framework. As self-interested individuals, they will contravene their commitments every time this increases their expected utility. In concrete model building, however, post-Walrasian economics treats these two figures asymmetrically: one is the supervisor, the other the supervised, one is the principal, the other the agent; and the 'scientific problem' is to find effective incentive mechanisms to push the agent to serve at best the interests of the principal. Implicitly or explicitly, capitalists' interests are transformed into social goals.

Starting from a symmetrical conflict, post-Walrasians introduce an asymmetry and put themselves at the service of one of the conflicting parties. There is no theoretical reason why the economist should take the viewpoint of the capitalist, rather than that of the worker. But once this theoretical choice has been taken, implicitly or explicitly, all issues of 'cheating', 'shirking' and 'laziness' follow naturally. This is why, in this literature, the lazy one is the worker, who works seven hours and 55 minutes (having 'shirked' 5 minutes in the toilets), not the capitalist who does not work at all.

### *Neoliberal cultural hegemony*

Theoretically, there is no obstacle that prevents neoclassical economists from developing also the social consequences of capitalists' opportunistic strategies against their employees. If this occurs rarely it is because the scientific community has its own internal logic. As Antonio Gramsci (1929–1935) pointed out in his study of cultural hegemony and the role of intellectuals, dominant ideology tends to impose the viewpoint of the ruling class as a cultural norm.

Post-Walrasian economics is both a cause and an effect in this process. On the one hand, its scientific problem is a product of capitalist ideology: the problem is to monitor and discipline labour. On the other hand, by transforming the capitalist's problem (the worker's opportunism) into a social problem, it reinforces the ideas that workers' discipline is a universal goal, and that all studies developing explicitly the standpoint and interests of the worker are politically biased and hence, according to the dominant conception, not really scientific.

Before Marxists converted to neoclassical methodology (and neoliberal ideology) took this route, the scientific defence of capitalists' interests in the workplace was not hidden behind questions of Pareto efficiency and second-best solutions. Both Marxists and bourgeois economists agreed that a greater effort at work was in the interest of capitalists and went against those of the working class.

When in 1911 Frederick Taylor wrote *The Principles of Scientific Management* – in which he studied how to increase workers' productivity and extract as much labour as possible from their labour power – its impact in the political and scientific debate was unambiguous: his work was appreciated not only by capitalists – which is quite obvious – but also by mainstream economists. Rapidly, scientific management affirmed itself as a new research program, with new university teachings and specialized academic journals. In the Marxist camp, this managerial approach was openly criticized, both theoretically and politically, with the development of the so-called *labour process debate*.

Taylor of course was not a Marxist and was perfectly aware that his fortune was due to his ability to put science at the service of the capitalist class. Less evident, by contrast, are the real intentions of the new radicals, who accept neoclassical economics as a matter of pure methodology, without discussing the relations between methodology and ideology.

To be clear, to be incapable, or unwilling, to develop Marx's conception is surely not a capital sin. But having missed the scientific mission of an epoch is a more serious blame. Because the concrete effect of post-Walrasian radicalism is straightforward: in a historical context, in which the labour movement was trying to unite and organize in the workplace and in the overall society, radical post-Walrasians have contributed to rationalize the everlasting problem of the capitalist class – to discipline labour and organize it according to capitalists' needs – and to reinforce a conception in which power is a simple interpersonal relation, which develops naturally, for personal convenience. Some of them have been rewarded with prestige and academic power for their theoretical contributions. But only by other academicians and bourgeois institutions, not by people struggling against capital chains.

## Economists as servants of power

The 1968 movement remains today one of the most advanced radical, revolutionary movement with a worldwide impact. Those people who fought the power in different spheres of social life and in different angles of the globe had in mind a radically different society.

Italian workers shouted: 'We want everything!' ('Vogliamo tutto' is the title of a political document about the struggles of 'Potere operaio' (Balestrini, 1974)). French militants echoed with 'Let's be realistic, demand the impossible!' ('Soyons réalistes, demandons l'impossible!' was one of the most striking slogans of the May 1968 movement, often attributed to Che Guevara). Feminism, black power, anti-fascism, anti-imperialism, anti-war, anti-nuclearism, anti-prohibitionism, ecologism, homosexuality, peoples' self-determination, in the sixties and the seventies, all aspects of social life were object of collective critique and political struggle. In workplaces, in schools and universities, in the streets and in prisons, everywhere institutionalized power was questioned and overtly fought. Strikes, occupations, self-organization, counter-culture, music, art, drug, sport became all means to react collectively against the forms of oppression and domination of capitalism. Struggles developed everywhere, in a common effort to change the material conditions of this class society, discard the coercive nature of bourgeois hegemonic culture and rethink the rules of social interaction.

For the first time in Western societies, a mass student movement played a major role in social struggles, joined the claims of workers and created a fusion with the civil rights movement in a process of radical critique and social emancipation. The student movement disrupted academic equilibria and imposed a radical reaction against mainstream thinking in all social sciences. In the United States, these processes led to the birth of the radical school, an academic project based more on common progressive political goals than on a general method and conception.

The academic debate on power is largely a product of these social and political movements. Forced by the contradictions of society and by overt political struggles, social scientists have been called to take position: on the one hand, those who tried to hide, justify or rationalize the existing forms of power, domination and coercion; on the other, those who criticized them and searched the way to attenuate or supersede them. It is within this historical context that some progressive academicians have developed this curious theoretical exercise, wishing to 'rehabilitate' Marx within mainstream economics.

Like old revisionisms, post-Walrasian radicals start by formally declaring sympathy for Marx, but soon after distance themselves from his method and critique. Rather than developing a theoretical conception of power that might give coherence to the collective struggles growing in society, post-Walrasians have developed a framework in which power is good for the individual and collective action is only a deplorable form of monopoly. Students and society demanded critical thinking and attacked frontally all institutionalized powers, including academic hierarchies. 'Radical' teachers and researchers answered by developing a theoretical framework in which 1) the greatest worldwide wave of collective struggles appears simply as an irrational, scientifically unfounded, reaction against an only imaginary world of social coercion and 2) the sole rigorous science of power has to do with isolated individuals fighting for themselves.

To affirm this general conception of power, post-Walrasian economists have worked hard. They have developed an abstract, universally valid, framework and have applied it to all fields of social interaction, from grocery shopping to international relations. Radicals, in particular, have pushed this conception very far and have concluded that power relations are practically ubiquitous. Curiously, however, they have never considered that, as scientists, they too are embedded in a community ruled by power relations and which reproduces itself by means of particular rules and mechanisms, whose effect is to shape and select scientific production. In their view – but this is a widely shared opinion even outside the academy – universities are the places of critical thinking, scientific autonomy and research freedom *par excellence*. Scientific rigour and technical skills, not power relations, class interests and cultural homologation, are the keys to academic success. *Voilà*, after a contradictory scientific path, the last contradiction of this academic approach to power, which pretends to be radical: power is everywhere, but in the academy.[11]

Historically, university professors have not been very inclined to criticize the system of power that gives them economic privileges and social recognition. Instead, they have shown high degrees of adaptability to all kinds of economic and political powers. When, in 1931, Benito Mussolini imposed the fascist oath in Italian universities, out of more than 1200 academicians, only in 12 refused it (and were thus excluded from their roles).[12] And when today European university teachings and researches are redefined, under the international coordination of the so-called 'Bologna process', to meet the needs of international capital restructuring, professors and researchers are again adapting meekly to their new economic and social functions. In market-oriented university systems, then, the role of power relations is not really weaker: apparently, political power is less invasive, but only because universities are already under tight control of economic power. And when explicit disciplining mechanisms are not enough, there comes the omnipresent Soros, with his *Institute for New Economic Thinking*, to direct economic research in the name of pluralism (of bourgeois science), attracting to himself all the 'heterodox' economists ready to do anything to get a slice of his lavish funding.

Although university systems work and reproduce themselves according to different mechanisms in different countries, they all play a delicate role in scientific and cultural production. Only in the head of the scientist, who does not recognize his/her social and economic role, can university be conceived as 'free' and science as 'neutral'. Only such a scientist can think that the success of his/her theory of power has nothing to do with the real power relations existing in society. It is not by chance, however, that the sharpest critique of intellectuals was developed by Gramsci – while he was paying the price of his radical thinking and political coherence in fascist prisons – not by a progressive economist believing in science neutrality.

Gramsci (1929–1935) explained that 'All men are intellectual' since 'There is no human activity from which every form of intellectual participation can be excluded'. His critique, therefore, is not about intellectuals as such, but about the social function of this professional category. In his revolutionary strategy, the problem is to create a 'new stratum of intellectuals', whose mode of being consists in 'active participation in practical life', in social struggles within the masses, in expressing the feelings and the instances of social movements. Only such an intellectual can play a revolutionary role against traditional intellectuals and their intrinsic conservatism.

But, of course, this process does not develop out of class relations, but within them, with open clashes between different class cultures and practices. Without conscious resistance, the interests and values of the ruling classes tend to prevail and to appear as interests and values of the whole society, so that even dominated classes identify their own good with the good of the ruling classes. This why, under the title of the weekly *L'Ordine Nuovo*, co-funded by Gramsci, a slogan reads: 'Educate yourself, because we'll need all your intelligence. Agitate yourself, because we'll need all your enthusiasm. Organize yourselves, because we'll need all your strength'.

'Cultural hegemony', for Gramsci, is not the *ex post* result of freely competing cultures, but a political strategy on both sides of class struggle. It is indifferent the good or bad faith of the individual scientist. The rise of post-Walrasian economics is part of this hegemonic process, which characterizes the neoliberal era. The project itself to force Marx's revolutionary ideas into mainstream economics is a manifestation of the role of cultural hegemony in science as well. Rather than rehabilitating Marx, these projects do in fact exclude his conception from the set of what they define rigorous science. Post-Walrasian economists pretend to fly higher than Marx because of their scientific rigour and neutrality. Without understanding that it is only their being part of a hegemonic process that makes them appear as scientifically neutral.

Post-Walrasian radicals not only miss the bourgeois nature of their theories but do not even grasp the political role they actually play. In their 'neutral' conception of power, the power of the capitalist over the worker is in the interest of the worker. And the objective need (for capital and for its master, but apparently for its sycophant too) to force the pace, the intensity and the overall effort of the worker, again, is only for the own good of the latter. This is what leftist economists affirmed while Thatcher and Reagan were starting the neoliberal program.

Although post-Walrasians might be convinced that their academic success is only a matter of science, when the mechanisms of academic production and reproduction are put in relation with the social and economic function of the university and other scientific institutions within the capitalist system, a more linear explanation emerges: the appeal of this approach is not necessarily in its self-proclaimed scientific superiority, but in its ability to incorporate even the most radical critique of capitalism within the more convenient framework of neoliberal culture and politics, thereby depriving it from all its subversive and revolutionary contents.

In 1974, before engaging actively in post-Walrasian economics, Bowles wrote an article titled 'Economists as servants of power', in which he discusses the 'immense . . . possibilities for socially concerned economists', if only they decide to work with social movements, and criticizes 'conventional economists', by dividing them in two groups: the 'Engineers' – 'neo-Keynesian stabilisers' and other economists working 'to "rationalize" production and increase profits for the large corporation' – and the 'Priests', 'neoclassical theorists for the most part', playing a 'less useful, but no less important' ideological role, whose impact is 'to obfuscate the sources of social problems, locating the roots of inequality and hierarchy in the nature of man (preferences) or the state of nature (technology), thereby denying the possibility of a substantially better society'.

It is hard for an economist to choose between these different roles. Only a theory of power based on the spontaneous maximization of workers' effort, under the principle of economic efficiency, could aspire to have it both ways.

## Conclusions

In his contribution for the *Journal of Economic Perspectives*, referred to at the beginning of this chapter, Joseph Stiglitz (1993) discusses explicitly the relations between the radical approach of Bowles and Gintis and the mainstream development of Walrasian economics, based on imperfect information and costly contract enforcement. He argues that there are striking parallels between the two approaches, that they use the same method and set of assumptions and that they deal basically with the same problem. The difference, in his view, is only about terminology:

> Mainstream economists have not only found concepts like exploitation and power to be useless in explaining economic phenomena, but they worry about introducing such emotionally charged words into the analysis. But

that is presumably precisely why the radical economists choose to use such words: they want the analysis to motivate action.

(Stiglitz, 1993, p. 112)

It is not very surprising that the winner of the Nobel Prize considers exploitation and power as emotionally charged words, rather than scientific concepts, and that, by contrast, he considers efficiency – the key word of the neoliberal political program – as a value-free notion.[13] But this is only a confirmation that value judgements are easily detectable only when they break the beliefs that form the cultural hegemony of a given time. Otherwise, they may appear neutral, even though the very possibility of pure objectivity in social research is a highly controversial issue.

Apart from this consideration, I share fully Stiglitz's conclusion about the internal compatibility of this research program. This is, however, only half of the story. The second half regards the relation with Marx. In this chapter, I have thus explicitly espoused a Marxist perspective and I have submitted to critique the methodology, ontology and ideology of post-Walrasian economics.

Let me recap my conclusions by starting from the pre-scientific choices of post-Walrasian economics. In the analysis of the capitalist – worker relationship, post-Walrasians – from ultra-liberals to radicals – have unanimously focused on the capitalist's standpoint and have thus helped to rationalize and solve its economic problem. In this way – perhaps, in some cases, involuntarily – they have transformed a problem of a part of society into a problem of the entire society. This choice involves a stronger role for ideology than is the case for Walrasian economics. The latter is only an attempt to formalize the virtues of market interactions among atomized individuals. Post-Walrasian economics goes further. Within the same individualist framework, which assigns no role to class relations, it introduces social classes surreptitiously by defining 'the economic problem' as 'the problem of the capitalist'. This ideological degeneration of radical thinking – I suggest – is the outcome of two interdependent processes: 1) the tendency to uncritically accept neoclassical methodology in the scientific community and 2) the consolidation of the neoliberal hegemony in culture and society.

Post-Walrasian methodology is based on two main ingredients: imperfections and opportunism. These ingredients are defined ahistorically. The resulting conception of power is ahistorical as well. The different forms that power takes in the history of capitalism are not objects of scientific inquiry. The goal is rather to show that there is a valid alternative to competition, under certain conditions. The result is a theory of power in which, by construction, competition is power-free. In post-Walrasian economics, the coercive law of capitalism is not competition, as Marx thought, but the lack of it.

This methodology imposes new conditions on the implicit ontology of Walras' model. In post-Walrasian economics, capitalists and workers are not social entities, but individuals with innate qualities. Their eventual power relation depends only on these qualities and on their fit with an imperfect decision-making context. The fact that one is a capitalist and the other a worker is irrelevant. They might also be a bank and a firm, two states, or a customer and a grocer. As long as the parameters of the models coincide, the nature of the power relation is the same. And as power arises in circulation, where only exchanges of equivalents occur, the interpersonal asymmetry before the exchange must be assumed to be favourable to the worker if one wants to prove that, after the exchange – when individual advantages have been monetized – power is in the hands of the capitalist.

When we move from the formal claim that 'post-Walrasian economics has demonstrated that the capitalist has power over the worker' to a discussion of the causes and the mechanisms of this power relation, the result is not so Marxist. Rather, it is a logical development of the mystified conception formalized by Walras. The proof is that, in these models, power is a form of capital and, as such, is treated as productive. But this also confirms that post-Walrasian economics is only a sophisticated version of the old bourgeois conception criticized by Marx, in which all forms of capital are conceptualized as productive. My conclusion is that, overall, post-Walrasian economics is a coherent extension of perfect exchange to contested exchange. The obvious consequence, however, is the addition of new contradictions to an already contradictory conception.

## Notes

1 I have criticized post-Walrasian economics in Palermo (2016a).
2 My critique of Williamson's theory and new institutional economics developed in Ankarloo and Palermo (2004). In Palermo (1999), I criticize the attempt to incorporate Austrian theory into new institutionalism, arguing that it is based solely on a common neoliberal political stance that does not, however, come to terms with the profound methodological distance that separates the two traditions of economic thought.
3 I have discussed the debate on power in Palermo (2007a, 2014).
4 In Palermo (2000), I argue that new institutional economics fails both in its attempts to characterize theoretically the capitalist firm and to analyse the power relations of capitalism.
5 Williamson (1994, p. 325) criticizes explicitly this position, by affirming: 'Firms can and do exercise fiat that markets cannot do', and characterizes intra-firm relations precisely by the asymmetry between employers and employees.
6 In Palermo (2007b), I develop an ontology of economic power in capitalism, inspired by Marx's conception, by focusing on the relationship between power to act and power over somebody and by investigating the coercing mechanisms and the constraining and conditioning structures that govern the reproduction and development of both power to act and power over somebody in society.
7 Bowles and Gintis distinguish between 'perfect competition' and 'perfect Walrasian competition': the former does not imply market clearing, the latter does (and coincides with what in the literature is generally called 'perfect competition'). Ultimately, this is why they can claim that power relations exist even in a regime of perfect competition (with non-clearing markets).
8 During the socialist calculation debate, Austrian liberals raised two arguments against socialist planning: the impossibility to process huge fluxes of information and the lack of incentive schemes for workers. We have already discussed the first argument in chapter 3. As concerns the second argument, neoclassical market socialists replied to anti-socialists by developing the same principal agent framework used to monitor workers in capitalism. Although academically effective, this reply shows that market socialists take alienation for granted even in their ideal models of 'socialism'.

9 Within modern Marxism, Fourie (1989) has criticized transaction costs economics, by arguing that its explanations of hierarchy in production rests on a theoretical confusion between production and exchange. Before him, Engels (1878, part II, ch. 1) had noticed: 'Production may occur without exchange, but exchange – by the very fact that it is only an exchange of products – cannot occur without production'.

10 I have developed the complex relations between coercion and competition in the Marxian conception in Palermo (2016b). From this analysis I have then developed a Marxist conception of competition and power in Palermo (2017, 2019) respectively.

11 With the notable exception of Pierre Bourdieu (1984), academicians have rarely tried to apply their theories of power to the university system in order to criticize its internal mechanisms and its economic and social functions. I have tried to contribute to this critique by discussing the Italian university system as a system of power in Palermo (2012).

12 The fascist oath was preceded by discriminations against women and was followed, in 1938, by the shame of the 'racial laws'. From exile, professor Gustavo Colonnetti (1973, p. 54) commented the easygoing reaction of his 'colleagues' by calling it 'prostitution of science'. Roberto Finzi (1997) reconstructs the stories of the victims of political and racial discriminations and points out that – except for rare but significant exceptions – the whole university system created a curtain of indifference or even contempt against them, which lasted even after the fall of fascism, fearing that their readmission in role might upset the new power balance within faculties. In Palermo (2011), I discuss the role of academic power in the evolution of the social and economic goals of Italian universities since national unification.

13 Rigorously speaking, Stiglitz's efficiency wages theory has more to do with exploitation than with efficiency, for total output is not increased by holding inputs constant, but by increasing one of them: the amount of labour extracted from workers' labour power.

## References


Akerlof, G. and Yallen, J. (1986) *Efficiency wage models of the labour market*. Cambridge, England: Cambridge University Press.

Alchian, A. and Demsetz, H. (1972) 'Production, information costs and economic organization', *American Economic Review*, 62(1), pp. 777–795.

Ankarloo, D. and Palermo, G. (2004) 'Anti-Williamson: a Marxian critique of new institutional economics', *Cambridge Journal of Economics*, 28(3), pp. 413–429.

Balestrini, N. (1974) *Vogliamo Tutto*. Milano: Garzanti.

Bourdieu, P. (1984) *Homo Academicus*. Paris: Minuit.

Bowles, S. (1985) 'The production process in a competitive economy: Walrasian, Marxian and Neo-Hobbesian models', *American Economic Review*, 75, pp. 16–36.

Bowles, S. and Gintis, H. (1988) 'Contested exchange: political economy and modern economic theory', *American Economic Review*, 78, pp. 145–150.

Bowles, S. and Gintis, H. (1990) 'Contested exchange: new microfoundations for the political economy of capitalism', *Politics and Society*, 18(2), pp. 165–222.

Bowles, S. and Gintis, H. (1993a) 'Power and wealth in a competitive capitalist economy', *Philosophy and Public Affairs*, 21(4), pp. 324–353.

Bowles, S. and Gintis, H. (1993b) 'The revenge of homo economicus: contested exchange and the revival of political economy', *Journal of Economic Perspectives*, 7(1), pp. 83–102.

Bowles, S. and Gintis, H. (1994) 'Credit market imperfections and the incidence of worker-owned firms', *Metroeconomica*, 45(3), pp. 209–223.

Bowles, S. and Gintis, H. (2000) 'Walrasian economics in retrospect', *Quarterly Journal of Economics*, 115(4), pp. 1411–1439.

Bowles, S., Gintis, H. and Gustafsson, B. (1993) *Markets and democracy: participation, accountability and efficiency*. Cambridge, England: Cambridge University Press.

Braverman, H. (1974) *Labour and monopoly capital: the degradation of work in the twentieth century*. New York: Monthly Review Press.
Cheung, S. (1983) 'The contractual nature of the firm', *Journal of Law and Economics*, 26(1), pp. 1–21.
Coase, R. (1937) 'The nature of the firm', *Economica*, 4(4), pp. 386–405.
Colonnetti, G. (1973) *Pensieri e Fatti dell'Esilio (18 Settembre 1943–7 Dicembre 1944)*. Roma: Accademia Nazionale dei Lincei.
Dugger, W. (1992) 'An evolutionary theory of the state and the market', in Dugger, W. and Waller, W. (eds.) *The stratified state, radical institutionalist theories of participation and duality*. London: M. E. Sharp.
Edwards, R. (1979) *Contested terrain: the transformation of the workplace in the twentieth century*. New York: Basic Books.
Engels, F. (1844) *Outlines of a critique of political economy*. Available at: www.marxists.org
Engels, F. (1878) *Anti-Dühring: Herr Eugen Dühring's revolution in science*. Available at: www.marxists.org
Finzi, R. (1997) *L'università Italiana e le Leggi Antiebraiche*. Roma: Editori Riuniti.
Fisher, F. (2011) 'The stability of general equilibrium – what do we know and why is it important?', in Bridel, P. (ed.) *General equilibrium analysis: a century after Walras*. London: Routledge.
Foucault, M. (1977) *Discipline and punish: the birth of the prison*. London: Allen Lane.
Fourie, F. (1989) 'The nature of firms and markets: do transaction cost theories help?', *The South African Journal of Economics*, 57(2), pp. 142–160.
Gintis, H. (1989) 'Financial markets and the political structure of the enterprise', *Journal of Economic Behavior and Organization*, 11, pp. 311–322.
Gramsci, A. (1929–1935) *Prison notebooks*. Available at: www.marxists.org/archive/gramsci/prison_notebooks/index
Greenwald, B. and Stiglitz, J. (1988) 'Pareto inefficiency of market economies: search and efficiency wage models', *American Economic Review*, 78(2), pp. 351–355.
Greenwald, B. and Stiglitz, J. (1993) 'New and old Keynesians', *Journal of Economic Perspectives*, 7(1), pp. 23–44.
Grossman, S. and Hart, O. (1986) 'The costs and benefits of ownership: a theory of vertical and lateral integration', *Journal of Political Economy*, 94(4), pp. 691–719.
Hahn, F. (1982) 'Stability', in Arrow, K. and Intriligator, M. (eds.), *The handbook of mathematical economics*, Vol. II. Amsterdam: North Holland.
Hart, O. (1995) *Firms, contracts and financial structure*. Oxford, England: Clarendon Press.
Hart, O. and Moore, J. (1988) 'Incomplete contracts and renegotiation', *Econometrica*, 56, pp. 755–785.
Hart, O. and Moore, J. (1990) 'Property rights and the nature of the firm', *Journal of Political Economy*, 98(6), pp. 1119–1158.
Jensen, M. and Meckling, W. (1976) 'Theory of the firm: managerial behaviour, agency costs and ownership structure', *Journal of Financial Economics*, (3), pp. 305–360.
Kantorovich, L. (1939) *Matematicheskie Metody Organizatsii i Planirovaniia Proizvodastva*, Leningrad: Leningrad University Press. English translation (1960). 'Mathematical methods of organizing and planning production', *Management Science*, 6(4), pp. 363–505.
Marglin, S. (1974) 'What do bosses do? The origins and functions of hierarchy in capitalist production, part 1', *Review of Radical Political Economics*, 6(2), pp. 60–112.
Marglin, S. (1975) 'What do bosses do? The origins and functions of hierarchy in capitalist production, part 2', *Review of Radical Political Economics*, 7(1), pp. 20–37.
Marx, K. (1857) *Outlines of the critique of political economy*. Available at: www.marxists.org
Marx, K. (1867) *Capital: critique of political economy, Vol. 1: The process of capitalist production*. Available at: www.marxists.org

Marx, K. (1885) *Capital: critique of political economy, Vol. 2: The process of circulation of capital*. Available at: www.marxists.org
Marx, K. (1894) *Capital: critique of political economy, Vol. 3: The process of capitalist production as a whole*. Available at: www.marxists.org
Moore, J. (1992) 'The firm as a collection of assets', *European Economic Review*, 36(2–3), pp. 493–507.
Palermo, G. (1999) The convergence of austrian economics and new institutional economics: methodological inconsistencies and political motivations, *Journal of Economic Issues*, 33(2), pp. 277–285.
Palermo, G. (2000) 'Economic power and the firm: two conflicting problems', *Journal of Economic Issues*, 34(3), pp. 573–601.
Palermo, G. (2007a) 'Misconceptions of power: from alchian and demsetz to bowles and gintis', *Capital and Class*, 92, pp. 147–185.
Palermo, G. (2007b) 'The ontology of power in capitalism: mainstream economics and Marx', *Cambridge Journal of Economics*, 31(4), pp. 539–561.
Palermo, G. (2011) *L'Università dei Baroni: Centocinquant'Anni di Storia tra Cooptazione, Contestazione e Mercificazione*. Milano: Punto Rosso.
Palermo, G. (2012) *Baroni e Portaborse: I Rapporti di Potere nell'Università*. Roma: Editori International Riuniti.
Palermo, G. (2014) 'The economic debate on power: a Marxist critique', *Journal of Economic Methodology*, 21(2), pp. 175–192.
Palermo, G. (2016a) 'Post Walrasian economics: a Marxist critique', *Science and Society*, 80(3), pp. 346–374.
Palermo, G. (2016b) 'Power, competition and the free trader vulgaris', *Cambridge Journal of Economics*, 40(1), pp. 259–281.
Palermo, G. (2017) 'Competition: a Marxist view', *Cambridge Journal of Economics*, 41(6), pp. 1559–1585.
Palermo, G. (2019) 'Power: a Marxist view – coercion and exploitation in the capitalist mode of production', *Cambridge Journal of Economics*, 43(5), pp. 1353–1375.
Samuelson, P. (1957) 'Wages and interest: a modern dissection of Marxian economic models', *American Economic Review*, 47, pp. 884–912.
Shapiro, C. and Stiglitz, J. (1984) 'Equilibrium unemployment as a worker discipline device', *American Economic Review*, 74(3), pp. 433–444.
Stiglitz, J. (1993, Winter) 'Post Walrasian and post Marxian economics', *Journal of Economic Perspectives*, 7(1), pp. 109–114.
Sveriges Riksbank (1991) *The Sveriges Riksbank prize in economic sciences in memory of Alfred Nobel 1991*. Available at: NobelPrize.org
Taylor, F. (1911) *The principles of scientific management*. New York: Harper & Brothers.
Williamson, O. (1975) *Markets and hierarchies: analysis and antitrust implications*. New York: Free Press.
Williamson, O. (1985) *The economic institutions of capitalism: firms, markets, relational contracting*. New York: Free Press.
Williamson, O. (1994) 'Visible and invisible governance', *American economic review, papers and proceedings*, 84(2), pp. 323–326.
Williamson, O. (1996) *The mechanisms of governance*. New York: Oxford University Press.

# 6 Market values

## The universalization of market values

Most of the theoretical and empirical problems I have raised so far are not really original. They are in fact long-debated issues that have unfortunately lost their centrality in economic discourse as critique as a scientific research method has faded. The neoliberal economic policy itself was the subject of harsh criticism during the years of Ronald Reagan and Margaret Thatcher, although later that same ultraliberal model became the hard core of the unique thought to which even left-wing (in some cases ex-communist) parties adhere without too many caveats today. Regardless of the effectiveness of the critique and rebuttals made on a scientific and political level, the neoliberal theory has achieved an important political result by affirming market values as universal values. In addition to the impact at the level of economic policy, the general values on which the political strategies of the new ultraliberal right are based have taken root at the cultural level: here and there it is acknowledged that the market can fail; however, the market is now the benchmark, the value system, that has imposed itself so widely even on the left that it appears, at times, universal and natural.

According to the arguments of the new right (and the new left), the market is the only institution capable of administering justice in the economic sphere: only the laws of the market are suitable for regulating relations between individuals. Economic conflicts must therefore not be resolved through an explicit discussion in terms of political positions and value judgements, but must be left to the market, which does justice through its economic laws.

However, the fact that market justice is value-neutral is not evident at all. Market laws, being valid only in the capitalist mode of production, reflect the values on which capitalist social interaction is based. In economic systems other than capitalism, market laws do not apply, and the rules of individual behaviour and social interaction reflect values other than those of the market. And, even within the capitalist system, if one recognizes its class division, it is easy to realize that the values presented as universal are actually those of the dominant class: the bourgeoisie. Engels (1877, part 1, ch. 9) wrote as follows:

> We therefore reject every attempt to impose on us any moral dogma whatsoever as an eternal, ultimate and for ever immutable ethical law on the pretext

DOI: 10.4324/9781032726168-7

> that the moral world, too, has its permanent principles which stand above history and the differences between nations. We maintain on the contrary that all moral theories have been hitherto the product, in the last analysis, of the economic conditions of society obtaining at the time. And as society has hitherto moved in class antagonisms, morality has always been class morality.

The values of the market are simply the values of the bourgeoisie, and if they are presented as universal, or even cease to appear as values (in the sense that, by becoming unanimously shared, they cease to give rise to conflicting judgements, which instead characterizes value judgements), it is only because we implicitly take the capitalist system as given and espouse the views of its ruling class.

The market imposes its laws as general and invariable laws from which there is no escape (unless the market itself is abolished). The reduction of the level of abstraction from the analysis of different modes of production to the analysis of the capitalist mode of production makes the general characteristics of the capitalist system appear as universal. This is also the case with values: the values that inspire capitalist institutions instead of being general (i.e. valid for the totality of capitalist-type systems, observed from the perspective of their ruling classes) appear as being universal (i.e. valid for any economic system and any social class).

The identification of the conditions of efficiency, rationality or desirability of the market is presented by bourgeois economics as a merely technical problem, to be tackled without introducing value judgements, as a condition of scientificity. The shift from the analysis of modes of production to the analysis of the capitalist mode of production, with the resulting universalization of market values, however, transforms the ban on introducing value judgements into economics into a ban on the use of value judgements other than bourgeois ones. This is obviously not methodologically correct when comparing different modes of production or different class cultures.

What interests me, however, is not so much the methodological correctness of the operation. Rather, I am interested in a particular consequence of the operation of universalizing market values, namely the annihilation of the possibility of discussing market ethics. The assumption that the values on which market interaction is based are universal implies that, precisely because of their universality, they must be taken as given and cannot be discussed. In bourgeois theory, the generality of market laws thus spills over into the value system that market laws enact, which is objectivized and, thanks to this, placed outside the sphere of moral enquiry. The (bourgeois) values of the market cease to be questioned.

Market values are based on individualism, meritocracy and competition. *Individualism* originates in modern bourgeois theory as a methodological foundation (the principle that all economic phenomena must be explained starting from the individual) to become immediately afterwards, albeit without any scientific reason, also an ideological foundation based on a double principle: 1) the individual is the best judge of himself and 2) society must only be judged on the basis of the evaluations of individuals endowed with economic resources (let us recall that it is on this double principle that Pareto's efficiency criterion is founded). *Meritocracy*, in a theoretical context that denies the existence of power relations, actually conceals the principle of the law of the strongest and makes the results of class selection appear as individual failures or successes. *Competition*, which in itself is not a value, becomes one precisely because of the objectification of market values: if the law of the market establishes that competition is won by the best (i.e. the strongest), the law of the strongest becomes, for bourgeois economists, the (obviously implicit) foundation of justice in economic relations.

The success of the new liberal right with respect to the objectification of market values is so overwhelming that it has also raised doubts on the left about the validity of the reasons for going against the market. Whereas in other fields of social interaction, laws are established on the basis of guiding principles derived from explicit moral and political discussion (in which political parties, trade unions, movements, associations, religious communities intervene), in the economic field the laws of the market, being objectively given, are considered immune to discussions in terms of values.

Think of the liveliness and harshness of the debates on issues such as abortion, euthanasia, and drugs, and compare this with the absolute and inescapable dictates of the law of the market regarding so-called structural reforms, the dismantling of the welfare state, the race to abolish pensions and public healthcare, flexibility and worker mobility: on the right to terminate one's pregnancy, to experiment the alterations of drugs on oneself, or to end one's existence with dignity, it is perfectly normal to have different opinions (although usually, it is those who would not enjoy such rights in any case who want to impose their principles on others, which is not exactly a liberal principle); on the duty to conform democratic institutions (won in years of struggle) to the law of profitability and on the duty of the worker to bend to the will of the market, instead, there is nothing to be said; these are only external constraints, against which, not only neoliberals, but, more generally, lovers of the *new* and of *progress* (i.e. in words, everyone), know that there is no point in battling.

The fact is that, once the logic of market relations has been accepted, it is difficult to submit the values implicit in market laws to a coherent critique. Bourgeois economics, by affirming the principle of universality of the market and of its laws, has thus subtracted large spaces, in the analysis of social relations, from the discussion in terms of values, making market values the indisputable reference point on which to base all economic relations.

All this undermines the left, which, being unable to propose a reflection on the modes of production or, simply, being unwilling to renounce the capitalist foundations of social interaction, finds itself accepting as given a system of values that historically does not belong to it and yet finds it difficult (or uninteresting) to question. To give three examples of the hegemony of market culture, let us think of the unfortunately increasingly topical problems of immigration, education and labour.

The discussion on immigration, in circles that are succubus (or promoters) of market culture, does not touch on moral issues at all. It is like people 'without feet on the ground' to investigate the moral values by which persons from poor countries should be allowed or denied entry into rich countries. The subject of the discussion is not the fact that in fleeing their countries of origin, immigrants risk their lives in the sea or are crammed into inhuman settings as in the days of the deportation of slaves from Africa (the difference being that for the slaves then it was a nightmare imposed by force and weapons, while for those of today it is a dream that, at the current market prices, only a few can afford). The fact that these new deportees 'freely' choose to undertake the most uncertain journey of their lives and that they are also relatively 'lucky' compared to those who instead remain in the misery and oppression of their countries of origin does not induce any reflection on the absurdity of the world capitalist system, nor does it produce any discussion of the fundamental rights of the individual in self-proclaimed civilized countries. On the contrary, the consideration that these people are 'free' and 'fortunate' only serves to pacify consciences (and shows that, after all, the economist who takes the initial endowments for granted only expresses the culture of his/her time). The only real problem being discussed (from barber's chats to parliamentary debates) is that of the market's demand for labour at different levels of qualification and the risk of jobs being lost for people with full rights. The stories experienced by (would be) immigrants and the conditions from which they try to escape (for which host countries often bear great responsibility) are irrelevant. What matters is a residence permit and a work contract. These are the conditions that the law of the labour market sets for entry into the North.

Education is increasingly oriented towards production. Schools themselves have become small competing businesses. Universities are instead institutions governed internally by almost impenetrable co-optation mechanisms, whose main external task is to supply specialized personnel to companies, passing on the costs of training to society and the families of individual students. All this in order to allow companies to defray personnel training costs from their budgets and thus reduce production costs. What could be better for a company than to find a nice army of qualified unemployed people on the market from which to draw according to the needs of the economic situation? But beyond the economic aspect, the biggest problem with this business-oriented model of education is that it also places strong conditions on the content and form of teaching. The purpose of schools and universities is not to form people with a critical sense, capable of forming their own ideas by comparing different visions and cultures (with the risk, perhaps, that one day they may even criticize the very mechanisms of the educational and production system). Instead, education serves to impart notions useful for production, and the only criticism considered legitimate concerns the fact that often the things learned are of no use in finding a job. In short, the contents of education are not criticized for their subordination to the needs of the market but, on the contrary, for the fact that this subordination is considered insufficient. The discourse on the right to study is not about the basic values according to which people should be provided with the tools and time to think and deepen their interests. Instead, the debate is about whether education meets market demand. As for the form of teaching and learning, woe betide those who refuse to passively assimilate the notions imparted and even believe that they can question them. There, selection is immediately triggered. Not as a social evil, but in the pure interest of the student (future worker): how could someone who is already at school or university would like to discuss and criticize as a method of learning and emancipation fit into the productive society? The demands of the labour market are other: discipline, obedience and respect for one's superior, these are the values that make a worker desirable. And so, authority, selection and hierarchy become the general forms even in teaching, taming the student before the final metamorphosis into a docile worker.[1]

The right to work is denied in fact. But what is worse is that even in theory it is considered a harmful remnant of a path towards a model that is now judged to have failed irretrievably. Work as a moment of fulfilment for the individual is then a discourse that, after being defeated on the ground, has lost even its utopian characteristics, to become, quite simply, anachronistic. Flexibility, mobility, wage moderation are today's buzzwords in the world of work. It is not production that serves the needs of people, it is people that serve the needs of production. It is the worker who must flex and displace and who must be able to make do with a wage determined by the game of competition. And if this game, as even economists know, pushes wages down, there is nothing to be done. These are the objective rules of the market. Trade unions themselves, having accepted the logic of the market and competition, have little to protest against the watchwords of capital: after all, their very existence is a blatant violation of the competitive model, which leads them to question the very culture of solidarity from which they were born. Faced with the drama of unemployment, then, they make capital's concerns their own, because, as we know, if capital worries, it does not invest and does not employ workers. In the absence of an alternative scheme to counter the competitive market model, the demands of the grassroots – clearly incompatible with the diktat of perfect competition that wants wages at subsistence level – also become extremely uncomfortable at the negotiating table with the bosses. Flexibility and mobility – which for the worker and his/her family don't exactly equate to greater autonomy and a few trips out of town – are thus accepted as an objective requirement of the production process, not as the subjective aspiration of every capitalist, and for this very reason are not even really opposed. The trade unions' concern is no longer to wrest the maximum from the capitalist counterpart, but to convince the base that that minimum achieved in negotiation is actually a lot (even if it is in fact little). Sometimes, then, completely addicted to the market culture, convinced in this way to fight unemployment, the unions even propose the reduction of real wages. The simple truth is that the new capitalist left has no longer anything to offer the workers. Only the rights of the individual now matter. The most radical campaign uniting all progressives of individualism today is the one in defence of the LGBTI movement. Anyone who raises doubts about the real emancipatory character of this movement, lavishly financed by Soros, is a conservative, an enemy of individual freedom. Social emancipation of the exploited classes is no longer on the agenda. Emancipation is now only an individual process, which concerns the individual's relations with his/her/its body, not the social relations that imprison the individual in exploitative conditions.

If 'feet must remain on the ground', values might fly a little higher. And it is certainly not in the interest of the right to open the discussion. A large part of the left has thus ended up accepting the political message of the new right, according to which the market is the supreme institution of justice in economic matters. While on other political issues, the right and the left maintain their cultural and ideological differences, on the most important issue, that of economic relations, the new right and the new left converge towards a common model (which is ultimately that of the old neoliberal centre) in which the only tolerated value system is that of the market.

## Moral values and economic interests

The affirmation of market values as universal values goes through a general process of mystification that leads to representing the culture and values of the ruling class as unanimously shared. The process of economic mystification thus leads to the economic interests of one section of society being concealed behind the objectivity of science and the theory of the common good. Parallel to this process of objectivizing market values, mystification also operates on the values of politics. Political mystification consists in masking economic interests that guide political action behind high moral values. In the political sphere, the problem is that those values that are presented as inspiring the various actions actually disguise economic interests that often have nothing to do with the declared values.

The debate, if one can call it that, on the Gulf wars or the Balkan wars or on the need to finance the Ukrainian coup government and its armed forces (also made up of battalions explicitly inspired by Nazism) so that it can send its people to die against a decidedly superior economic and military power in the name of defending European democracy, has developed and is developing as if the stakes consisted exclusively of the highest moral values (freedom, justice, democracy, civilization) and very little is known about the economic interests of the opposing forces. The fact then that, if it were really a matter of defending moral values, the behaviour of the moralizing forces (NATO and the United States in the lead, but right behind the European Union and its states) would be highly contradictory, may at best leave us puzzled as to the real objectives pursued, but it certainly does not help us to understand the Gulf crisis, that of the former Yugoslavia, the war in Afghanistan, the Russian-Ukrainian conflict or the Palestinian question (problems that could instead be brought into much better focus by having at hand a nice map of the oil fields, pipelines and other key resources of capitalist development and investigating the strategies of the imperialist powers to appropriate everything).

The problem of the relationship between politics, moral values and economic interests also invests less dramatic and spectacular aspects of our lives: for example, issues such as the environmental disaster and the quality of life only hit the headlines when it comes to launching the new electric cars or encouraging the transition to economically uncompetitive energy sources alternative to hydrocarbons. Here again, the problem is posed in terms of almost universal values: who can afford to speak out against protecting the environment, a common good owned by us all? Even a 15-year-old girl with diagnosed autism like Greta Thunberg, who instead of going to school, started a lonely protest in front of the Swedish Parliament and found herself catapulted to give lectures to the whole world from the highest headquarters of the United Nations, the World Economic Forum and the Vatican, understands this. The environment is sacred and green corporations are social benefactors. In this way, a strictly economic problem, that of the development of particular industrial sectors and of the growth of the profits of the companies that operate in them (through questionable instruments such as state incentives at the expense of the community), is also transformed into a highly moral problem and politics is presented as the instrument of moralization and the pursuit of the common good.

Regarding the fate of the young lone fighter, of course, it did not cross the mind of any environmentalist or progressive, right-wing or left-wing, radical or moderate, that perhaps a young girl suffering from Asperger's syndrome would have been better integrated into her community by attending school with her classmates, instead of running from one seat of power to another, without knowing their role and history. The little Greta, sacrificial victim of the most spectacular media operation, surrounded and pampered by the strong powers, known and loved all over the world, fed to finance by her own parents while she was trying to get out of her autism, convinced by now to be the star of the green, is actually more alone than ever. This, from a human point of view, is the Greta phenomenon: the instrumentalization of children turned into a struggle for progress, under the applause of public opinion. And green investors.

The discrepancy between declared and actually pursued objectives has long since moved beyond the sphere of action of those directly involved and has established itself at the cultural level so widely that it is difficult to identify. It is intuitive to understand why those directly involved have a particular interest in mystification: it enables the pursuit of real goals without the need to discuss them, let alone make them explicit. It is more difficult, however, to explain how mystification affirms itself even where the actors involved do not derive a direct benefit from it. Sometimes the values associated with certain news, especially in the economic field, seem to escape even those who make a moral issue out of them. A sports journalist would not dare to state that fortunately AS Roma beat Juventus or that disgracefully AC Milan is third in the standings. Economic news, by contrast, seems to respond to a precise moral code, which its spokespeople do not hesitate to display publicly, as if it were unthinkable not to share it: in what sense is the appreciation of the dollar a *positive* fact (beyond its algebraic meaning)? How can it be argued that wage increases are *dangerous*? And, above all, dangerous *for whom*? For workers perhaps? In what sense is the rise in stock market prices a good thing and their fall a bad one? Who pays the shareholders' capital gains when the stock market goes up, and what does it matter to us worthless people when the stock market goes down? According to what accounting nonsense can it be argued that millions of dollars are 'burned' when the stock market falls?[2]

No one explains it to us. But politicians, journalists, economists (and shareholders!) are all happy when the stock exchange goes up, while they are all desperate when it goes down, and it seems that we should be too. Fortunately, there is now Jerome Powell, the chair of the Federal Reserve. He at least says it loud and clear: there is no room to lower interest rates in the event of unemployment, which, as we know, would trigger the usual dreaded wage-price spiral. But when the Nasdaq collapses, he takes interest rates to zero in an instant to prevent at all costs the 'too big to fail' companies from failing all together.

In both political and economic mystification, the economist bears important responsibilities: in the case of political mystification, the economist's responsibility is mainly passive and consists in too often uncritically accepting the motivations expressed by politics, without adequately informing public opinion of the economic repercussions and partisan interests of the interventionists; in the case of economic mystification, instead, the responsibility is entirely active, since it is bourgeois science that provides the universal ethical code, proclaiming the existence of the common good and claiming to provide the best instruments for its pursuit. Thus, although political and economic mystification are two aspects of the same phenomenon, consisting of the pursuit of undeclared goals, it is in the economic sphere that mystification fully enters into the very perception of reality and this thanks to the force conferred on it by bourgeois science and its absolute hegemony in the centres of knowledge and indoctrination. However, once certain economic principles have been allowed to pass (the rationality of the market and the consequent superiority of the Western model over all other economic models, the right-duty to extend market relations to the maximum and to impose such a model on others), they also become the guide for politics proper, which ceases to be discussed on the basis of the obvious hypothesis of conflicting interests and also becomes a simple instrument for pursuing the common good.

The game is tough: on the one hand, the various power groups, exploiting our intellectual laziness, hammer us with value judgements that do not belong to us and that we end up feeling as ours; on the other hand, relying on our values (or, which is the same thing, on the values we feel as ours), they ask us for our consent to policies that serve their purely economic interests (and, very often, go against our own interests).

If the capitalist system seems to emanate its own value system, it is not because it has been constructed on the basis of a particular moral system, but because different and changing economic interests are intertwined in it. And this is why, when we try to analyse this hypothetical value system proper to capitalism, it appears so contradictory: because we naively seek its coherence in an imaginary ethical system, whereas it simply reflects the changing economic interests of the ruling classes (which not even the rationalizing lenses of the economist can really recompose). Thus, for example, in the face of so much military interventionism by the West, on so-called humanitarian grounds, we cannot explain the silence on the Israeli occupation of Palestine and on the genocide of the Palestinian people, where not even children are spared. Or, in the face of so many warnings of 'wage moderation' in periods when the oil price rises (because of the inflationary pressures this triggers), we do not understand why, at least for the sake of consistency of reasoning, there is no recommendation of 'wage exaggeration' in periods when, instead, the oil price falls. The fact is that the ethical system we imagine and whose internal coherence we would like to understand does not actually exist (except as a mystified product of the economic interests of the time).

The recipe, then, can only be that of the utmost scepticism towards all value-based arguments. Far more important, instead, is the identification of the economic interests at stake. Only when economic interests are wedded to a certain system of values will we hear about the latter, and those who will speak to us about it will appear to be the priests (or gendarmes) of these values, and it is on these values that we will be called upon to express ourselves.

This process of mystification originates from the very association between capitalism and democracy, two aspects of modern economic-political systems that appear almost synonymous to us even though they are actually in contradiction with each other: capitalism is based on the pursuit of self-interest according to the logic of the economically strongest, democracy is based on the equal participation of all in social decision-making processes. Where popular consent is not necessary, there is no need for mystification, economic force is sufficient. Where force is not enough (or is simply not economically convenient), power has no other way but mystification. Thus, through mystification, we see fundamental values born and die, which only take on meaning to the extent that they are instrumental to the pursuit of the interests of the ruling classes. Health, the environment, respect for human rights and the rights of other living species, the preservation of the artistic heritage, and democracy itself are all values that have no importance in themselves (and it is the history of capitalism that teaches us this); they become fundamental, however, as soon as an economic interest is aligned with them, in order to ride them to the achievement of the set (but undeclared) goal and then dump them when the mission is accomplished.

The dependence of the guiding values of politics on the evolution of economic relations is very evident in the debate on international relations: values such as pacifism, respect for political borders, and the right to self-determination of peoples today leave room for the new universal values of the superiority of the Western institutional model, the fight against drug trafficking and terrorism, (asymmetrical and selective) respect for human rights, and security (of the United States and its most loyal allies), which are more congenial to the changed economic and geopolitical interests of the capitalist centres and more in line with the changed power relations at the social and political level.

The formation of a political consciousness through which to resist mystification and intervene in the sphere of material relations is a laborious process, itself dependent on the sphere of values. It is indeed by restarting a general reflection on the guiding principles of our society and the possible ways to transform them that it is possible to resist the current neoliberal drift disguised as economic and political progress.

The need to resume reflection on the moral principles of our economic system by the different cultures participating in this process of resistance would seem to clash with the need to look sceptically at those innovators whose arguments are all developed on moral grounds (without any reference to underlying economic interests): on the one hand, it would seem necessary to forcefully resume discussion in terms of values, on the other, the risk is to discuss values which, in reality, conceal completely different interests. However, the contradiction is only apparent and is resolved by correctly interpreting the theoretical role of demystification: the demystification of declared values, whether in economics or politics, serves to lay bare the interests at stake, not to assert an alternative system of values, and it is only once the true stakes have been determined that the discourse on values can be properly addressed.

From the economic point of view, neoliberal thinking constitutes the most advanced form of mystification, all aimed at making the entire sphere of economic relations appear to be governed by objectively rational principles necessary to achieve the highest moral values of individualistic ideology, and it is this economic mystification that provides the guiding values of political action and makes possible the absurdity of a political discourse conducted entirely in the name of the common good. Demystifying the mechanisms of bourgeois society is therefore a necessary (though clearly not sufficient) step in resisting bourgeois ideology and the material basis from which it derives. Critical reflection on the values implicit in our social system is an indispensable moment in the debate on alternative ways of regulating social and economic relations. However, it is obvious that, in the constructive phase of such a debate, different social models and different moral conceptions can be confronted as proposals for overcoming the limits of the market model. In this sense, the demystification of bourgeois economic theory does indeed constitute the basis for a political reflection as well, but the political implications that can be drawn from it do not derive from a particular *ex ante* ideological approach, but from a scientific analysis of the validity of the various hypotheses of neoliberal theory and the rigour of the method through which it derives its normative and political implications.

## The cultural victory of the new right

While at the political level and in heterodox economic research there are various signs of dissatisfaction with the market model and the representation of it provided by bourgeois economic theory, the latter proceeds straight ahead. As we have seen, bourgeois economics claims the rationality of the market by asserting (in a theoretically questionable way) its independence from any moral system. In fact, bourgeois economists impose an explicit prohibition on themselves against introducing value judgements, on pain of losing scientificity of the theory. The paradox is that despite this prohibition, it is precisely on the discourse of values that the new right affirms its triumph.

Since an open confrontation on the issue of values is not possible, it is on the terrain of the analysis of competition and cooperation that the debate on the desirability of the market takes place. In fact, competition – that is, the market's own coordination mechanism – does not necessarily produce efficient results, so that forms of cooperative-type interaction, inspired by values of solidarity, might become convenient (again from the point of view of efficiency). This approach only apparently allows the discourse of values to be avoided; in reality it leads to the affirmation of the individualistic value system on which the philosophy of the new right is based as the only scientifically admissible value system. Let us see how.

Competition and cooperation are not values; they are economic mechanisms. However, in some cases, they tend, albeit erroneously, to appear as values, insofar as they guarantee economic efficiency: in cases where the cooperation mechanism leads to allocations that are superior, from the point of view of efficiency, to the solutions obtainable through the competitive mechanism, the impression is given that solidarity can be economically justified with respect to individualism; in the opposite cases, individualism is considered to be economically justified. These, after all, are the messages respectively of the 'visible hand' and the 'invisible hand' theorems that have attracted so much attention from economists since the birth of the political economy.

According to the invisible hand theorem, under certain conditions, purely individualistic behaviour leads to socially desirable situations (the expression 'invisible hand' refers to the well-known metaphor of the classical economist Smith). The visible hand theorem, on the other hand, originates as an explicit critique of the invisible hand principle and shows the superiority, under certain circumstances, of explicit forms of coordination of the actions of individualistic agents over automatic forms of coordination based on the competitive mechanism ('The visible hand' is the title of a famous book by Alfred Chandler (1977)).

Thus, under the conditions in which the invisible hand theorem applies, individualism is transformed into a social virtue and the competitive mechanism assumes the role of an efficient (and, therefore, value-positive) instrument for the realization of this prodigy; under the conditions in which the visible hand theorem applies, instead, it is solidarity that acquires value, and the cooperative mechanism acts as an efficient instrument.

A new theoretical stimulus in the analysis of the effects of competitive and cooperative interactions has been provided relatively recently by 'game theory'.[3] Game theory is a set of logical-mathematical models analysing the interaction between decision-makers whose actions are interdependent and in which the outcome of their interaction depends on the strategies chosen (the random element, if present, is not the only factor determining the outcome of the game). One particular game that has attracted much attention from economists is the so-called 'prisoner's dilemma'.[4] The 'game' is between two men caught with stolen goods and accused of theft. However, there is insufficient evidence for conviction unless at least one of the two confesses. In the absence of a confession, the two prisoners can only be convicted of the lesser offence of possession of stolen goods. Individualism, the inability of the two prisoners to agree on a common strategy and a specially designed system of incentives lead both prisoners to confess the theft and betray their comrade, thus ending up providing the decisive proof of their own guilt.

In mathematical terms, the game has the following structure. Consider two prisoners named *Alby* and *Billy*. Each is faced with two alternatives: to confess or not to confess. There are therefore four possible cases in all: *Alby* and *Billy* both confess, neither confesses, *Alby* confesses, and *Billy* does not, *Alby* does not confess and *Billy* does. By hypothesis we assume that when a prisoner confesses, he also betrays the co-defendant. Let us then analyse the incentive system put in place to induce the two prisoners to confess.

If *Alby* confesses (and betrays) and *Billy* does not confess, *Alby* is immediately released from prison, while *Billy* is punished with the maximum sentence (5 years in prison). Symmetrically, if it is *Billy* who confesses (and betrays) while *Alby* does not confess, *Alby* gets 5 years and *Billy* goes free. If, instead, *Alby* and *Billy* both confess, they each get three years in prison (since, in that case, the betrayal of the partner does not provide a useful service to justice). If both do not confess, as there is no evidence against them for the major offence, they get 1 year sentence (for minor offences).

Individualism and the impossibility of co-operating with each other in a credible manner lead both prisoners to confess (thus taking three years each). The reason is as follows. Let us put ourselves in *Alby*'s shoes. If Billy confesses, it is better for *Alby* too to confess (and get 3 years instead of 5); if, conversely, *Billy* does not confess, *Alby* will still find it convenient to confess (and thus be released rather than serve 1 year). In short, whatever *Billy*'s behaviour, *Alby* will find it convenient to confess. The game being perfectly symmetrical, *Billy* will do the same reasoning and find that the optimal choice is to confess. The result is that both confess and take a three-year sentence each. The Pareto-efficient solution, however, is the one in which both do not confess and take only one year each.

The reason why left-wing economists like this game so much is that it shows how individualism and competition do not necessarily lead to the common good but can backfire on the decision-makers themselves. In short, as with market failure theory, the visible hand and the prisoner's dilemma emphasize the inadequacy (with respect to efficientist goals) of the pure competitive mechanism and the possibility that the cooperative mechanism may be more effective, thus justifying the rationality of solidarity as a value of conduct (for if the two prisoners could cooperate, they would immediately realize that it is in their common interest not to confess).

But solidarity and individualism are social attitudes of ethical derivation and must not (and cannot) be discussed and justified on the basis of their effects on economic efficiency. Not least because, in doing so, the same discourse of values is subjected to the efficientist scrutiny of the market, giving rise to circular reasoning, since the efficiency of the market itself presupposes, as we have seen, a well-defined system of values based on individualism. In other words, by making the justification of solidaristic behaviour depend on the economic effects that this behaviour produces in the market system, we forget that as a yardstick for judgement we are using precisely the individualist yardstick of the market. In this way, solidarism ceases to be an alternative (and, in my opinion, ethically superior) value system to the individualistic value system to become merely an efficiencyist by-product of individualism itself. Solidarity is not valued as such, but only justified to the extent that it is efficient (according to individualistic logic).

All this, of course, occurs implicitly, since, as mentioned earlier, the economist is forbidden to talk about values. Through the discussion of the mechanisms of competition and cooperation, the economist thus takes his revenge by addressing with the utmost scientific rigour precisely those topics that provoke the closest emotional reactions to the discourse of values. In this contradictory attempt at a scientific discussion of values, the new right is not alone. The left also participates, thus making the attempt to characterize the different theoretical schemes ideologically and scientifically increasingly difficult. And this aggravates the identity crisis of the left. In order to curb the spread of the market, left-wing economists work to highlight all those cases where the market fails, the visible hand beats the invisible one, cooperation is superior to competition from the Pareto efficiency point of view, and the dilemmatic and individualistic prisoner betrays and is punished, in the belief that this serves to undermine the neoliberal principles of economic policy.

As a minimal strategy, all these attempts work because they show the limits of a system based solely on competition and the logic of the strongest. However, they do not question the logic of the strongest as such, if anything they legitimize it. The result is that while attempting to slow down the advance of the market, they deal the final blow to those attempts to question the logic of the market itself and, with that, give validity to an internally contradictory logical operation (the objectification of market values) that sanctions the cultural victory of the new right in the scientific field.

## Appearance and essence in market relations

If, on the one hand, the assertion of market culture in society is influenced by the hegemony of neoliberal thought in economic theory, on the other hand, the economist's view of economic relations and society in general is itself a reflection of the objectification of market values. In this dialectical process, the bourgeois economist plays the role of a conservative apologist, self-assigning himself the task of making existing economic and social mechanisms appear to meet high criteria of rationality. In this sense, the cultural success of the new right should not be ascribed to any particular strategic skills of its political leaders or obscure conspiracies on the part of scientific research institutions. On the contrary, in addition to the obvious reasons related to the processes of change in existing material relations, it has its foundation in the mystified perception of social relations induced by the contrast between formal equality and substantial inequality that characterizes the economic relations of capitalist democracies, and the sole responsibility of the bourgeois economist is to rationalize this contrast, describing social relations as they appear (based on the principle of formal equality) instead of as they really are (of substantial inequality).

From a Marxist perspective, if there were no difference in reality between the *appearance* and the *essence* of social phenomena, there would be no reason to undertake scientific research. If the essence of problems were self-evident, science would just be a collection of commonplaces: there would be nothing to discover and there would not even be a need for experts because everyone would see for themselves what there is to see. While bourgeois theory attempts to recompose the existing contrast between formal and substantial aspects of economic relations by presenting formal appearance as the true essence of the problem (and treating the existence of substantial asymmetries as secondary), Marxism, in its critique of bourgeois society, argues instead that it is possible for formal equality and substantial inequality to coexist peacefully, and that appearance and essence are perfectly compatible and form different aspects of the same reality, that of capitalism. If there is a contrast to be recomposed between formal and substantial aspects, this must take place, in fact, not in theory: it is not by describing a given reality as rational and just that it becomes rational and just. Instead, the transformation must take place directly in reality and, from this point of view, the first contribution of theory consists in demystifying appearances, in determining the essence they conceal.

The greatest contrast between appearance and essence in capitalist relations probably lies in the perception of market prices as an expression of relations between objects, rather than as an expression of relations between people. The fact that a refrigerator has a certain price and a washing machine another seems to be a direct attribute of the relationship between the two appliances, in the same way that they have different sizes and different weights. Market prices thus appear as direct attributes of the objects, not as products of the system of economic and social relations, and this makes it appear that these relations are entirely natural. However, if the refrigerator and the washing machine have a market price, it is only because they are *commodities*, and their being commodities is a consequence of the particular way they are produced and exchanged in the capitalist system. The contrast between *appearance* and *essence* is therefore that prices simply appear as the exchange relations that exist between *commodities*, but this appearance is only made possible by the existence, in bourgeois society, of particular relations between *people*, who produce and exchange these commodities through the market.

There is not much difference in substance if, at the end of the year, the peasant hands over 20 sacks of grain to the feudal lord, keeping ten for himself, by virtue of a feudal order imposing it on him/her, or if he/she hands over all 30 sacks to a capitalist – having freely chosen, at the beginning of the year, to sign a contract with him/her to sell his/her labour power – and then buys ten of them back on the market with the wages received. In both cases, the farmer and his/her family do not eat part of the grain they have produced, and both systems function neatly only because institutional rules guarantee and impose the transfer of sacks of grain from one subject to another, as a condition of the system's survival. But, in the first case, the transfer of resources from those who produce them to those who consume them *appears* to us as the result of a political relationship of domination and exploitation, while, in the second, everything *appears* to us as harmonious and as the result of free economic choices. Nevertheless, behind this different *appearance* lies the same *essence* of (perfectly legal) appropriation of the product of others' labour. And, on closer inspection, it is precisely the legality of the appropriation-expropriation process that produces a contrast between appearance and essence.

The economic relations existing in the capitalist and feudal systems appear to be of freedom or of oppression, depending on whether the respective systems of institutional rules (which protect and guarantee the ruling class) are taken as a given or not. In the capitalist system, worker and capitalist are both free to bargain over the sale of labour power by the former and its purchase by the latter, but they are only free within the capitalist rules that guarantee and enforce the buying and selling of labour power. And this system of rules establishes that the capitalist has full right to demand a share of the total product, even if he has not worked to produce it. Similarly, in the feudal system, workers are free to retain for themselves the product of (their own) labour performed on servile lands, once they have secured work on the master's lands, as dictated by the rules of feudalism. And, according to that system of rules, the feudal lord is fully entitled to demand the product obtained from the master's land, even without having worked on it. This is why the capitalist system is the system of the bourgeoisie just as the feudal system is the system of the feudal lords.

If we take the institutional rules of a system as given, the relations established within it are, by definition, free. It is only by questioning these rules that it becomes possible to truly discuss freedom and oppression. If feudalism appears to us as a system of exploitation and domination, it is only because we analyse it with the bourgeois lenses of the capitalist system (i.e. with lenses external to feudalism); and, similarly, if capitalism appears to us as a system of freedom and equality (even if only formal), it is because, once again, we are unable to have any other lenses than those of the class that dominates capitalist relations.

Analysing the rationality of capitalism on the basis of the market price system is a contradictory operation in itself. The price system established under capitalism expresses nothing more than the exchange relations (between commodities) necessary for the product to pass from the hands of those who work to those who have the right of ownership and consumption, and the rationality of the price system can at best express the conditions for this product transfer to take place in a smooth and orderly manner. But then, the rationality of market prices is simply the manifestation of the relations of exploitation of the working class by the bourgeois class.

A second problem, then, is that even taking the capitalist institutional system for granted, market prices are by no means the result of a competitive confrontation between the different actors in the game, as assumed so far. Instead, they are, to a large extent, controlled and planned prices. Thus, while market prices continue to appear as the natural expression of relations between things, over which it is not possible to intervene, they are in reality the most effective and least visible instrument to exploit and dominate social classes, countries and entire geographical areas. And to do this, it is not necessary to have an absolute control of the price system. The important thing is to have primacy in the key sectors with high value added and to impose on others – through economic pressure, first of all, but also through political or military pressure, if necessary – productions with a high labour and raw material content. Cocoa is African and Latin American, but chocolate is Swiss. The lithium used to power electric car batteries is mined in Chile (by exploiting child labour) but Tesla is headquartered in Texas (and sells its cars in the name eco-sustainability). Sportswear is produced in Korea, but Nike and Adidas are United States and German, respectively. In the world of multinationals and international bodies that impose restructuring plans, economic and social reforms, production specialization models, import and export constraints, market prices are administered prices, direct instruments of power. The control of price dynamics is the most painless tool to impose relations of domination, dependence and exploitation.

But the real problem with market prices as a value system regulating relations between people is not in the fact that it is in the hands of a handful of companies or countries. Whether or not there is direct control of price dynamics, if the price system expresses conditions of exploitation and domination, it will certainly not be the absence of a monopolist subject to be criminalized that will alleviate the objective conditions of the exploited and oppressed. If anything, if one truly believes that manipulative subjects do not exist and that the dynamics of market prices are beyond control, this should demonstrate the need to radically rethink the role of the market as an uncontrolled mechanism with undesirable effects. And indeed, as demonstrated in Marxist literature, monopoly aggravates the conditions of exploitation, but the latter is also present in the realm of perfect competition.

In short, whether market prices are an instrument of power in the hands of particular subjects (as even part of mainstream economics recognizes), or a completely uncontrolled phenomenon (as full bourgeois economics would have it when it mythologizes and prescribes the model of perfect competition), does not change the substance of the existing relations of exploitation, nor does it change the solution to the problem, which in any case passes through their abolition. If economic relations regulated by the market are relations of exploitation, of inequality between those who work and do not earn and those who earn and do not work, the abolition of such conditions can only imply the abolition of the instrument that allows their perpetuation: the market. Thus, today's struggle against the symbols of capitalist domination personified in particular multinationals or in certain states and international organizations, although necessary to develop critical reflection on the inspiring principles of capitalist relations, risks also not being sufficient ('when one Pope dies, another Pope is made'), if it does not also produce a change in the rules of the game and if it does not question the institutional set-up that gives strength to the subjects being fought. The real change produced by bourgeois revolutions lies not in the heads they inevitably knocked off, but in the institutional progress they produced. And today the institution around which everything else revolves and from which the powerful derive their strength is the market.

The appearance of capitalist relations as relations between free people, hiding the essence of exploitative relations (which are precisely established on a free and voluntary basis, given the existing constraints, of course), only complicates the process of emancipation, aiding the spread and intensification of the objective conditions of exploitation and hindering the political processes of market control. The fact that market relations, summarized in commodity prices, appear as natural and universal makes it appear that capitalist society is not the product of human beings but the product of superior forces, to be indulged (and not, eventually, fought). According to market culture, economic and social relations must not be organized according to man's conscious design but must obey the divine design of the market. Just as in religion one must genuflect before the God identified as true, so in economic and social relations one must accept the will of the only God that exists today, the market God.

## Notes

1 In Palermo (2012), I develop a Marxist critique of the Italian university system, its power relations and its economic and social functions from the Unification of Italy to the present.

2 Without any pretence at providing an exhaustive answer to these questions, the issue of share price fluctuations nevertheless deserves a closer investigation. Let us consider the following example. In the economic system, there exist 3 assets, $x_1$, $x_2$, $x_3$ whose prices are $p_1$, $p_2$, $p_3$, owned by subjects *A*, *B* and *C* respectively. By selling part of their goods each subject can buy part of the goods owned by the other subjects. It is clear that, if the price $p_1$ rises in proportion to the prices $p_2$ and $p_3$, subject *A* (owner of $x_1$) will be able to obtain larger quantities of the goods $x_2$ and $x_3$ by giving the same quantity of $x_1$ in exchange. Who pays for this net gain achieved by *A*? Obviously, *B* and *C*, who will see their total purchasing power reduced by exactly the same amount. Whether $x_1$, $x_2$, $x_3$ are physical goods, services, stock market securities or something else makes no difference: when the price of an asset you own rises (relative to the prices of other assets) you have an increase in your real wealth; when the price of an asset you do not own rises you have a decrease in real wealth (which goes to finance the capital gains of the subjects owning the asset).

Apparently, one might think that the stock market's performance only concerns investors in the first instance, and that workers may at most have an indirect interest in the stock market since when investments go wrong, demand for labour is reduced. In reality, this is not the case. Suppose, in fact, that asset $x_1$ is a share, asset $x_2$ is a consumer good, and asset $x_3$ is the labour power (subject *A* is then a shareholder, subject *B* is the company that produces the consumer good, subject *C* is the worker who only has his/her own labour power to sell). Let us also assume that the worker is only interested in buying consumer goods and not also stock market securities (because, for example, he/she is too poor to buy them). As we have said, if the price $p_1$ (the price of the share) rises, subject *A* (the shareholder) becomes richer and can therefore buy increasing quantities of all other goods, including the consumer good $x_2$. As a consequence, subject *C* (the worker), even if completely extraneous to the stock market performance, will nevertheless see his/her own consumption of $x_2$ decrease, by an amount equal to the increase in consumption by subject *A* (the shareholder). In general, therefore, when the stock market rises there is a redistribution of wealth to the advantage of shareholders, while when it falls the redistribution benefits all other subjects. All this without there being any creation of value in one case, or destruction of value (or 'capital burning', according to a jargon invented by journalists specialized in financial matters without any basis in political economy or accounting) in the other.

After that, many considerations can be made: if stock prices go up, capitalists become more optimistic, investment increases, output and employment grow, and in the end, neoliberal economists maintain, everyone benefits. Other economists, instead, contend that when the stock market rises, financial investment becomes more attractive than industrial investment and, as a result, output and employment instead of growing fall. But these are just economic theories that may or may not be valid. Instead, the redistribution of wealth between shareholders and non-shareholders is an incontrovertible accounting fact.

3 Game theory is one of the research fields in which the support of the US Department of Defence and the *Rand corporation* have been decisive. Indeed, game theory has applications in a large number of different fields, yet it was its military applications (especially in the context of the Cold War) that attracted the largest research funding.

4 The logic of this game was first developed in 1950 by two *Rand corporation* mathematicians, Merril Flood and Melvin Dresher. The name 'prisoner's dilemma' and the story describing the mathematical game as an interaction problem between two individualist thieves were introduced by Albert Tucker, also a consultant at *Rand*.

## References


Chandler, A. D. (1977) *The visible hand.* Cambridge, MA: Belknap Press.

Engels, F. (1877) *Anti-Dühring: Herr Eugen Dühring's revolution in science*. Available at: www.marxists.org/archive/marx/works/1877/anti-duhring/index.htm

Palermo, G. (2012) *Baroni e Portaborse: I Rapporti di Potere nell'Università.* Roma: Editori Internazionali Riuniti.

# 7 What is to be done?

The problem of realizing a world in which it is the needs of people and not the 'purchasing power-preferences' combination that determine collective choices is certainly complicated, but the point today is to figure out how to set in motion a process that goes in this direction. At least on the objective (the direction of the process), however, we must be clear. In a world where the division of labour and specialization have reached today's levels, it is simply unrealistic to imagine that the complicated relationships that bind us to each other can be regulated by themselves. Certainly, the market is a mechanism that, in one way or another, solves the problem by keeping the system going. The point is that it solves it badly, because the market regulates according to the logic of profit and capital accumulation and all the rest (poverty, misery, inequality, crisis, exploitation, alienation etc.) is just a set of side effects.

In the climate of triumphalism over the West's market-driven economic successes, the first thing to do is to reverse the process. Economic (and profit) growth, employment recovery (with stagnating wages), and fiscal consolidation (by dint of spending cuts and privatization) are not economic successes. They all express a retreat in the conditions of workers and citizens in general and an advancement of corporations and their bosses.

## Class struggle and economic policy

Growth without inflation and inflationary surges in the presence of stagnating wages are only successes of capital. The resumption of employment under harsher, more precarious and less protected working conditions (with productivity nevertheless on the rise) only expresses an increase in the rate of exploitation: if in a family only one person used to work, now two or three work, and the standard of living is the same because, in addition to falling real wages, with the reduction in public spending, services once offered by the state now have to be paid for in cash.

The balancing of public budgets is then as absurd as it gets. How can anyone think that a person's health can be subordinated to the profit logic of a hospital company? The functioning of public services, whether privatized or still in the hands of state administrations, has become all about business: local health companies,

DOI: 10.4324/9781032726168-8

hospitals, schools, railways, public utilities, all have to respect the principle of a balanced budget (or, preferably, a surplus), as in any efficient company.

Reducing inflation is good for the banks, which obtain higher real interest rates, not for the workers, who cannot even keep their real wages (given that the containment of inflation is achieved precisely through so-called 'wage moderation', the true pivot of economic policy in the last decades, and given the impossibility of linking wages to price increases because of the damage this would do to the overall efficiency of the system); not to mention the fact that, with the existing balance of power, workers have even stopped aspiring to at least a share of the proceeds deriving from the increasing productivity of their own labour.

Let us consider the latest data and the actual lines of economic policy in the US-led world.

2021 is a black year for US inflation: from 1.4 per cent in January, it rises to 7,0 per cent in December (Trading Economics, 2024a). With a nominal interest rate of zero, an inflation rate of seven per cent means a real interest rate of –7 per cent (the real interest rate is equal to the difference between the nominal interest rate and the inflation rate). Negative real rates of these magnitudes were not even seen during the lows of 1974 and 1980, following the oil crises, and one has to go back to the period between 1947 and 1951 to encounter such low figures (Longtermtrends, 2024).

With negative real rates, banks lose, not gain. A bank that lends 100 dollars at a nominal interest rate of two per cent receives 102 dollars after one year. However, if in the meantime the price of bananas has risen from one dollar to 1.07 dollars (seven per cent inflation rate), with those 102 dollars the bank will no longer be able to buy 100 bananas, as it did at the time of the loan, but only 95.3 (102 dollars divided by 1.07). In nominal terms, the bank has gained two dollars; in real terms, it has lost five bananas.

Since the financial crisis of 2007–09, triggered by the bankruptcy of Lehman Brothers (then considered a too big to fail bank), interest rates in the United States have been at zero and the Federal Reserve has flooded the markets with liquidity through its quantitative easing programmes (large purchases of securities of various kinds by the central bank). Certainly not to stimulate economic growth and reduce unemployment (problems that existed even before the banking crisis) but to support the markets and prevent a chain of bank failures. Since then, every time the Federal Reserve has tried to raise interest rates, stock markets have shuddered, and the Fed has quickly backtracked. With the 2020 crisis triggered by the so-called anti-pandemic interventions, then, quantitative easing blew up the Fed's balance sheet. From values around 800 billion dollars in 2008, the Fed's balance sheet got close to nine trillion dollars in 2022 (Federal Reserve, 2023).

For many years, in a stagnant economic climate, increased money supply through quantitative easing remained mainly in the financial markets, causing stock and bond prices to explode, with limited effects on commodity prices. With the first hints of a post-pandemic recovery, however, things change rapidly. Now there is nothing else the Federal Reserve can do: if in 2008 it had to lower rates to zero to save the banks, now, again to save the banks, it has to raise them and it has to do it decisively.

Monetary tightening begins on 17 March 2022, with an initial increase in the key interest rate, the federal funds rate, by 25 basis points, followed in May by a further 50 basis points, and four interventions of 75 points each before the end of the year, before slowing the pace of tightening, reaching 5.25–5.50 per cent in July 2023 (Trading Economics, 2024b).

In the press conferences following Fed decisions, where the chair's words make the Nasdaq move in real time, Powell talks about defending families, workers, pensioners and small savers, and blames inflation on Covid and Russia. So far, the markets are standing still. It is when he comments on the timing of the Federal Reserve's balance sheet reduction strategy, after years of quantitative easing, and the speed with which interest rates are to go into the tightening zone, that the markets move.

The last time the Fed implemented such an aggressive interest rate policy was in the 1980s. From 1979 to 1987, the chair was Paul Volcker, remembered as the man who defeated inflation. His motto was 'No pain, no gain' (also taken up by Arnold Schwarzenegger): the former of course was for capitalists and bankers, and the latter for workers. The monetary squeeze was in fact coordinated with the class attack initiated by Reagan and Thatcher in the name of the free market.

There, too, a major paradigm shift was at stake: the worldwide transition to the neoliberal paradigm, with its attendant social and cultural changes. These processes, for those who know the history of capitalism, are always violent and entail high and asymmetrical social costs, which fall particularly on the least protected sections of the population. But back to the present: while the Fed closed the credit spigots, US inflation peaked at 9.1 per cent, in June 2022, before abruptly falling back to 3.0 in June 2023.

The European picture is similar. In most of the European Union, the post-Covid recovery is slower than in the United States and so is inflation. The eurozone is coming from negative inflation rates in the second half of the 2020s: the lockdown had disastrous economic effects in Europe and deflation is the consequence. Here too, the recovery encounters the same problems of money overhang and bottlenecks in the production chain. Inflation only starts to rise more significantly in the last quarter of 2021, explodes in March 2022 with the sanctions on Russia, surpasses that of the United States in July 2022, at 8.9 per cent, and peaks in October, at 10.6 per cent (Eurostat, 2023). The European Central Bank (ECB) must, therefore, also join in the monetary tightening, which is now underway in all countries of the dollar area. Of course, after the eurozone countries have started their recovery plans, entirely on debt, when interest rates were at zero.

In this context, the annual Jackson Hole Symposium in August 2022, where central bankers, politicians and economists from all over the world, at the invitation of the Federal Reserve in Kansas City, can take note of chair Powell's indications on how central banks should coordinate in managing monetary tightening, takes on special significance. Indeed, the United States is concerned that the hike in domestic interest rates, if not accompanied by similar measures by other central banks, will result in an excessive appreciation of the dollar and reduce the competitiveness of US companies in international markets. This is how the ECB also starts the new phase of credit tightening: after an initial increase of 50 basis points at the end of July 2022, from September it accelerates the tightening, with further increases until the interest rate on main refinancing operations reaches 4.50 per cent in September 2023 (European Central Bank, 2024). As in the United States, the effect on price dynamics is strong, with inflation returning to 2.4 per cent in November 2023.

Problem solved, then? Yes, but only for banks, which, despite being at the heart of the crisis, have meanwhile resumed making profits. Indeed, in the inflation/recession ballet, it is always the workers who pay, with part of their wages during inflation and with their employment during the recession. A couple of years of ten per cent inflation before returning to sound anti-inflation policies and workers lose a fifth of their real wage forever. In fact, when inflation stops, prices do not go down to the starting level. One does not need to be an economist or a worker to understand this, it is sufficient to enter a supermarket. But while workers perceive the fall in their purchasing power, due to processes over which they have no control, with hunger and cuts in primary consumption, for the economists who contend for the helm of the economy, everything is fine and they go on talking about the 'inflation/unemployment trade-off', with the neoliberals more concerned with the former and the Keynesians with the latter, as if inflation and unemployment were not both borne by the working class.

Of course, pumping and draining money is of no use unless the economic conditions from which banks and capital in general make profit change. Powell himself says this between the lines when he talks about the wage-price spiral: inflation is fought by cutting wages. So, alongside monetary policy, fiscal policy is also intensified, again in the name of the common good, at least formally, though in fact at the expense of the exploited class.

After decades of restrictive measures, international stability pacts to curb public spending, deficits and debt, spread blackmail and structural plans for those who get out of line, thanks to the 'Covid crisis' (or more correctly the crisis induced by so-called 'anti-Covid interventions'), the sacred principles of budgetary rigour are being overturned to allow states to embark on a huge public investment plan in support of private capital, putting themselves at the service of the global industrial restructuring strategy led by the large high-tech financial groups.

Unfortunately, public money has long since run out and the only way for states to finance private capital is through debt. So, in the midst of the pandemic crisis, while there was no money to create a few more hospital beds, nor to help workers get through the month, the United States, the European Union and all the capitalist countries allocated trillions of dollars to digitalization, technology companies and the green economy, the real winners in the economic war unleashed in the shadow of the pandemic. Finally, we are back to that lovely Keynesianism, which spends a lot and spends in debt as if there were no tomorrow. As Keynes (1923, p. 80) himself stated: 'The long run is a misleading guide to current affairs. In the long run we are all dead'. Unfortunately, with these policies, it is mainly workers who die and when tomorrow effectively comes the neoliberal economist of the day will tell the survived ones that they have consumed too much and worked too little and that it is time to tighten their belts.

This is the beauty of the alternation between left and right in the governing of capitalism: with the neoliberals, profits are privatized, with the Keynesians, costs are socialized. And if for some reason capital dictates that the U-turn should take place in the middle of the ECB president's term of office, Mario Draghi takes five minutes to change his mask, going back on all the principles of budgetary rigour advocated for decades to place himself at the head of the new army of interventionists, with his now famous phrase 'whatever it takes'. The men of international finance are ready to do anything to save the international financial system, so long as the workers foot the bill.

Thanks to the new public interventionism in favour of finance, workers lose rights and wages, precarious jobs increase, and the very way of working gets transformed, forcing workers to adapt quickly to the new technological-social paradigm. From this point of view, the refinement of the means of control and social discipline deployed in the 'fight against the pandemic', from which derives the further fragmentation of all social movements and the workers' movement in particular – divided by now even according to a vaccine or a green pass, which sadly resembles the fascist party membership card, without which one could not work – define a framework of social relations objectively favourable to capital, aimed at shifting the entire burden of the economic crisis onto the working class.

In this way, the crisis passes from the banks to the workers, with the aid of the state. The banks are in fact the main creditors of states. They have long been in crisis and states and central banks have always done everything to save them. But when financial speculation attacks the indebted states and forces them into controlled default, it is they, the banks, through the international organizations, who dictate the structural reforms to better squeeze workers.

In this process of power redistribution, the state is left with coercive and repressive functions towards its people and limited economic powers. The latter are in fact assumed directly by international organizations and international creditors. Workers are left with nothing but to work harder, under worse conditions, for lower wages, as a condition for repaying the debts that the state has contracted in their name. Of course, in defence of their health and democracy in Europe.

## The right, the left and the common good

The market logic of perfect competition wants every worker to stand alone at the bargaining table in front of his/her boss, and at this table it is precisely the law of the market that sets the price. Levelling wages on individual productivity is the real goal of capital, the necessary condition for cost minimization and profit maximization. Having reduced the bargaining power of workers, their purchasing power and their rights, the neoliberal offensive would now like to prevent, with theoretical arguments, any wish to reconstitute the workers' front. The conditions of systemic efficiency are in fact incompatible with trade union unity, and even the trade unions themselves seem to have bowed to this logic for some time now. The employment question is no longer considered a key factor (an instrument) in the emancipation process of the workers' movement, but simply an objective in itself. In order to increase employment, the left-wing politicians and trade unions are ready to do anything: reduce real wages (because it is through the creation of profit opportunities for capital that employment is increased), increase flexibility (because it is by accommodating market demands that full employment efficiency is realized), decrease guarantees (because these are costs for companies).

Even then, the theoretical confusion between employment, as an indicator of the strength of the workers' movement, and employment, as a statistic index of desirability in itself according to the parameters of the new market left, leads to waving the processes of the emergence from the black market as great economic successes. Whereas these are nothing more than the transformation of the rules of the labour market: in this way, what was illegal has been made legal, declaring legitimate the conditions of exploitation that the legislator had wanted to prevent (and which the black market had managed to achieve anyway), turning the legislator into the mouthpiece of the market and subordinating the laws of the state to the laws of the market. This is exactly the design of capital. Having beaten the workers on the ground, accustoming them to long periods of recession as the price to pay for the Europe of capital, capital now demands the regularization of abuses: not just an amnesty on the past, but new lasting rules for the future. If before it was necessary to hire an off-the-books worker in order to be able to pay him/her little and fire him/her at will, now the bosses want special laws that allow them to pay little and fire at will in the sunlight. And since the process has already reached an advanced stage, here is the competition between centre-right and centre-left to claim paternity for these 'great successes' on the employment, inflation and public accounts fronts, successes that all point to the increase in the conditions of labour exploitation and the worsening of the conditions of unemployment sustainability.

More and more workers are being forced to accept working conditions and wages that they could previously afford to refuse (thanks also to the retreat of the state on the front of services deemed essential). In the general mystification, the left has also embraced the mystification of employment as a goal in itself, forgetting that a society in which people work hard, but profits remain in private hands, is the society of capital, not that of labour.

In this process of retreat of labour vis-à-vis capital, Europe lags far behind the American model. There, the industrial relations system has perfectly adapted to the dictates of the market, breaking the inverse relationship between unemployment and wage dynamics: even with prolonged periods of low unemployment rates, the US labour market no longer produces any upward push in wage earnings (as is generally the case) and this only thanks to the profound weakness of the labour movement, which, perhaps, is no longer even a movement, but has truly become a set of isolated individuals. In this way, the United States has managed for years to grow at relatively high rates (compared to Europe), allowing US capital to turn growth in production and productivity entirely into growth in profits, without any possibility for workers to raise their heads. And now that the question of government spending has arisen again, this is not in response to the unmet needs of the population (which have increased in tandem with the general retreat of the state from the economy), but as a necessity to finance wars – both those in which the United States is directly involved, and those it conducts through proxies, arming states and private battalions – and to defend US companies in the economic war against China. The naivest commentators see in this resumption of public spending a reversal of the neoliberal model and a return to the Keynesian-style policies that characterized the decades following the Second World War. But in a context of reversed power relations between social classes compared to those years, the resumption of public spending has nothing to do with social spending. It only serves to compensate private companies for the lack of profits (compared to their expectations) and to create the conditions for private profits to grow again at sustained rates. Thus, in keeping with the principle of the common good, the common enemy also emerges, a role assigned once to Saddam Hussein, another to Slobodan Milosevic, then to Osama Bin Laden, then back to Saddam Hussein, Muammar Gaddafi (and family), to finally arrive at today's enemy number one: Vladimir Putin. It is only for these noble goals (*killing* terrorists and eliminate those whom the West calls dictators), made of common good and common evil, of friends and foes of all, of wars in the name of God (with respect to which, however, even the Pope openly expresses his dissent), that United States today revises the guiding principles of its public budget policy. There is no place for class struggle in a country all united against the common enemy and all committed to defending, on behalf of the whole world, the good against the evil.

In Europe, by contrast, the dissolution of social confrontation for the benefit of the common good is still proceeding slowly because, despite the backwardness and mystifications, the workers still retain the memory of the conquests obtained in the years when class struggle was explicit and fought openly, with the awareness that the common good, in capitalism, does not exist and that an advance in working conditions is a retreat in the remuneration of capital. However, under the authoritative warnings of central banks and international institutions, which intervene in every economic, political and social field (albeit without any popular legitimization), it is becoming increasingly difficult to question the imperative to catch up quickly and finally give way to the accumulation of capital as a goal in itself.

This violent offensive of capital means one thing above all: increasing commodification. More and more our lives are commodified and more and more society bends to the demands of the market. Where there is a space, a market is created and where there is a market, the rules that obstruct its law, that of the richest and the strongest, are removed. Free areas become paying car parks; beaches, private resorts; hospitals, health markets. And every time a market is created, a new price to pay and a new discrimination against the community are introduced, as guarantees that those who can afford it will not lack anything: less time wasted looking for a place to park, fewer people on nice beaches, the best doctors at one's service.

Countering this tendency means first of all making the clash explicit and rejecting the logic of efficiency and the common good. The bourgeois mystification of market relations geared to the collective good serves the strategic interests of capital since it allows class struggle to be waged without any explicit declaration of war. And this is how citizens, but above all workers, not even being called to arms, lose the struggle without even fighting it.

The left has made the entire story of market rationality its own, out of either incompetence or political expediency (in the frenzied pursuit of the centre, the petty and middle bourgeoisie and, why not, big capital, sometimes supporting particular financial and industrial groups just because they compete with the groups sponsoring the centre-right). My feeling is that behind this theoretical convergence towards the neoliberal model, on the part of the left, there are no great political strategies, but only much ignorance and too much opportunism.

## Market prices and administered prices

The great theoretical discovery of bourgeois economists less confident in the market's ability to realize social goals is that the prices of commodities can be controlled: by lowering the price of a commodity, consumption is stimulated and by increasing it, there is a disincentive effect. In this way, the idea takes shape that, by appropriately playing with the price system, it is possible to recompose the existing contrast between the criterion of rationality expressed by the market and the social values that one would like to guarantee. Faced with a society that expresses an equivalent valuation for a life-saving medicine and a bottle of wine, the morally motivated bourgeois economist proposes to sell the bottle of wine at a higher price and to subsidize the supply of medicine by making it more accessible to consumers.

There is no doubt that the introduction of political prices for commodities related to health, education or other values considered socially important makes it possible to respond better to the needs of the population than is the case with prices determined in unregulated markets. Indeed, by intervening appropriately in the price system, it is possible to affect the valuations that society implicitly expresses through the market and resolve some of the most serious contradictions between market valuations and social objectives. What is more, in a context such as the present one, where market laws are interpreted as the supreme expression of capitalism's rationality, price controls may actually prove to be a useful tool to reduce some of the perverse effects of market interaction. Faced with the contrast between the values of the market and the values of society, there is no reason why politics cannot claim the right to influence exchange relations, correcting market valuations instead of pandering to them (as the most extreme neoliberals would have it).

However, two questions arise here. Firstly, if one accepts that the defence of health is incompatible with the mechanism that determines the market prices of medicines, one cannot then demand the balancing of the public budget, since, with the parameters of market efficiency and competitiveness, the supply of medicines at political prices implies a deficit in the state budget. And this applies to every commodity linked to the realization of social values whose market valuation is not satisfactory. Second, one should not confuse a partial and largely ineffective remedy with the solution to the problem.

The reason why the remedy can only be partial is that, in any case, whatever the political price of medicine, the sick person without money will continue to be unable to buy it. The only way to get him/her the medicine he/she needs will be to provide it at zero price, which is tantamount to abolishing (at least for certain sections of the population) the medicine market. The reason the remedy is ineffective is that, where the market exists, price dynamics follow the laws of capital accumulation, not those of public morality. The economic laws of capitalism are autonomous from the will of politics. The politics of bourgeois society can ride or counter the dynamics imposed by the law of capital accumulation (according to which society must satisfy the needs of capital valorization, not the needs of the population), but it cannot abolish them because this would mean abolishing itself, that is, erasing the logic of capitalist interaction.

Thus, all efforts to control the price system by, for instance, making medicines cheap will be hampered by the functioning of the market itself, which, firstly, will tend to put the public budget in crisis (unless the state finances the deficit generated by the subsidy to medicines with redistributive policies to the detriment of other sectors or other sections of the population, which, of course, is a principle alien to the market) and, secondly, it will tend to generate a black market in which medicines will be traded at (higher) market prices, thus allowing those with purchasing power to grab the medicines even when the sick with no money are most in need.

A rich bodybuilder may have a high willingness to pay to be able to inject himself/herself with GH – the so-called 'growth hormone' – even if objectively in less need than a poor person suffering from dwarfism. This fuels the black market in anabolic drugs, making them available to those with more economic means and effectively depriving those who need them most. In this process, the individual athlete improves his/her sports performance, but at the same time becomes himself/herself more and more a commodity. Indeed, if the individual athlete does not have the money, but the sports clubs see in him a potential source of profit, it is the sports clubs themselves that provide him with the hormones to become the strongest and best paid footballer . . . and the tallest dwarf in the world. After all, if capitalism has turned a ball game into a planetary business, what's so strange about a sports club continuing to bomb its athletes initially affected by dwarfism until they are 1.70 metres tall (when the average height of men in the world is 1.71 metres)? (Our World in Data, 2024).

Obviously, these are problems that admit of various solutions at a legal-administrative level, but the point is that these solutions, to be effective, must corner the market, not exploit its mechanisms.

When a state imposes an exchange rate that is not in line with market valuations, a black market in foreign exchange develops. When the state increases the price of cigarettes relative to the standards set by the market, smuggling develops. And when international sports commissions ban doping, sports clubs with greater economic resources develop more sophisticated forms of doping that pass doping controls and allow them to translate their greater economic power into better sporting performances from which to make greater profits.

These phenomena, whether welcome or unwelcome, are a consequence of the fact that the market, even when placed under political control, remains an allocative mechanism with its own laws. State interventions in a market context can at most attempt to achieve a compromise between the objectives of politics and those of the market, that is, they can attempt to guide the market, but they cannot abolish its economic laws. But one might ask: why seek a compromise with a mechanism that only responds to its own logic, when that logic is only that of the accumulation of capital (which has nothing to do with the values that democratic society claims to be inspired by)?

The attempt to resolve the irrationality of the market system (with respect to social values) through price controls is therefore only palliative. As such, it is still better than nothing (i.e. the deregulated market). But it cannot be confused with the solution to the problem. This means that the opposition between the values that society explicitly wishes to enforce and the values that the market implicitly realizes cannot be recomposed by exploiting the market mechanism (i.e. by playing on the moral evaluations implicit in its prices), but by opposing it, by preventing it from functioning.

## Basic income, precarious work and commodification

In recent years, in the wake of the economic crisis, the proposal of a 'basic' or 'universal income' has matured among economists who consider themselves progressive: an income that the state should provide to all its citizens or, according to some less radical proposals, to certain categories of people.

Technically, this is simply one of the many possible social buffers aimed at dampening the economic cycle. Politically, this instrument is defended in particular by economists of the Keynesian school. According to them, basic income supports aggregate demand, economic growth and employment. The most radical, those who wink at Marx, add that it also promotes emancipation from wage-labour and constitutes a real instrument of anti-capitalist struggle.

Let us instead see why basic income not only cannot achieve these goals, but actually ends up going in the opposite direction: worsening the crisis, developing neoliberalism and accelerating the processes of job precarization and commodification of society.

To begin with, it is worth remembering that this proposal, which is so popular today among the radical left and the more interventionist Keynesians, practically coincides with the 'negative income tax' proposal popularized by the champion of neoliberalism Milton Friedman in 1962. The idea of a negative tax, that is a state transfer to citizens, is in fact as old as neoclassical economics and Pareto already discussed how, in his view, state transfers could combine allocative efficiency and distributive justice.

Since this type of policy is now mainly defended by Keynesians, let us start with the alleged expansive effects of basic income on economic growth and employment. According to the 'multiplier theory', it does not matter who you give the money to, the important thing is to increase the disposable income of households, so that they increase spending and consumption, stimulating production growth. This at least is what Lord Keynes (1936) says.

One of his colleagues, less known to the uninitiated, Michal Kalecki (1934), observes, however, that those who consume the largest share of their income are the workers (who with their wages certainly cannot save), while capitalists, especially those with multi-figure fortunes, while consuming more than workers, necessarily save a significant share of their income. Therefore, while remaining within the Keynesian logic, he suggests supporting lower incomes, which end up almost entirely in consumption; if, on the contrary, money is given to those who already have plenty, it increases savings, not consumption. Giving money to everyone equally, therefore, is not only ridiculous in terms of distributive justice, it is also nonsense as a means of supporting aggregate demand: because money given to the rich will not increase their consumption (which is already at desired levels) but their savings (which will generate interest and further increase their wealth).

But let us set aside the differences between Keynes and Kalecki and see whether these transfers to households (rich or poor) really have an expansionary effect on aggregate demand.

Technically, a transfer of money to households has the same expansionary effect as a tax cut (it is indeed a negative tax). However, the same multiplier theory states that an increase in public spending of the same amount has a greater expansive effect. So, if austerity is the problem, basic income is by no means the appropriate instrument; public spending is more effective. If then, the financing of basic income takes place precisely through cuts in public spending, the overall effect ends up being even recessive.

Let us examine this process step by step. Suppose the state distributes a total basic income worth 1,000 dollars. Suppose further that part of this additional income is consumed – say 4/5 – and the remaining fifth is saved. Consumption thus increases by 800 dollars and saving by 200 dollars. It does not matter here whether it is workers, capitalists or both who consume. For both Keynes and Kalecki, the increase in overall consumption stimulates firms to expand production by the same amount (this is of course the most optimistic hypothesis since firms might decide to increase, at least in part, prices instead of production).

Assume, for example, that this additional consumption of 800 dollars is directed towards the purchase of books and bottles of wine and that therefore the producers of books and wine increase their production to match the increase in demand. This means that the companies producing books and wine and the workers they employ will see their income increase by 800 dollars overall (with a parallel reduction in unemployment if the increase in production is achieved by hiring new workers). But the process does not stop.

Part of these 800 dollars received by those involved in the production of books and wine will in fact be consumed, while the remainder will be saved. 4/5 of these 800 dollars (i.e. 640 dollars) will thus be spent on consumption and 1/5 (i.e. 160 dollars) will be saved. It matters little whether these new persons will also buy books and wine or different goods, for example, records and beer. In the latter case, it will be the producers of records and beer who will expand production, resulting in an additional income of 640 dollars.

If then the record and beer producers want to use the new income to buy houses and medicine or candy and chocolate, from the point of view of aggregate demand the question does not change. 4/5 of 640 dollars (i.e. 512 dollars) will translate into increased production and income and 1/5 (128 dollars) will go into savings. And the process continues.

If we retrace the process from the beginning, on the day the basic income is introduced, nothing happens at all: production remains unchanged, and households simply see their disposable income rise. Immediately afterwards, however, as soon as the new income earners start spending, consumption and national income increase first by 800 dollars, then by 640, then again by 512, and so on. Of course, these are smaller and smaller income increases, which will eventually tend to zero. But the fact that Keynesians emphasize is that the sprinkling of 1,000 dollars generate a much larger increase in national income. With the data of our example (with a consumption share in income of 4/5), national income will have increased by 4,000 dollars at the end of the process. In formal terms, denoting by $c$ the fraction of income spent on consumption, one dollar of basic income generates an increase in national income equal to $c/(1 - c)$.

At the same time, however, the public accounts of the state worsen by 1,000 dollars. Trying to recover these 1,000 dollars through taxes is a contradiction in terms. If you give with one hand and take away with the other, disposable income (i.e. income after taxes and transfers) does not change and, consequently, neither does consumption. The whole expansionary process stops before starting. At the aggregate level, there is no demand stimulus.

The only real alternative is then to cut public spending. However, as we said, according to Keynesian theory, public spending interventions have a greater impact on income than monetary transfers to households (or tax cuts). So, when the state has to cut public spending to finance basic income the net effect will be recessionary.

To understand this point well, let us consider the effects of an increase in public spending. A reduction of it will obviously have symmetrical effects. Let us imagine that instead of giving 1,000 dollars to households, the state allocates 1,000 dollars to build a bridge. With these 1,000 dollars, the state hires new workers and buys the materials and machinery needed to build the bridge (or it launches a tender and then private companies will hire the workers and buy what is needed). Suppose the construction of the bridge takes one year. During this year, the income of the workers and those selling the resources needed to build the bridge increases by a total of 1,000 dollars. The increase in public spending of 1,000 dollars therefore immediately begins to generate an increase in national output and income. But, again, the process does not end there.

Of this additional 1,000 dollars in the pockets of those who participated in the construction of the bridge, 800 will be spent on the purchase of consumer goods and 200 will be saved. As before, it makes no difference whether these people want to consume wine, beer, books or records. At the aggregate level, total demand increases by 800 dollars and so does the production of wine, beer, books or records.

And without going through all the steps, the producers of wine, beer, books or records will increase their consumption by 640 dollars and so on. These effects induced by the initial increase in public spending are identical to those induced by the basic income. The only difference between the two manoeuvres is the direct impact on income of the 1,000 dollars involved in building the bridge, which is not there in the case of the basic income. At the end of the process, with the same assumptions as before, the increase in national income is in fact 5,000 dollars. In formal terms, one dollar of public expenditure generates an increase in national income of $1 / (1 - c)$.

Not only does this prove that a Keynesian should focus on public spending instead of cash transfers if he/she wants to sustain demand. But it is also clear that if we finance basic income by cutting public spending, the two processes do not cancel each other out at all: in the end, we will have a lower national income. By how much? Exactly by the amount of the manoeuvre.

In the Keynesian tradition, this important result is called the 'balanced budget multiplier', also known as Haavelmo's theorem (Haavelmo, 1945). Its implication is simple and straightforward: to increase income without affecting the state budget, government spending and taxes must increase, not decrease. Decreasing taxes (or distributing basic income) in the presence of a balanced budget constraint, or debt limits, produces recession, not economic growth. And the nice theoretical thing is that there are not even so many calculations to be done because the net effect on national income is known a priori: one dollar (or one billion dollars) of basic income and one dollar (or one billion dollars) of public spending cuts reduce national income by one dollar (or one billion dollars). From a mathematical point of view, the difference between the basic income multiplier and the public expenditure multiplier is –1. In formulae: $[c/(1 - c)] - [1 / (1 - c)] = -1$. The conclusion is simple: when you fix the size of the basic income you also fix the size of the recession!

So far, we have been reasoning in the abstract. In reality, however, the constraints on state indebtedness are very concrete and interest expenditure on public debt constitutes a burden for the state, especially for the most indebted ones. The assumption that the state must cut public spending following every tax cut or direct transfer to households and enterprises is indeed a constant in the history of capitalism. In the name of stimulating demand and combating the crisis, these policies have always ended up compressing demand and aggravating the crisis, as the neoliberal wave unleashed by Reagan and Thatcher in the 1980s shows.

But proceeding with the critique and moving onto an even more concrete terrain, the idea of basic income must be framed in the context of class relations, which are anything but static in capitalist systems and have been characterized for decades by the weakening of the working class and the rise of precarious work.

In capitalism, competition pushes the wage down, towards the subsistence level. In times of crisis, when competition gets tough, it can push it even lower. In the era of precarious work, then, the subsistence wage loses its minimum wage features as the reproduction of the working class becomes an individual problem: if the wage is not enough, it is up to the individual worker to find other small jobs to get through the month. The dividing line between employed and unemployed becomes a problem of statistical definition. But with existing labour relations, all precarious workers know that with a part-time, apprenticeship or on-call contract there is no way out of poverty.

In such a framework, basic income does not improve workers' conditions at all. Instead, it serves to rationalize precariousness in a context of crisis. No one breaks free from the blackmail of wage-labour. On the contrary, the overall design is that of a labour market tailored to corporations, with multiple and intermittent jobs for workers, according to changing business needs, and lower and lower wages as a condition for corporations to invest again. By providing everyone with a monetary base to rely on, basic income helps institutionalize the new labour model and accompany the fall of wages below the subsistence level.

The worker's remuneration becomes the sum of two components: the proper wage, which is in free fall, and a government subsidy to make ends meet. Both components, of course, are produced by the worker but the worker's voice can only be heard on the first part of the income, the state decides about the other. Thus, the role of the trade union struggle diminishes and that of the treasury increases. Why struggle in the workplace? Better to work in silence and wait for the state contribution. What can be granted to workers is determined by the Ministry of the Economy. Instead of dampening competition between workers, basic income thus helps to structure a world in which the labour movement does not exist and there are only isolated individuals competing for precarious jobs, with the help of the state.

Workers' rights are outdated, now there are only the rights of the bourgeoisie, those that are exercised by buying. The market is the new uncontested yardstick of rationality. This is ultimately what basic income is for, to enable services from which the state gradually withdraws to be purchased on the market and to develop private capital in the name of the common good.

Basic income thus helps to complete the process of disintegration of the working class. After the atomization of its internal relations through the war of all against all, the disappearance of the external antagonist: when we buy, there are no workers and capitalists, we are all consumers. Workers fighting each other in the workplace, but united with the bourgeoisie in the supermarkets.

According to the logic of basic income, rights are enforced by buying commodities. As workers, therefore, we count less and less, but as consumers we are the new sovereigns (even if, with the existing distribution of income and wealth, some consumers are definitely more sovereign than others). In the new consumer-based society, the customer is always right, and the worker is always wrong. People work in silence and raise their voices when the service is not good. Basic income weakens the worker (who produces everyone's income) and strengthens the consumer (who just spends the income), sacrificing the rights of the former and sanctifying those of the latter. Therefore, if the transport worker goes on strike, it is not his/her demands that matter but the inconvenience he/she creates for the traveller. This is repeated to us on every occasion by newspapers and televisions, which give no space at all to the reasons and sacrifices of the workers in struggle but carefully report the testimonies of weary travellers protesting the cancellation of trains.

The new market left does not like to dirty its hands with workers' struggles in the places of production. The new radical-chic front of social struggles is now in the places of consumption. Thus, as wealth polarizes and workers have a hard time making ends meet, there is a growth in 'critical consumption' campaigns: the conscious abstention from consuming certain commodities because they do not conform to the moral standards of the new bourgeoisie. Who knows what else those who don't have a cent in their pockets have to abstain from! Without even knowing the techniques of workers' struggle, based on boycotting production, by exposing their bodies and lives to risk, the new critical consumerists talk about boycotting this or that commodity, by doing nothing at all, by simply abstaining from buying it. Consumer sovereignty and the 'one dollar, one vote' logic are fully espoused by those who believe they are fighting the system. Without even realizing that nine out of ten critical consumption campaigns are launched and financed by companies competing with the targeted ones. And indeed, no supporter of critical consumption really intends to generalize his/her 'form of struggle' to the entire commodity world. They give up one commodity only to buy another.

While the crisis bites and workers pay the price, the new left in general and supporters of basic income in particular pursue the common good. In the face of soaring profits and falling wages, they promise income for all. Because the important thing is to buy – or, more correctly, to sell – commodities, even if they are soaked in workers' blood. Working conditions worsen, but commodities shine on supermarket shelves. This is the common good in consumer society: hell in production and heaven in exchange (for those who can afford it).

But let us take one step further in our critique. If on the supply side, basic income is part of the new model of exploitation based on precarious work, on the demand side, it favours the process of commodification of society, facilitating the always delicate phase of selling commodities and developing the role of the market. On the one hand, it increases the rate of exploitation during the production process, on the other hand, it fluidifies the realization of profits at the time of sale and expands the role of private capital.

In general terms, the state can intervene in the economy in various ways. It can, for instance, decide to provide certain services directly, such as education and health care or even transport, telecommunications and all the rest. Or it can leave the satisfaction of social needs to private capital. But one should be under no illusions. If one follows this second path, the satisfaction of the needs of the population is subordinate to the maximization of enterprises' profits: we may believe that we are putting capital at our service and direct it towards the production of what we need but, in the end, it is we who have to organize ourselves to satisfy capital's needs. Capital has its own mechanisms, its logic is that of profit, the rest are side effects.

The basic income proposal fits into this second approach. It does not develop public services, it provides money with which to buy private services, commodities. It is not the tax system that finances public spending, it is cuts in public spending that finance basic income. The commodity is not seen as the cell of the capitalist system, the production of which presupposes class exploitation and subjugation to capital, but as the instrument to satisfy individual and social needs. The production of commodities and the subjugation of society to capital are thus not combated but expanded. The state must withdraw from the production of goods and services and become a mere supplier of money. The satisfaction of needs is taken care of by corporations, compatibly with profit maximization.

The problem is twofold. First, when goods and services are provided through the market, by definition, they cannot be universally accessible. As we have already said, whatever their price, there will always be people who need them but cannot afford them. Second, when relying on the market, the imprint of capital transforms the very nature of goods – it makes them commodities – subordinating their use value to the logic of profit and exchange value.

As market relations grow, rights are emptied of content and are progressively subordinated to purchasing power, leaving the least well-off excluded for the benefit of the better off. It is not the urgency of need that counts, but the capacity to spend. Milk is produced to be sold, not to feed children. If it actually ends up in the baby's bottle, all the better. But if it ends up in the bowl of the Siamese kitten of the bourgeois lady, that's fine too. And the same goes for medicine, housing, transport and everything else. If one looks at needs, medicines should go to the sick and houses to the homeless. If purchasing power counts, everything goes to the richest. The right to income – so hailed by the supporters of basic income – does not add a right, it limits all the others. Income becomes universal and rights become on payment. No longer equal services for all but services according to census, just as Friedman wanted.

The second problem is no less serious. The more the market develops, the more the needs of men and women – but also those of other species and the ecosystem – cease to matter. Everything and everyone become an appendage of capital. In this process, it is the nature of the commodity itself that is transformed because instead of satisfying human needs, it must satisfy the needs of capital. Every year, internet connections become more powerful and faster, and every year, security keys are perfected to prevent connections from running at full speed. What a disaster it would be if a user connected to the internet without paying! Instead of investing in maximizing access to the service, investments are made to restrict access, to exclude those without money. Result: one hundred internet connections in the same neighbourhood (without anyone ever seriously checking the damage they cause) and ten wretches in the same neighbourhood who cannot even check their e-mails. This is how the internet develops under the drive of capital. The same need for communication could be satisfied by the state with open connections, at a lower cost. Instead, states first privatized their telephone companies and then pushed citizens to buy services from the new private enterprises. And now the supporters of basic income urge them to transfer money to the people to increase the profits of these huge enterprises.

Of course, we cannot blame the supporters of basic income for the commodification of the world. Ultimately, they are themselves cultural products of the commodification process even when they believe they are fighting the system. But it is precisely this uncritical acceptance of the market – from which derives the political proposal to expand it further – that makes them dangerous political opponents.

In a world where everything is achieved with money, the sick, the hungry, and the homeless do not ask for medicine, food and a home, but for money. We cannot all be economists. We are just sons of this system and many of us do not even have the time to criticize or study it. Those who do not even meet their basic needs ask for money to be able to buy paracetamol, bread and pay rent. Instead of locating the problem in the fact that paracetamol, bread and housing are commodities produced only on condition of creating profit, the problem appears to them as a shortage of money with which to buy these commodities. As we have seen, however, Marx (1894, ch. 13) explained well before the new radical economists launched their campaign for universal income that 'Everything appears reversed in competition, and thus in the consciousness of its agents. . . . The vulgar economist does practically no more than translate' these appearances 'into a seemingly more theoretical and generalized language, and attempt to substantiate the justice of those conceptions'.[1]

Supporters of basic income do not even try to criticize the rationality of the market. They take it as given. And where the market hiccups, they call upon the state to unblock it and develop its role. Instead of suggesting a process of decommodification of medicine, food and housing, which would allow these goods to finally be produced by looking at the needs they have to satisfy and not at the profits they have to guarantee, the new income fetishists would like to increase recourse to the market and proceed at a faster pace along the undermined road of commodity production, which is then the same road that enriches the capitalist and impoverishes the worker in the distributive sphere.

The market is the circulatory system of capital. Without it, capital cannot impose its law. Extending its role simply means expanding the realm of commodities and compressing that of rights: capital advances and society retreats. In the market, it is capital that rules, it is like Mike Tyson in the ring. To extend the different aspects of our social life to the market believing we are fighting capital is like breaking up an oral altercation with Tyson and inviting him to put the gloves on to settle the matter.

Basic income cannot act as an instrument for the emancipation of the working class. Workers emancipate themselves from the slavery of capital through wage growth, the recognition of rights and the decommodification of social relations, not through new incomes that accompany the fall in wages, the loss of rights and the commodification of society.

The sick does not need money but a health system that works well and for free. Medical research cannot be at the service of profit if it must guarantee health, and medicine cannot be a commodity if it must reach those who need it. Boys and girls must be provided with schools that make them think, not that teach them to bow down to the capital. They must be given sports facilities where they can grow up healthy, educate their bodies and have fun. To reduce gender asymmetries, domestic work, which is still too much for women, must be socialized, not monetized. In order to give a concrete response to the needs of the population, goods and services must be provided, outside the market circuit and outside the logic of profit. Society must be de-commodified, not commodified further. This is the conclusion reached by Marxism after criticizing capital and its mechanisms. There is no room for any basic income in this path.

## Unmet needs and overproduction

In its ambitious mystifying enterprise in defence of the market and its oligarchic rationality based on the principle of 'one dollar, one vote', bourgeois economics ends up forgetting the real problems that afflict capitalism, not so much as a system capable of realizing the common good, but rather as a system capable of self-regulation. Despite all the theoretical efforts made, the market's constant inability to provide the commodities actually needed is there for all to see. With large sections of the population unable to satisfy their basic needs, the paradox is that capitalist production is characterized by continuous crises of overproduction.

From a moral point of view, the problem would seem to be that of producing and supplying the needy with the goods and services to satisfy their unmet needs, but from the point of view of the survival of the system, the problem is instead that of the excess of production of commodities in relation to the capacity of the holders of purchasing power to absorb them.

The current social division of labour and wealth, both domestically and internationally, is characterized by the contradiction that where people work more there is less capacity to spend, while enormous wealth is concentrated in hands that will never be able to spend it. When I wrote the first edition of this book (2004), the three richest people in the world had a combined wealth greater than the gross domestic product of the 48 poorest countries. The 497 billionaires (in dollars) recorded in 2001 had a combined wealth of 1.54 trillion dollars. This wealth was greater than the gross domestic product of all sub-Saharan African countries (929 billion dollars), the gross domestic product of the oil-producing countries of the Middle East and North Africa (1.34 trillion dollars) and the combined income of the poorest half of the world's population (Anderson and Cavanagh, 2000). Today, the number of billionaires has risen to 2,640 and their total wealth to 12.2 trillion dollars. Six men own more than 100 billion dollars each, for a total wealth of 822 billion dollars (Forbes, 2024).

It may not be a Pareto move, but if we left the billionaires just one billion dollars each, their standard of living would probably not be affected except marginally, while 9.56 trillion dollars (12.2 trillion – 2.64 trillion) would be freed up to benefit the community. But these are just abstract speculations. Reality evolves in the opposite direction: the rich accumulate wealth and the poor poverty.

The contradiction of our society is that we work too much (and produce too many commodities that cannot be sold) and, at the same time, the needs of those who work are not met. If this situation cannot change through the automatisms of the market mechanism, it is because a general redistribution of property and purchasing power on the basis of a unanimous consensus – according to the Pareto criterion, so to speak – is clearly unthinkable. If one has no economic means, one has no weight in the collective decision-making processes regulated by the market and this even prevents oneself from expressing his/her needs. It is this contradiction between the distribution of needs and purchasing power that makes possible the paradox of the simultaneous scarcity and overabundance of production in capitalism. However, while the existence of unsatisfied needs has no direct repercussions on the economic functioning of the system (it may have them indirectly, through channels of social and political struggle), unsold production means crisis.

The problem of capitalist production is not so much the minimization of production costs (that can always be achieved by squeezing wages), but rather the sale of products. The biggest trade battles (and many of the military wars) are waged to secure control of the markets where to sell the products (as well, of course, as where to find the raw materials needed for production). And so, investments continue to be made in the production of the commodities most needed by those with purchasing power (while continuing to force their absorption rate), whereas those goods that are needed by those who cannot pay are simply not produced.

Capitalist overproduction affects entire sectors. Technological products have production costs that are too low to justify the high prices at which they are sold. The computer they sell to you today at a high price extolling its technological properties will, within a year, be reviled by the same sellers as an archaeological relic incompatible with all the new advances in technology. There is no reason for an individual to have three computers or four mobile phones, but since the technology industry produces computers and mobile phones and the potential buyers of these commodities are only limited sections of the world's population, it is they who must be forced to throw away their old, prehistoric computers and mobile phones and buy a new one. The technological development of these commodities, of course, is fixed at the drawing board: there would be no reason to put a new model on the market every year, if not to make the previous one obsolete and thus create an outlet for a production that otherwise could not be sold.

If one acted in the name of rationality, it would seem more logical, since the well-off have been provided with computers and mobile phones, to turn to other segments of the population, new countries, which could enjoy such commodities. But market rationality says instead that, at this point, new services are produced for computers and nicer mobile phones are made to replace the old (perfectly functioning) ones.

The automobile market in advanced countries has been saturated for decades now: everyone who can afford it has one or more cars, and yet, in the most absolute short-sightedness, new cars continue to be produced all the time, even knowing that private transport, precisely for reasons of efficiency and sustainability, can only have a hard time. According to industry studies, the key to the success of the various car manufacturers in snatching each other's market shares (in an industry that is in crisis overall) lies in the average launch period for a new model. So, every three to four years, all car manufacturers cease production of the 'old' models and start production of the new ones, which obviously must not look too much like the old ones; otherwise how could car owners be induced to change cars more and more often? And if the principles of marketing are not enough, then the state and international organizations step in to impose new supposedly safety and ecological standards so that cars on the road are taken to the scrap yard on their own wheels, to be replaced by new super-ecological cars that will be rendered obsolete within a few years.

In the face of such productive irrationality, market signals and incentives do not go in the direction of an industrial reconversion that solves the problem of over-production of cars and eliminates the waste of a system that produces commodities made to last 20 years but which the system itself makes obsolete after four; on the contrary, market incentives lead to interventions that only serve to postpone the problem for a few years, in the hope that the whole of society will eventually have to bear the burden, according to the usual logic of privatizing profits and socializing losses. So now capital calls on the state, demanding scrapping incentives, tax breaks, financial aid and laws forcing car drivers to change their cars even when there is no reason to do so, just in order to sell more and more cars, all of which will get stuck in traffic.

This is how we see the emergence of high moral values in public intervention policies, such as safety and respect for the environment (which in reality only serve to make us throw away our old car so that we can buy a new one, preferably with an electric engine), which we then see die as soon as it comes to work safety and industrial pollution (since, in the latter case, these values clash, rather than marry, with those of profit maximization and capital accumulation).

## Social rationality and planning

If the system has so far avoided the biggest crises and has been able to remedy the crises that have occurred, it is, paradoxically, precisely thanks to the massive intervention of the state (or, rather, of the states, given the international dimension of the markets). The state and the international institutions intervene by favouring particular technological developments and preventing others, supporting sectors in difficulty, absorbing surplus assets and rescuing, from time to time, opportune industrial and financial groups in crisis. The very functioning of the market rests on the centralized intervention of the state and international bodies, which, with different weights and instruments, define the rules of the game, actively intervene with fiscal, industrial and trade policies, participate in relations between social actors and, in so doing, govern and direct the process of capital accumulation.

While neoliberal economists are all about defending the deregulated market, it is public planning (by the state and international bodies) and private planning (by multinational corporations) that prevents the final collapse of the market. Obviously, this is a planning that seeks to rationalize production while remaining within the logic of profit and whose effectiveness, at best, is aimed at the orderly functioning of the system and the creation and exploitation of ever new opportunities for profit. But, if the state intervenes in defence of profit, it is only because, in so doing, it defends itself. The (public or private) rationalization of the process of (private) capital accumulation is in fact the primary condition of survival of the capitalist system and its institutions.

However, if public and private capitalist institutions are capable of rationalizing production according to capitalist logic, that is, according to the objectives of capital accumulation, production can also be rationalized according to the logic of the democratically determined goals, reflecting the needs of the population. This means addressing the production problem through the instrument of planning, starting with a democratic procedure of defining the public objective function.

So let us see more clearly what the problems of a planner are, who seeks to rationalize production in response to the needs of his people, rather than in response to the needs of capital accumulation. Bourgeois theory does not really contest the ability to produce with the same technical efficiency as the market. The same techniques used by capitalist enterprises could in fact be used by socialist enterprises. Nor can it be argued that the socialist enterprise is less productive than the capitalist enterprise because of lower performance incentives since this is tantamount to admitting that the capitalist enterprise exploits the workers more, that is, that higher levels of productivity are obtained through greater effort on the part of the worker, that is, through an increase in the input 'labour', which has nothing to do with efficiency, which presupposes that the maximum output is obtained for the same input.

Nor can the rationality of planning be contested in relation to the efficient allocation of resources: in the market system, it is the objectives of individual consumers, weighted according to their purchasing power, that guide the allocation of resources; in a planned system, the allocation of resources is instead guided by the objectives of the planner. The problem of planning therefore has nothing to do with issues of irrationality or inefficiency; it is simply a matter of pursuing different goals than those pursued in the market society – in one case it is the goals of those with purchasing power that matter, in the other it is the goals of the planner – but in both cases the goals set can be realized efficiently, with the minimum use of available resources.

Rather, the real critique of bourgeois theory concerns the planner's (in)ability to actually know what is to be produced based on the (objective) needs and (subjective) preferences to be satisfied.

As far as needs are concerned, the criticism is not very relevant. Since these are objective facts, science and a little common sense would suffice to resolve the issue: it is not so difficult to understand that a hungry person needs food, a cold person needs clothes and a home, and a sick person needs care and medicine. On the other hand, as far as 'higher' social needs are concerned, we know by now that education, sport, culture cannot be considered luxuries at all, once the strictly basic needs have been met.

So let us come to subjective preferences: here indeed, without the participation of the interested party who freely expresses his/her opinion, it is difficult to imagine how a planning authority can satisfy the varied preferences of its citizens. But is it then true that the market does it better? After what we have said about the coercion imposed by individual budgetary constraints, does it still make sense to define the market as a place where preferences are freely expressed? And then, what do the market sensors that Austrian economists insist on so much actually detect? Perhaps that a rich man prefers a Jaguar to a Mercedes, but not that a penniless person prefers pasta to rice (or a Mercedes to a Jaguar), or that an African child prefers milk to flies on his/her nose. Not to mention the fact that when market sensors detect a preference for milk, there is no chance that it will end up to African children who need it to survive. More likely, with the current distribution of income and wealth, it will end up instead to the kittens of bourgeois ladies. And, if this is the case, why should an outline vote (with appropriate voting and political discussion criteria) on social priorities and the goods and services to be produced not suffice to give the planner an idea of the wishes and aspirations of his people?

Moreover, this insistence on individual preferences only reflects the aspirations of the bourgeoisie (the freedom to buy this or that product, or even the freedom to dismiss this or that worker), hiding them, once again, under the guise of the common good. In the society of consumerism, it may seem provocative, but I must make these three considerations. Firstly, I do not see the point of talking about preferences when we are still far, in too many cases, from satisfying basic needs. Second, I do not find the right to choose a car so important, when for many people this choice will simply never arise due to lack of purchasing power. Thirdly, preferences expressed in individual choices reflect an unacceptable underlying asymmetry: for some, the problem of choice concerns first and foremost the particular boss on whom to make their very existence dependent; for others, instead, the choice concerns only the type of car or the brand of dress since for them the day when they will see their existence dependent on a boss who is not their relative or their father's friend will simply never come.

But, if the criticism of planning really boils down to the problem of making one person get the yellow shirt and another a red one according to their preferences, then it does not seem to me that there are any insurmountable technical problems: it would suffice to produce a certain overabundance of coloured shirts, which, moreover, in the current market system happens in all sectors where preferences count (without this being considered in any way a social problem, since excess supply is the guarantee of demand satisfaction).

From a practical point of view, a planning process that respects socially expressed needs and preferences must determine a value system that defines the criteria of economic rationality. This process of defining social values to inspire the production and distribution of goods is obviously compatible with various procedures of individual and social participation in political life. In this sense, planning – the conscious direction of the economy – can be achieved through different models of democracy, identifying the most appropriate venues in which to allow stakeholders to express their needs and desires and thus participate in defining society's goals. In this respect, the issue of the voting system is only one aspect of the problem. Alongside models of representative democracy, different models of participatory democracy can be imagined (and implemented). Whatever the democratic model of political participation, it is in any case sufficient to determine the value system that serves as a guide for economic action. On the basis of this value system, the entire production and distribution apparatus must then be reorganized.

It is obvious that the transition to a planned mechanism implies a radical redistribution of voting rights compared to the current market-based distribution. Therefore, it is normal to expect that the exchange relationships between commodities, expressed today in market prices, will be revolutionized. If in market society we spend 50 dollars to produce a medicine that can save a life and another 50 dollars to produce a good wine, it is not because we have publicly discussed and decided that the value of life is equivalent to that of a good drink, but because, in aggregating individual needs and preferences through the market the desires of the holders of purchasing power prevail, who – perhaps because they are healthy, perhaps because they are alcoholics, or perhaps because they are rich enough to afford both medicine and wine – are willing to spend the same amount on a life-saving pill as on a glass of wine. This does not happen in the planned system: through production planning, the goals to be pursued by society are explicitly determined and can be the subject of democratic discussion.

## Use and exchange values

The transition from market to planning can be achieved according to different dynamics. The more important the needs to be satisfied, the more urgent is the replacement of the market's 'rationality' criteria with rationality criteria actually defined from the needs of the population. In this process of expanding the economic sphere under the conscious control of society, the spontaneous dynamics of the market must be explicitly fought, leaving room for democratically established social values. The laws of the market can therefore in no way be taken as the yardstick by which to judge. This means that the production of goods and services must be progressively decommodified, that is, it must be aimed at the direct satisfaction of needs, not at sale on the market.

From a theoretical point of view, maximizing the allocative space managed by planning on the basis of a democratic criterion of rationality and minimizing the allocative space managed by the market (according to an oligarchic criterion of rationality), use values will tend to prevail over exchange values. Let us take a closer look, then, at what *use values* and *exchange values* are.

The *use value* of a good derives from the particular properties of the good that make certain uses of it possible. Water has a use value because it thirsts, pasta because it feeds, a computer because it helps in writing a book. The *exchange value* (the price), on the other hand, expresses a relationship between goods: on the market ten litres of water are exchanged for a kilo of pasta and 1,000 kilos of pasta are exchanged for a computer. In capitalism, these exchange relations are not occasional, they are instead the very goal of production: goods and services are not produced to be directly consumed by the producer but to be sold on the market. In this sense, their very nature gets transformed since the exchange value rather than the use value becomes the very goal of capitalist production.

If bourgeois economics talk about 'goods' as if their nature were the same in all modes of production, Marx (1867, ch. 1) opens *Capital* precisely by discussing the nature of the 'commodity' in capitalist production and the issue of its value. Use value is obviously an essential prerequisite for exchange value: a good that has no use value will never receive a market valuation simply because no one is willing to give up anything in exchange for it. However, once it is established that commodities that are exchanged in the market necessarily have a use value, the relative importance of their different uses is not sufficient to determine their exchange values: water is essential for life (and therefore has a great use value) but in many market economies it has a very limited exchange value, compared for example with that of diamonds (whose use value is certainly secondary from the point of view of survival).

In the realm of commodities, it is not the use value that drives production but the exchange value. Nobody cares if the internet is truly accessible to all and if security keys are an unnecessary expense. In capitalism, it is all about making profits. Therefore, research focuses on technologies to exclude service and appropriate profits, not to expand access. If the best pastry chefs compete to make the best chocolate cake, Nutella goes straight into the toilet. But if you want to build the greatest fortune in Italy you have to make a low-cost crap that everyone likes. Chocolate stops being made with cocoa and becomes a mix of palm oil, cocoa butter and marketing. Originally, it served to satisfy our taste, now it serves to enrich those who sell it. Use value succumbs to exchange value. Worshipping Nutella is trendy, and a country with a worldwide culinary reputation is now better known for its industrial cuisine than for the taste, variety and quality of its food . . . and the Ferrero family is the richest in Italy.

In this process of commodification, the intrinsic characteristics of goods are moulded by capital to best suit its needs and all that remains of the original good is its name. By their nature, chocolate and an internet connection have nothing in common. However, when their production takes place on a capitalist basis, they become almost identical: for capital they are both means to make profits; and if in order to maximize these profits, the connection slows down and chocolate becomes a fatty paste, the problem lies with men, not with capital. And if food corporations have been able to transform the very nature of chocolate, what is so strange if now they pompously launch insect flour, the new source of protein for those who can no longer afford a steak?

Whether it is basic necessities or superfluous things makes no difference. If chocolate is not a political priority for anyone (although the commodification of food affects the concrete lives of all of us in the deepest way), the problem becomes more serious when it comes to the right to education or health. Because while neoliberals and Keynesians would like to develop the market through state subsidies and incentives to households and firms, these rights are increasingly denied in practice by the very lack of public funds. Thus, thanks to the advance of the market, state schools and the national health system are shrinking, and private schools and clinics are growing instead. The latter, however, have no interest in developing the cultural and scientific growth of young people and developing an organic approach to health because critical study and medical prevention match badly with the logic of profit. If we already complain about the commodification of these sectors vital to the satisfaction of basic needs, by expanding the role of the market, commodification accelerates.

In a commodified world, given equal effort in production, if commodity *X* is produced instead of commodity *Y*, it is not because *X* is more important than *Y* from the point of view of the uses to be made of it, but because it has a higher value on the market, which allows greater quantities of other commodities to be obtained in exchange. In a planned system, by contrast, production is driven directly by society's assessment of the uses of different goods and services. The real problem, then, is to ensure that society can express its evaluation in a democratic manner, by collectively establishing its priorities and consciously defining criteria of economic rationality to replace the criteria of market (ir)rationality summarized in the price system.

## Bourgeois and communist values

Once the criteria of social rationality in production have been established, the question arises as to each individual's participation in the production process and the sharing out of the product. In the market society, the package of commodities each individual receives depends on his/her economic capabilities, not on the actual need for those goods. In other words, market society gives *to everyone according to his/her economic capabilities*, not according to his/her needs. But even if one were to stick to the mystified representation of bourgeois economics, according to which the market gives *to everyone according to his/her ability* (understood as individual dexterity, rather than spending capacity), in what sense can such a criterion be considered a purely efficiencyist matter? It actually incorporates a strong and counterintuitive value judgement: why should the capable have more resources to pursue their interests? One could, for instance, argue – on the basis of a different value system – that one who is incapable should be given more (e.g. because an incapable might need more resources to satisfy his/her needs or even because he/she might simply have more needs). But this only confirms that the bourgeois economy's concept of efficiency is an ideological concept, laden with value judgements.

It should also be added that, in the market system, participation in the social process of production, work is a (formal) right, but not a duty: this means that those who are not in need are de facto exempt from the drudgery of work, while the imperative to work hard and in the most humble and risky conditions is imposed on the very ones in need. This means that the contribution that each individual makes to total production is not proportional to his/her ability, but to his/her needs.

If Marx (1875, ch. 1), in the Critique of the Gotha Programme, stated that 'in the highest phase of communist society (. . .) society inscribe on its banners: *From each according to his ability, to each according to his needs!*', the bourgeois motto (obviously not made explicit) is: *From each according to his needs, to each according to his abilities!* If one then recognizes that the main ability that matters in the market is the spending capacity, we can get even more precise: *From each according to his needs, to each according to his spending capacity!*

Extending the realm where it is the law of the market that regulates social relations means extending the realm where this double allocative principle applies, which takes from those in need and gives to those who already have. Realizing a society in which it is the needs of individuals and the community that drive production and the allocation of resources means, on the contrary, subtracting space from the market: abolishing market prices and their presumed rationality (which only assumes meaning in the logic of 'one dollar, one vote'), letting the values democratically expressed by society guide economic choices, and redefining the very meaning of economic rationality on an expressly social basis, which, in the current stage of advancement of the social division of labour, is only possible through conscious forms of control of production.

All this should also lead to a general rethinking of the values on which social interaction is based and of the meritocratic logic itself (on which the market's incentive mechanism is based). Meritocracy is not only a mystification of the law of the strongest – in the market, the strongest wins, not the best – but above all a principle incompatible with the communist ideal of a world in which it is our needs (duly determined and democratically expressed) that guide productive activity, not our supposed prowess.

## Decommodification, democracy and communism

In the market the rule 'one dollar, one vote' applies, in the political sphere of collective decisions the rule 'one head, one vote' applies (despite all the imperfections and flaws of the representative mechanism). The first principle is not democratic, the second is. And so all that needs to be done is to progressively reduce the field in which it is the impersonal market mechanism that regulates our relations and extend the field in which it is our conscious wills on an equal footing to form a collective choice. The thing is very feasible (albeit wretchedly countercultural): all we have to do is to take space away from the market, decommodify goods, things, people, making them simply goods, things, people, instead of commodities, and, in so doing, allow society to express its own evaluations on alternative uses of resources without any respect for the logic of exchange values imposed by the market. As long as there is a market, there will be a violation of democracy, and the larger the market space, the more serious this violation will be.

The realization of democratic principles, in a context in which the limits of the market are recognized, therefore passes, in my opinion, through four interdependent conditions:

1. The establishment of democratic procedures for political confrontation to determine the social priorities and economic goals to be pursued. (In the current system, social priorities are determined by the autonomous and socially irrational forces of the market.) This means extending the mechanisms of collective decision-making based on the democratic principle of 'one head, one vote' to

the various fields of economic interaction, effectively preventing the development of the oligarchic principle of 'one dollar, one vote' in force in the market. At the institutional level, the realization of a system of real economic democracy requires radical changes to truly assert the dominance of politics over economics in both the real economy and finance. All economic decisions (first the strategic ones and those regarding most urgent needs, then gradually all the others) should therefore pass under the control of democratic institutions (and not institutions lacking popular legitimacy and pretending to be *super partes*, such as central banks and other national and international financial bodies).

2. The expansion of the economic space regulated through the conscious instrument of planning, starting with a democratically determined objective function, as a means of providing citizens with the goods and services deemed socially necessary, according to the priorities expressed by society.
3. The progressive replacement of the bourgeois principle from each according to his needs, to each according to his (spending) abilities in force in the market, with the communist principle from each according to his abilities, to each according to his needs in force in a state that rationalizes production according to the needs of its people (and not according to the needs of capital accumulation). On the side of public expenditure, this means ensuring the supply of essential goods and services for free, or, if not feasible, at a political price dependent on the priority level of the needs that these goods and services have to satisfy. On the side of tax revenues, this means sharply increasing the tax burden (a necessary condition for financing the expansion of public services) through a strongly progressive system that penalizes capital income.
4. The progressive decommodification of the various spheres of our lives: food, health, housing, education, culture, sport, transport and, of course, labour (labour power in Marxian terms), which is the real turning point towards a socialist society. From the material point of view, this means directing the production of goods and services related to these social objectives towards the direct and free satisfaction of the needs of the population, while at the same time countering the production of goods and services for sale on the market. From the people's point of view, instead, it means extending the rights and protections of all weak subjects in market interaction, starting with workers.

All this means confining the market to ever narrower scopes and finally abolishing it.

## Note

1 In his critique of capital, Marx insists that competition is the vehicle for this reversal between essence and appearances. In this passage, he notes in particular that the capitalist who, under competitive pressure, expands production and reduces costs, actually sees his profits rise, but does not realize that, in doing so, he contributes to the fall of the general profit rate. The vulgar economist instead of explaining the origin of profit (as labour extorted from workers) and the causes of its fall (the over-accumulation of capital) presents profit as value created by capital (through the competitive stimulus) and illudes himself/herself that he/she can counter its fall by further developing competition and capital accumulation.

## References


Anderson, S. and Cavanagh, J. (2000) *The rise of corporate global power*. The Institute for Policy Studies, pp. 1–14. Available at: www.iatp.org/sites/default/files/Top_200_The_Rise_of_Corporate_Global_Power.pdf

European Central Bank (2024) *Key ECB interest rates*. Available at: www.ecb.europa.eu/stats/policy_and_exchange_rates/key_ecb_interest_rates/html/index.en.html

Eurostat (2023) *Inflation in the Euro area*. Eurostat. Available at: https://ec.europa.eu/eurostat/statistics-explained/index.php?title=Inflation_in_the_euro_area

Federal Reserve (2023) *Recent balance sheet trends*. Available at: www.federalreserve.gov/monetarypolicy/bst_recenttrends.htm

Forbes (2024) *World's richest people*. Available at: www.forbes.com

Friedman, M. (1962) *Capitalism and freedom*. Chicago: University of Chicago Press.

Haavelmo, T. (1945) 'Multiplier effects of a balanced budget', *Econometrica*, 13(4), pp. 311–318.

Kalecki, M. (1934) *Essays in the theory of economic fluctuations*. London: Allen & Unwin.

Keynes, J. M. (1923) *A tract on monetary reform*. London: Macmillan.

Keynes, J. M. (1936) *The general theory of employment, interest and money*. London: Palgrave Macmillan.

Longtermtrends (2024) *The real interest rate*. Available at: www.longtermtrends.net/real-interest-rate/

Marx, K. (1867) *Capital. A critique of political economy, Book 1, The process of production of capital*. Available at: www.marxists.org/archive/marx/works/1867-c1/index.htm

Marx, K. (1875) *Critique of the Gotha programme*. Available at: www.marxists.org/archive/marx/works/1875/gotha

Marx, K. (1894) *Capital. A critique of political economy, Book 3, The process of capitalist production as a whole*. Available at: www.marxists.org/archive/marx/works/1894-c3/

Our World in Data (2024) Available at: https://ourworldindata.org

Trading Economics (2024a) *United States inflation rate*. Available at: https://tradingeconomics.com/united-states/inflation-cpi

Trading Economics (2024b) *Euro area inflation rate*. Available at: https://tradingeconomics.com/euro-area/inflation-cpi

# 8 Conclusions

In this book, I have tried to highlight the unfoundedness of the widespread belief that the market is a desirable, efficient or rational allocative instrument. The illusion that this belief rests on rigorous scientific foundations is, in my opinion, one of the main reasons for the affirmation of the neoliberal culture far beyond the boundaries of the groups, social classes, countries and geographical areas that directly benefit from market interaction.

Market culture, with its claimed (and unfounded) neutrality, is today the biggest obstacle one faces when trying to reason openly about other possible worlds. Over and over again, even in many critical circles, the conviction re-emerges that the market can be ridden, governed, directed, and this not as a lesser evil with respect to the most extreme neoliberalism, but as a solution to the problems of a world in which everything is transformed into a commodity (to be exchanged indeed on the market). When an object or an aspect of our life (work, health, education, the environment, sport, sex, art, culture, scientific research) becomes a commodity, it is subjected to the impersonal laws of the market and the community loses its right to determine the most appropriate guiding values to regulate its production and distribution according to the needs of the population, because the only value that counts in the market is profit.

In an attempt to counter market culture (which justifies and idealizes the process of increasing commodification) I have first of all tried to show the groundlessness of its scientific foundations. My conviction (or perhaps only hope) is that by opening up the discussion on the scientific foundations that would claim to support the entire neoliberal system, it is possible to appreciate how the defence of the market is now a simple act of faith and how bourgeois economics, while claiming to want to conform to the rigour of exact sciences, has in reality come ever closer to a religion, with its own God to be idolized and to whom to sacrifice those nine-tenths of the world's population who only pay the costs of the market.

My remarks against the defence of the market by bourgeois theory have been articulated on two levels: one of internal critique, the other of external critique.

On the internal critique level, I first showed the particular significance of the supposed rationality, efficiency, desirability and necessity of the market, highlighting the ideological and biased content these terms take on in scientific discourse.

DOI: 10.4324/9781032726168-9

The first problem concerns the individualistic ideological approach which, in bourgeois economics tends to overlap with methodological individualism. It is one thing to say that all phenomena must be explained from the individual (a methodological principle that is, moreover, highly questionable), quite another to say that rationality, efficiency and social desirability must necessarily be expressed in terms of the absolute sovereignty of the individual. This principle also takes on a strong conservative connotation in economic discourse through the definition of the Pareto criterion as a normative yardstick since the individuals whose values are considered supreme and inviolable are not abstract individuals but the concrete individuals that make up market society. In this way, each individual is endowed with veto power over every possible change, and only those changes that receive unanimous approval are considered normatively legitimate (Pareto criterion), whereas the status quo is implicitly accepted as legitimate without being subjected to any approval by the sovereign individuals.

In bourgeois theory, moreover, the sovereignty of the individual takes on an arbitrary and quite particular form according to which the individual is sovereign only in the act of consumption. Individualistic ideology thus merges with the consumerist one, resulting in normative prescriptions that are explicitly at odds with the founding principles of capitalist democracies themselves.

Thanks to the myth of the fair market, without power relations, without classes and as a source of wealth and information, bourgeois economics then makes a virtue out of social differences, elevating the winners of the 'market game' to deserving triumphant and mortifying the others as despicable losers. Here the mystification and ideological intrusion are twofold: first, it is arbitrarily established that in the market the best always wins, whereas in general the strongest wins; second, it turns the fact that in capitalism each individual's remuneration is linked to his/her performance into an absolute moral principle (obfuscating the fact that meritocratic morality is not absolute at all, but specific to competitive modes of interaction). That remuneration depends on performance is a fact in market interaction, and by transforming a factual judgement into a value judgement, bourgeois economics commits a methodological malfeasance, violating the principle dear to David Hume that it is not scientifically correct to deduce what ought to be from what is (Hume, 1739). Moreover, having introduced meritocratic morality in a context of economically heterogeneously endowed agents, bourgeois economics implicitly espouses the political principle of 'one dollar, one vote', that is, the principle of the importance of the individual according to census.

Obviously, leaving aside the academic debate, all these critiques of bourgeois economics in its mystified treatment of the market translate into just as many critiques of the market itself. Regardless of the arguments of neoliberalism, in fact, the principle of consumer sovereignty, the fact that the 'market game' is not a game of skill and luck, but one of power and class struggle, and the principle that it is on the basis of census that individual preferences are aggregated in determining collective choices are all facts that apply in the market. If on the theoretical level the problem of bourgeois economics is the attempt to portray these facts as rational and efficient, on the level of communist action the problem is the need to change these same facts by abolishing the privileges and discriminations they express.

On the external criticism level, a first limitation of the market efficiency theory concerns the assumptions regarding the productive sphere: the presence of increasing returns to scale, externalities and public goods in reality prevents the realization of Pareto market efficiency.

A second order of problems then emerges on the demand side, if one reflects on the real world validity of the principle of consumer sovereignty and the assumption that individual preferences are actually innate or, in any case, determined outside the economic sphere.

The issues of economic power, social classes and exploitation can also be considered as elements of external critique as they are completely absent from the schemes of bourgeois theory but strongly present in capitalist reality. Connected to these issues is the critique of the attempt to portray the powerful captains of industry of modern capitalist systems as bold *self-made-men.*

In raising these critiques, all I have done is to make explicit what economists (neoliberal and otherwise) know (or should know). Mainstream bourgeois theory has chosen to use the terms of scientificity, rationality, efficiency, treating the problem of market interaction with the utmost analytical precision in a merely formal attempt to prevent ideological intrusions and value statements. But the truth is that these terms are themselves imbued with ideology since they are based on an implicit but precise value judgement consisting of the tacit approval of the distribution of purchasing power and its mechanisms of reproduction.

The uncritical acceptance by the 'market left' of these principles is, in my opinion, one of the root causes of its identity crisis. Starting from the rejection of the logic of exchange values (market prices) as an expression of rationality and social efficiency, I have therefore proposed, in line with Marxist thought, a criterion of rationality based on use values and democratically determined social priorities (which presupposes the decommodification of things and people and the planned direction of the economy). And, with it, the progressive extension of the political principle of 'one head, one vote' to all spheres of economic and social interaction – conditions necessary to realize a society that takes from each according to his/her abilities and gives to each according to his/her needs.

## Reference

Hume, D. (1739) *A treatise on human nature*. London: J. Noon. Available at: https://davidhume.org/texts/t/

# Glossary

**Allocation** Distribution of available goods among individuals in society.

**Analytical Marxism** School of thought within Marxism (existing only on an academic level) that adheres to methodological individualism and uses the analytical tools of neoclassical theory, in particular, those of game theory. It analyses some of the Marxist propositions (e.g. concerning exploitation and class relations) with the hypothesis of optimizing individual choices and explains social entities (e.g. social classes) as a product of the choices of rational individuals.

**Arrow-Debreu model** See: *General economic equilibrium model.*

**Arrow theorem** See: *Impossibility theorem of voting.*

**Austrian school** School of economic thought founded in 1870 by Carl Menger, dominated by the economists who held the chair of Political Economy at the University of Vienna until the 1920s. Together with the neoclassical school, it gave rise to the so-called 'marginalist revolution' in economic theory based on the subjective theory of value. Analytically, it differs from the neoclassical school in its rejection of formalism and its analysis of disequilibrium processes rather than the study of equilibrium positions. On the political and normative level, it came to be characterized by its critique of socialism and planning in general and its radical defence of the market mechanism.

**Basket of goods** Set of different goods in given quantities. For example, a basket of goods may consist of a kilo of bread, three onions and two bottles of wine.

**Budget constraint** Set of baskets of goods that a consumer can purchase with the monetary income at his/her disposal, given the prevailing price system. According to neoclassical consumption theory, the budget constraint is a datum of the consumer's problem. The existence of completely heterogeneous budget constraints between individuals is therefore not a phenomenon to be explained, but the datum from which to start. Among all the baskets of goods that respect the budget constraint, the consumer will choose the one that best responds to his subjective preferences (also to be considered as an exogenous datum to the model).

**Constant returns to scale** They are realized when a proportional increase in all inputs generates an equally proportional increase in output. In such circumstances, the size of the production plant is of no importance from the point of view of production efficiency: small and large enterprises are technologically completely equivalent.

**Consumer sovereignty** Normative principle according to which the assessment of the functioning of an economy must refer to the ability to realize consumer preferences (which are taken as given and are considered independent of social interaction). This principle is the foundation of all modern normative economics. It is actually a special case of the principle of individual sovereignty.

**Contestable markets, theory of** A monopolistic market is perfectly contestable when the costs of entry and exit from the market by potential rivals of the monopolist are zero. According to economic theory, in the case of perfect contestability, *potential* competition in a monopolistic market produces the same effects (in terms of Pareto efficiency) as those produced by *actual* competition. Indeed, the mere fear that a new firm might enter the market prevents the monopolistic firm from taking advantage of the monopoly benefits and forces it to behave as if it actually operated under conditions of perfect competition.

From the point of view of realism, the conditions of perfect contestability are certainly no better than those of perfect competition. On a theoretical level, however, the theory of contestable markets makes it possible to defend the market even when it violates the conditions of perfect competition (as in the case of monopoly). The greatest impact of this theory concerns the regulation of markets: according to the old guiding principles of regulatory agencies (anti-trust and sector-specific agencies), sectors characterized by few giant companies had to be reorganized or at least put under surveillance so as to re-establish competitive conditions. The theory of contestable markets undermines this simple principle by asserting that the existence of a monopoly in a given sector is not sufficient to eliminate the benefits of competition (and therefore does not necessarily require state intervention) since competition could still operate in a potential way.

**Critical consumption** Bourgeois-inspired campaigns aimed at discouraging the consumption of certain commodities on moral grounds. The logic of these campaigns, sometimes even presented as radical instruments of anti-capitalist struggle, is based on the acceptance of the 'one dollar, one vote' principle, the cardinal principle of market interaction in capitalism.

**Decreasing returns to scale** They occur when a proportional increase in all inputs generates a less than proportional increase in output. In such circumstances, the increase in the size of the production plant, instead of allowing a saving in the quantity of input per unit of output, leads to a deterioration in the technical conditions of production. The large enterprise is thus less efficient than the small one. This hypothesis is very widespread in the models of neoclassical theory (and, in particular, is fundamental in the general economic equilibrium model), despite its little, or no, empirical relevance and the problems of logical consistency that it poses (in fact, if reducing the size of the firm increases the efficiency of the firm itself, each firm would be inclined to divide itself into smaller and smaller production plants until it eventually disappears).

**Economic model** Simplified representation of reality used to describe and interpret an economic phenomenon. Generally, given the hegemony of the neoclassical school, the concept of model is restricted to mathematical representations.

**Economic power** Ability to condition the behaviour of other subjects through the use of economic instruments. The exercise of economic power may come about either through the ability to modify the decision-making constraints of other subjects or through the ability to influence the subjective criteria (e.g. preferences) that guide the decision-maker's choice within the existing constraints.

**Economies and diseconomies of scale** The former occur when costs per unit of output decrease as output increases. The latter when costs per unit of output increase as output increases. The concept of economies and diseconomies of scale is closely linked to that of increasing and decreasing returns to scale. The latter, however, only concerns technological aspects (the greater or lesser technological efficiency of the large plant compared to the small plant), whereas the concept of economies and diseconomies of scale also involves the prices at which the firm buys inputs. In the presence of constant returns to scale (i.e. with the same technological efficiency), the large firm might still be more economically efficient than the small one to the extent that, by buying large quantities of inputs, it is able to obtain lower prices than the small firm.

**Endogenous variable** See: *Exogenous and endogenous variable*.

**Endowments** Amount of assets possessed by different individuals before market interaction begins. According to neoclassical theory, the different endowments of individuals in the capitalist system constitute a starting point in economic analysis, not a phenomenon to be explained. In the general economic equilibrium model, in order for Pareto-efficient allocations to take place, it must be assumed that individual endowments respect the 'consumer survival' hypothesis, according to which the endowment each individual receives at birth is such that he/she can live even without market exchange. This is, of course, an assumption lacking any realism.

**Equilibrium** Situation in which no agent is interested in changing its behaviour. If the system is in an equilibrium position, it remains there, barring exogenous shocks on the data on which the equilibrium is defined. In neoclassical theory, the concept of equilibrium depends directly on the axiom that agents make their economic choices by solving constrained optimization problems. Neoclassical equilibrium is obtained when all agents optimize their objective function given the constraints of their decision problem. Under such circumstances, in fact, no agent will have an interest in unilaterally changing its behaviour (since it is already obtaining the maximum possible).

From this general definition, the usual definition of equilibrium as the equality of supply and demand is obtained. The procedure is as follows. From the analysis of the constrained optimal problems of individual agents, it is possible to construct 'individual supply and demand curves' for each good, which express the optimal quantities that the individual agent is willing to buy or sell depending on the prices of the goods. For each good, the individual demand and supply curves are then aggregated to form the 'market demand and supply curves'. The former summarize the overall demand of all agents willing to purchase a certain good (resulting from the solution of their respective optimization problems). The latter, instead, summarize the total supply of all agents willing to sell the good. The intersection between the two market supply and demand curves thus expresses an equilibrium configuration in the sense that all agents in the system realize their optimal exchange plans.

**Equilibrium method** The analysis of reality using equilibrium models presupposes that the system is in its equilibrium position. For this to happen, it is first of all necessary that an equilibrium exists, that is, that the theoretical conditions for the existence of equilibrium are met in reality. In the case where more than one equilibrium exists (non-uniqueness), the problem then arises of which position the real system is in. Finally, in order to interpret reality as being located in its equilibrium position, it is necessary to analyse the conditions of stability: if in fact the equilibrium is unstable, even the slightest perturbation – which would cause the system to move out of its equilibrium position – would end up moving the system further and further away from equilibrium (thus making the hypothesis that the system is continuously in equilibrium impossible to defend). Only with these precautions does it make sense to analyse the problem of normative properties of equilibrium (such as the question of Pareto efficiency).

**Equity and justice** Equity is a principle of distributive justice. Procedural equity refers to the rules that govern the distribution of resources among individuals. Substantive equity refers instead to the resources actually received by each individual. In the presence of substantive inequality, in the distribution of resources, according to John Rawls' theory of justice, rules should favour the most disadvantaged groups. According to the approach of Hayek and Robert Nozik, distributive justice should instead be defined only in a procedural sense.

**Exchange value** See: *Use value and exchange value.*

**Exogenous and endogenous variables** When constructing an economic model, it is first necessary to specify the sets of variables that are exogenous and endogenous to the model. Variables that are exogenous to the model are those that are not explained within the model itself, but are instead taken as given, as a starting point for the explanation of other variables (the endogenous ones). From a methodological point of view, therefore, the exogenous variables are placed outside the sphere of economic investigation and simply constitute the starting data for the entire theory. Endogenous variables are instead the variables that depend on other variables in the model and are thus explained by the model itself.

**Exploitation** In Marxian theory, difference between the value produced by labour and the value of labour power. In the production process, the worker sells his/her labour power (he/she commits to work for eight hours a day) in exchange for a wage. During the working day, he/she produces commodities that thus incorporate eight hours of labour. However, with the daily wage he/she receives, the worker can purchase commodities that incorporate a smaller amount of labour (say five hours of work). The fruit of the remaining three hours of labour (surplus labour) ends up in the capitalist's pocket in the form of profit. The existence of surplus labour, as a necessary condition for the existence of profit, is the basis of Marx's theory of exploitation. According to Marx, exploitation characterizes all class-divided societies: in feudal society, it is evident and manifest; in capitalist society, it is hidden behind the veil of 'voluntary' exchange, which makes the (objective) relationship of exploitation appear as the result of 'free' subjective choices.

In neoclassical theory, the concept of exploitation has instead a completely different meaning: it expresses the difference between the actual market price and the (theoretical) price of perfect competition. It is worth noting that, contrary to the neoclassical axiom, in the Marxian conception exploitation occurs even in a capitalist system characterized by markets of perfect competition because capitalism in order to function must still guarantee positive profits for capitalists.

**Externalities** Effects of the economic activity of one party on the welfare of other parties that occur without the parties involved being able to negotiate these effects in a special market. These are, in a sense, 'side effects' of market interaction that are not subject to negotiation between the parties. A company that has two different techniques, one of which is 'clean' and the other polluting, will choose to use the cheaper one without any regard for its socially harmful effects. For their part, those affected by pollution have no means of inducing the company to use clean techniques. The result is that the level of pollution will tend to be higher than that compatible with Pareto efficiency. Externalities are thus a case of so-called market failures. Getting the state to intervene in order to re-establish Pareto efficiency, in any case, does not mean inducing eco-friendly production at all but simply producing the level of pollution desired by the holders of purchasing power.

**Game theory** It studies strategy games (chess, draughts, poker) in which luck, if present, is not the only factor determining the outcome (games such as heads or tails or the game of goose are thus excluded). At a formal level, it can be defined as a set of logical-mathematical models analysing the strategic interaction between rational subjects (i.e. optimizing a given objective function). It became widespread in the late 1950s and found applications in the fields of oligopoly theory, wage bargaining theory, economic policy and international cooperation. Outside the economic sphere, important applications concern military problems (developed particularly during the Cold War). Indeed, it was the military interests of the United States during the Second World War and the Cold War years that led to the development of this branch of mathematical economics.

**General economic equilibrium model** Mathematical model first formalized by Walras in 1874 and later developed in particular by Arrow and Debreu in the 1850s in which a complete system of markets is assumed to exist in which individuals exchange the goods they own with each other. The model is based on three fundamental givens concerning technology, individual preferences and the initial endowments with which each individual starts market interaction. The problems that are analysed through this model are those of existence, stability, uniqueness and Pareto efficiency of the equilibrium. From a theoretical point of view, the least encouraging results concern the problem of stability and uniqueness of the equilibrium. To date, however, the general economic equilibrium model remains the most organic and mathematically advanced attempt, developed by the neoclassical school, to study the functioning of a system of interdependent markets and to assess its normative properties.

**Goods and commodities** A good (or service) is anything (or activity) that has a use value (see: *Use value and exchange value*). It is a generic category, completely unrelated to the mode of production and its social relations. A chair serves to sit on in feudalism as well as in capitalism or socialism, and the use that can be made of it does not depend on how it was produced. A commodity, instead, is any good or service produced by human labour, destined for sale on the market. The commodity is thus a specific category of capitalism. In addition to having a use value, the commodity also has an exchange value. In capitalism, it is not directly the use value of commodities that drives production, but their exchange value, since production is for sale on the market. Thus, what is produced is not what is most needed, but what is most profitable. The ultimate goal of commodity production is not the satisfaction of people's needs through the production of the most appropriate goods but the maximization of capitalists' profits.

**Haavelmo theorem** See: *Keynesian multiplier*.

**Increasing returns to scale** They occur when a proportional increase in all inputs generates a more than proportional increase in output. In such circumstances, the large enterprise enjoys a technological advantage over the small enterprise. Increasing returns to scale constitute a case of so-called market failures. In the presence of increasing returns to scale, in fact, a market characterized by a multitude of competing small firms is inefficient because no single firm is able to exploit the economic benefits that accrue from increasing the scale of production. This prevents the realization of Pareto efficiency conditions. From the point of view of hypothesis realism, although increasing returns to scale are excluded by assumption from the general economic equilibrium model, they are certainly not the exception, but rather the norm.

**Individual's sovereignty** Principle according to which the individual is the best judge of his/her own needs and the most suitable means to satisfy them. On a normative level, according to theories based on the sovereignty of the individual, only the evaluations expressed by individuals must contribute to forming an assessment of social desirability, which excludes any consideration of a directly social nature in the definition of the common good of society.

**Invisible hand** Principle according to which, in a competitive environment, the individual who only pursues his/her own self-interest also contributes to the achievement of the public interest. The expression 'invisible hand' is due to the classical economist Smith. Today it is used loosely by much of neoliberal economic theory even when the theoretical framework used has little to do with the Scottish economist's conception of the market.

**Justice** See: *Equity and justice*.

**Keynesian multiplier** Theory stating that an increase in private consumption expenditure, investment expenditure or government expenditure increases national income by an amount greater than the initial increase in expenditure. The underlying idea is that an increase in any component of aggregate demand increases national income and induces an increase in consumption. This increase in consumption will in turn generate further increases in income in a process that goes on forever, while gradually dampening. The idea of a 'multiplier effect' was first proposed by Keynes' student, Richard Kahn, and later integrated by Keyens in his *General Theory*. Understood as an instrument of economic policy, this theory suggests that state interventions in government spending or taxes have impacts of different magnitudes. In the case of an increase in government spending, there are in fact two effects: a 'direct effect', since government spending is itself a component of aggregate demand, and an 'indirect effect', through the induced increases in consumption. By contrast, in the case of a tax reduction in order to stimulate demand, there is no direct effect and the final increase in income is only due to the indirect effect operating through the increases in consumption. If the two manoeuvres are combined with a simultaneous increase in government expenditure and taxes, thus leaving the state budget unchanged, the two indirect effects operating through consumption will cancel each other out and the result will be an increase in national income equal to the manoeuvre on government expenditure and taxes. This result is known as Haavelmo's theorem.

**Labour power** In Marxian theory, physical and intellectual capacities employed by workers in the production process, as distinct from the labour actually provided. What the worker sells to the capitalist is labour power, not labour. Extracting the maximum amount of labour from labour power is one of the capitalist's goals. The difference between the value of the product and the value of labour power (the value of the means of subsistence the worker receives in the form of wages) is called surplus value. The specificity of capitalism compared to other modes of production lies in the fact that, in the process of expanding markets, labour power itself becomes a commodity.

**Liberalism and neoliberalism** Liberalism originates as political-philosophical current of thought, which affirms the limitation of the powers of the state in the name of certain fundamental individual rights (including the right to property), considered as pre-existing the creation of society itself ('philosophical liberalism'). In its economic developments, liberalism is a set of theories that see the market as the most suitable instrument for harmonizing relations between individuals.

The theoretical roots of neoliberalism, as it stands today, can be traced back to the simultaneous emergence of the neoclassical school and the Austrian school at the end of the 19th century. The former gradually established itself as the hegemonic economic school at an academic level, contaminating even the heterodox schools of thought that were often critical of the market, and imposing its method and worldview in the most prestigious universities and scientific journals. The latter, while remaining confined to the so-called economic heterodoxy, played a decisive role above all at the cultural and political level in extolling the supposed virtues of the free market.

Politically, the neoliberal programme was launched in the 1980s by Reagan and Thatcher and quickly established itself as a model of economic policy worldwide in the following decades. By now, neoliberalism constitutes the cultural, scientific and political hegemony in much of the western world and is also embraced by the political left, which, in some cases, even presents itself as radical.

**Marginalist, school** School of thought born in 1870 with the almost simultaneous contributions of Walras, Jevons (founders of the neoclassical school) and Menger (founder of the Austrian school). The term 'marginalist' refers to the use of differential calculus. According to Schumpeter, what the neoclassical and Austrian schools have in common is the rejection of the classical and Marxian approach based on the objective theory of value and the proposal of a subjective theory of value. Instead, the use of differential calculus is only developed by the neoclassical school, as the Austrian school maintains a critical stance towards mathematical formalism. From this point of view, it would be more correct to speak of a 'subjectivist revolution' rather than a 'marginalist revolution'.

Mathematically, the marginalist approach proposes differential calculus as the universal method of analysing economic issues. According to Lionel Robbins' definition, economics is the science that studies human conduct as a relationship between ends and scarce means applicable to alternative uses. With this definition, economics loses its character as an essentially historical science (in the sense that it studies different forms of economic organization in different historical contexts functioning according to different principles and mechanisms) to become, or at least claim to become, a universal science valid, like the exact sciences such as mathematics or physics, in any context.

**Market** Place where economic transactions take place. In economic theory, the term does not necessarily refer to particular physical locations, but indicates a network of relationships between economic operators, even distant from each other, who exchange the same type of good.

**Market failures, theory of** Theory showing how, under certain circumstances (increasing returns to scale, externalities and public goods), perfect competition is incompatible with Pareto efficiency. From a regulatory point of view, this theory envisages the state intervening either by directly producing the goods for which the market is unable to realize Pareto efficiency on its own or by dictating rules that push market participants to reduce the degree of existing inefficiency. From a methodological point of view, this line of research belongs to the neoclassical school that has the general economic equilibrium model as its theoretical reference. The latter in fact defines the ideal (completely unrealistic) case in which the market of perfect competition produces Pareto-efficient allocations. The theory of market failures therefore plays a complementary role by focusing on the cases of Pareto inefficiency of the market. From the perspective of realism, market failures are certainly not the exception, but the norm.

**Market power** In the case of a seller, ability to set the price above the level of perfect competition without losing all its customers. Symmetrically, in the case of a buyer, ability to set the price below the level of perfect competition without losing all its suppliers. Market power thus denotes a degree of monopoly and implies a violation of perfect competition: in perfect competition, a seller setting a price above the prevailing market level would fail to sell anything and, symmetrically, a buyer offering a price below the market level would fail to make any purchase.

**Market socialism** Set of theoretical models in which the means of production are publicly owned and the allocation of resources follows market rules. On a historical level, the experiences of Yugoslavia and Hungary in the post-1960s reform period are the main concrete realizations of these models. As a school of thought, market socialism has strong affinities and overlaps with analytical Marxism and, methodologically, is a branch of neoclassical economics.

**Mathematical programming** Set of mathematical methods for optimizing an objective function within certain constraints. In the simplest case where the objective function and constraints are linear, it is called linear programming. Mathematical programming is the tool par excellence of economic planning.

**Methodological individualism** Principle according to which all economic and social phenomena must be explained by tracing them back to the action plans of the agents who have contributed to determining them. A scientific explanation must establish a relationship between observed social interaction and individual behavioural criteria. The starting point is therefore a set of isolated individuals, who are seen as totally independent of the social context in which they interact, and society itself, with its economic institutions and rules of operation, is seen as the result of spontaneous interaction between individuals. Society is not itself a cause of the individual, as assumed in sociological studies and holistically inspired economic theories. It is only a consequence of individual actions, which are the real driving force behind every social phenomenon. The individual therefore needs no explanation. The only phenomenon that requires a scientific explanation is the social interaction that develops when several isolated individuals enter into contact.

Very often, both in 19th century and more recent economic literature (including many economics textbooks), in order to emphasize the total independence of the individual from the social context, the figure of Robinson Crusoe, the character from Daniel Defoe's novel, is introduced as a narrative device. It is only when Robinson comes into contact with his servant Friday that the economic interaction between the two and the institutions that regulate its functioning develop. Among the modern schools of economics inspired by methodological individualism, neoclassical theory with its new institutional developments undoubtedly plays a central role mainly due to the academic hegemony it has gained. From a strictly theoretical point of view, however, the most strenuous defenders of methodological individualism are the economists belonging to the Austrian school. Marx used the term 'robinsonade' in a derogatory way to indicate this abstract way of giving 'explanations' without reckoning with history (see: *Methodological individualism, Marxist critique of*).

**Methodological individualism, Marxist critique of** Although the term 'methodological individualism' was only introduced in the economic debate in 1908 by Schumpeter, the idea that a satisfactory economic explanation must necessarily trace all social phenomena back to individual choices goes well before that. In fact, the critique of bourgeois political economy, as a set of theories that conceives of the relationship between the individual and society in a unidirectional sense instead of grasping their dialectical relationship, is one of the central aspects of the theory and methodology of Marx and Engels, who severely questioned the very idea that there can be an abstract human nature independent of the social context. According to the two authors, political economy, in its attempt to provide universally valid propositions, independent of historical context, does nothing more than assume as universal the human nature of bourgeois society, which in reality is nothing eternal, being itself the product of a particular mode of economic interaction, based on the progressive extension of market relations. Instead of studying the history of the different forms of social organization and the different types of individuals that develop in them, it represents contemporary society as a consequence of a universal human nature. For this reason, all the specific characteristics of capitalism (private property and the market above all) and of the human nature that develops in it (based on individualism) end up appearing as universal instead of as proper to this particular mode of production.

The method of bourgeois economic theory, with its robinsonades, thus reflects all the contradictions of an aprioristic and ahistorical method of analysis which, in defining the isolated agent as its starting point, ends up in fact already assuming in it the whole set of social relations that characterize the society it wishes to explain. The asymmetrical division of labour between Robinson and Friday, their propensity to exchange, the very language that enables them to communicate, are all aspects presented as original traits of the personalities of the two subjects, whereas they are actually the product of the social context from which they come. With these methodological premises, according to Marx and Engels, bourgeois theory deprives itself of the possibility of conceiving other economic systems apart from the capitalist one, which prevents it from grasping the development of society and the individuals of which it is made up in their historical and transitory dimension.

**Methodological individualism and political individualism** The former refers to a type of economic analysis that traces all social phenomena to the behaviour and choices of individuals, while the latter indicates a political programme aimed at promoting individual freedom. Although these two positions are often found side by side (at least on a formal level) in neoliberal theories, there is in fact no causal link between them: first, it is possible to defend individual freedoms without espousing the particular individualistic method of analysis; second, from the point of view of scientific rigour, the choice of a particular method of analysis should depend on a particular conception of reality (ontology), not on a particular political programme.

**Minimal benevolence principle** Ethical principle stating that 'it is good that people are better off'. This principle is used in neoclassical economics to transform positive propositions concerning Pareto efficiency into normative propositions about the desirability of achieving Pareto efficiency. At a closer inspection, however, this ethical principle proves to be neither minimal nor benevolent.

**Needs and preferences** Needs express necessities (biological, cultural, social), preferences tastes. The former are objective, the latter are subjective. Neoclassical and Austrian theory concentrate on the concept of preferences and ignore that of needs, which is instead the subject of analysis in Marxism and other schools of thought such as the 'old' institutional one.

In its analysis of preferences, neoclassical theory adopts the axiomatic method, which consists of imposing certain properties on individual preferences structures. On the basis of these axioms, it then develops the theory of consumption and demand and, from these, derives all normative prescriptions for market efficiency. Austrian theory, by contrast, rejects mathematical formalism and considers preferences as the object of a process of individual discovery that takes place precisely through market interaction. The strong element that the neoclassical and Austrian theories have in common is the principle that individual preferences must be taken as given (without therefore being explained economically).

Completely different, instead, is the approach of the theories based on the concept of needs. They consider the different needs of the individual as orderly in a hierarchical sense (first the universal needs of water and nutrition, those of physical and mental health, and then gradually those of a higher order and of a social and cultural nature, also dependent on the historical context). On the normative level, theories of needs suggest that it is the comparison between the structure of existing needs and unmet needs that determines the objectives of public intervention (regardless of whether the existing needs actually manifest themselves on the market).

**Neoclassical school** Together with the Austrian school, protagonist of the marginalist revolution of the 1870s, based on individualism and differential calculus. From the 1930s onwards, it tended to distinguish itself from the Austrian school by its strong inclination towards mathematical formalization and its focus on the study of equilibrium configurations. With the discovery of new mathematical techniques, the reference to differential calculus lost its importance and today the neoclassical school essentially coincides with mathematical economics. The term neoclassical was introduced in a derisive sense by one of its staunchest opponents, Thorstein Veblen. Today, the term has lost all critical connotations, and the neoclassical school is by far the dominant school at the academic level.

**Neoliberalism** See: *Liberalism and neoliberalism.*

**New institutional economics** School of thought that uses the neoclassical analytical framework to explain the nature and role of economic institutions of capitalism. The fields of application are among the most diverse and include economic history, positive economics and normative economics. In the field of history, the attempt is to interpret the evolution of capitalist institutions as a march towards the gradual elimination of all forms of Pareto inefficiency. In the field of positive economics, the theory assumes the market as a primordial, everlasting and natural institution, and attempts to grasp the *raison d'être* of the other capitalist institutions (the state and the firm in particular) by assuming that they emerged as spontaneous solutions to the problems of market failures. Contrary to all historical evidence, the theory asserts that hierarchical organizations themselves, such as the capitalist corporation, are the product of a spontaneous agreement between the parties (in the case of the firm, between the workers and the capitalist). In the field of normative economics, the theory portrays large corporations as driven by the efficiencyist principle of cost reduction and thus envisages a minimal role for public intervention.

**New Keynesian economics** School of thought that emphasizes the role of nominal rigidities (particularly wages), information asymmetries and, in general, market imperfections in the interpretation of employment dynamics and business cycles. Although it declares to be inspired by the theory of Keynes, from a methodological point of view, it develops the neoclassical conception, based on methodological individualism.

In the theoretical debate, this school is criticized above all by the so-called 'post-Keynesian' (or, simply, Keynesian) school, which argues that adherence to neoclassical methodological principles distorts the conception of the English economist. In fact, one of Keynes' great theoretical contributions lies precisely in having developed a consistent framework for studying the links between certain important aggregate variables, without having to assume methodological individualism and mathematical optimization (the so-called 'macroeconomics'). Keynes' own conception of the market economy as a system incapable of self-government has nothing to do with the problems of Pareto efficiency on which neoclassical theory (harshly criticized by Keynes himself) and the theories derived from it insist so much. On the contrary, in the Keynesian framework, it is the problems of aggregate demand that make public intervention in the economy necessary. From a practical point of view, moreover, the great advantage of Keynesian theory is that it provides some powerful theoretical tools for assessing the effects of economic policy without any need to analyse in detail the decision-making problems of each individual agent. New Keynesian economics, by contrast, aims precisely at micro-founding macroeconomics.

**Normative theory** See: *Positive and normative theory*.

**Objective function** Mathematical function expressing the objectives pursued by the decision-maker and their relative importance. In modern economic theory, all economic problems are represented as problems of optimization of a given objective function under certain constraints. Moreover, both the objective function and the constraints are taken as given.

**Ontological individualism** Ontological individualism refers to the proposition that it is individuals who create all social institutions. Collective phenomena, according to this ontological position, are not really real entities, but merely hypothetical abstractions. Such abstractions come from the decisions of individuals, who are the only entities of which economic reality is composed. Very often, this position on the nature of economic reality is accompanied by a particular methodological choice, according to which the scientific explanation of a social phenomenon must always start from individual choices (methodological individualism). From this point of view, all macroeconomic propositions that do not have a microeconomic foundation (i.e. the vast majority of traditional macroeconomics) would be devoid of scientific content.

As Mark Blaug notes, the fact that individuals create social institutions is trivially true. However, this does not imply that there cannot be an inverse relationship according to which social institutions can have an effect on the individual's behaviour. Nor, Blaug continues, does ontological individualism imply the existence of particular methodological rules to be followed in the study of collective phenomena, as proponents of methodological individualism claim.

**Optimization** Generic term for maximization or minimization of a mathematical function. According to neoclassical theory, the behaviour of any decision-maker can be represented as an optimization problem under certain constraints.

**Overproduction** Excess of production over the absorptive capacity of the holders of purchasing power. In Marxist theory, overproduction crises are an intrinsic factor of the capitalist system. Indeed, the very laws of capital accumulation, operating through the market mechanism, prevent a congruent development of supply and demand at the aggregate level. According to the dominant theory's representation of the economic system, by contrast, the market is a mechanism capable of automatically coordinating the demand and supply of each good, which also implies, as a special case, perfect coordination between aggregate demand and supply.

**Pareto efficiency** Situation in which the only way to improve someone's situation is to make someone else's situation worse. In a Pareto-efficient situation, therefore, no Pareto moves are possible (see: *Pareto move*). The extensive use of the concept of Pareto efficiency in economic theory is linked to the fact that moves that improve someone's condition by damaging someone else's can only be defended by introducing particular value judgements. The adoption of Pareto efficiency as a normative criterion is instead generally considered independent of any value judgement. However, this is wrong since the Pareto criterion presupposes the acceptance of the individualistic ideology and the principle of 'minimal benevolence' (see: *Minimal benevolence principle*).

**Pareto move** Change that improves someone's condition without worsening anyone else's.

**Partial and general equilibrium** In partial equilibrium schemes, the analysis of a single market is carried out by introducing the assumption that it is separated from the rest of the system. More precisely, it is assumed that the conditions prevailing in all other markets are given and do not depend at all on what happens in the market under consideration. Under these assumptions, the demand and supply of a good depend solely on its price. In general equilibrium schemes, by contrast, all markets are analysed simultaneously. The demand and supply of each good now depend on the prices of all goods. For example, an increase in the price of coffee in addition to causing a decrease in the demand for coffee could, indirectly, increase the demand for tea (as a partly substitute good for coffee). Even if one wants to focus on a single market (the tea market), the equilibrium conditions therefore also depend on the prices that are set in other markets (the coffee market). Furthermore, while in a partial context, equilibrium requires equality between supply and demand in a single market, in the general context, this equality must be respected in all markets.

Partial equilibrium analysis is, at best, only a first approximation of what actually happens in a system of interdependent markets. This approximation is all the more misleading the stronger the links of interdependence that exist between markets. On the other hand, the only way to assess the importance of existing interdependencies is to place them explicitly in a general equilibrium framework. In this sense, general equilibrium analysis is undoubtedly superior to partial equilibrium analysis from the point of view of logical-deductive rigour, and the only advantage of partial equilibrium schemes lies in their relative simplicity.

**Positive and normative theory** Positive economics studies the functioning of the economic system and the consequences of public intervention policies. Normative economics, instead, analyses the desirability conditions of the functioning mechanisms of the system and of public interventions. The former is descriptive in nature and deals with *what is*, while the latter is prescriptive in nature and deals with *what ought to be*.

According to the positivist philosophical conception, positive economics must be completely extraneous to all value judgements and be based solely on factual judgements. Conversely, value judgements are considered necessary only in the derivation of normative positions from the strictly scientific results of positive theory. The distinction between positive and normative economics generated a lengthy debate in which it was pointed out that even positive economics cannot in fact be considered extraneous to the ideological view and value judgements of the theorist.

**Preferences** See: *Needs and preferences*.

**Prisoner's Dilemma** Game theory problem in which the interaction between two subjects with conflicting interests produces an equilibrium solution that does not satisfy Pareto efficiency. Two prisoners believed to be complicit in a certain crime are faced with two alternatives: to confess or not to confess. The choice to confess (and to betray the co-defendant) leads to immediate release only if the other prisoner also does not confess as well. If, instead, the other prisoner also confesses, the 'service' rendered to justice by betraying one's partner is of little use to the prosecution, and both receive a three-year prison sentence. The prisoner who does not confess, when the other confesses, receives the maximum sentence (five years). If both do not confess, as there is no evidence against them for the major offence, they both receive a one-year sentence (for minor offences). Individualism and the inability to cooperate with each other in a credible way induce both prisoners to confess (thus getting three years each). The reason why both confess is that each prisoner knows that if the other confesses, it is better for him/her too to confess (and take three years instead of five); if, conversely, the other does not confess, it is still better for him/her to confess (and thus be released rather than serve 1 year). In short, in both cases, it is advantageous from an individualistic point of view to confess. The Pareto-efficient solution, however, is the one in which both do not confess (one year each). Of course, outside of individualistic logic and Pareto efficiency considerations, history provides us with numerous examples of perfectly rational individuals who were unwilling to betray their comrades, regardless of the consequences that awaited them under the 'incentive mechanisms' of the judicial system.

**Public goods** According to neoclassical theory, goods that have two properties: 1) the enjoyment of the benefits of the good by an additional consumer costs nothing; 2) the exclusion of an additional consumer from the enjoyment of the good is technically impossible. This is a purely theoretical definition that has nothing to do with whether the good is offered by the public sector or not. Public goods constitute a case of so-called market failures. In the presence of public goods, the market, if left to itself, does not lead to Pareto-efficient economic allocations.

**Purchasing power** Amount of goods and services one can purchase with the money at one's disposal.

**Radical school** School of thought critical of certain aspects of market society and dominant economic theory. At the academic level, its fundamental point of reference is the US association *URPE* (*Union for Radical Political Economics*), founded in 1968 by academics and political activists. It includes Marx sympathizers, the economics of feminism, studies on race and class relations, the analysis of economic and social inequalities, development and underdevelopment theories and various more or less radical critical contributions to neoliberal theories. From a methodological point of view, it is not entirely correct to characterize this convergence in the motivations behind scientific research as a true school of thought, since the methods of analysis employed are inspired by different (and, in some cases, mutually incompatible) schools of thought. From a methodological point of view, theories of radical inspiration have increasingly embraced the principles of neoclassical theory.

**Rationality** At the individual level, according to neoclassical theory, the principle according to which a person always pursues his/her own self-interest and uses the most appropriate means to realize the objectives he/she has set out. Full rationality is when the decision-maker optimizes a given objective function under existing constraints while bounded rationality is when the optimization process is not completed (e.g. because it is not possible to know exhaustively the existing choice options or because the decision-making process itself may be costly and time-consuming). Referring instead to the economic system as a whole, it indicates the existence of mechanisms of economic interaction that enable the realization of social ends that are deemed appropriate. If, as in neoclassical theory, social evaluation is inspired by the individualist principle of consumer sovereignty, the rationality of the economic system consists in the existence of instruments (market prices) that allow rational calculation at the individual level.

**Scientific neutrality of economic theory** Attempt to exclude all ideological and moral premises from economic analysis. In the positivist philosophical approach, the quest for scientific neutrality led to a clear distinction between positive and normative economics. Only the former, insofar as it manages to keep itself free from value judgements, takes on a fully scientific character. The latter, on the contrary, since it cannot do without value judgements, cannot aspire to express universally valid propositions.

**Scientific neutrality of economic theory, Marxist critique of** From a Marxist perspective, bourgeois economic theory is by no means scientifically neutral. It reflects, even in its strictly positive economic formulations, the vision, aspirations and concerns of the dominant class of capitalism, the bourgeoisie. The reason why the propositions of bourgeois economics appear value-neutral is that implicitly the theory takes the capitalist system as given and espouses the views of its ruling class. With these assumptions, only those moral positions that do not fall within the moral conception of the bourgeoisie truly appear as loaded with value judgements. According to Marxism, it is the bourgeois class that has an interest in presenting its moral conception as eternal and universal, and it is always the ruling class that has an interest in claiming the neutrality of its view of economic relations by claiming that its theory is based on the principle of the common good.

**Transaction costs economics** Branch of the new institutional economics according to which the evolution of the economic institutions of capitalism (in particular, the state and the firm) follows the principle of minimizing transaction costs, understood as the costs of operating the market mechanism. According to this theory, existing institutions are the result of a selection process of the most economically efficient institutions. Methodologically, this theory is derived from neoclassical economics. In fact, it is an attempt to analyse the economic institutions of capitalism through the tools of neoclassical theory.

**Use value and exchange value** Concepts developed from classical and Marxian political economy. Use value is the property of a good to satisfy a given need (see also: *Utility*). Exchange value (or market price) is the ratio by which a quantity of one good or, more precisely, a commodity, is exchanged on the market for quantities of other commodities (see: *Goods and commodities*). Use value is a presupposition of exchange value: a good that has no use value (i.e. a good that serves no purpose) cannot have any exchange value because no one is willing to give up anything to get a completely useless good in exchange. However, the use value is not sufficient to determine the exchange value: water is certainly more important than oil from the point of view of use value, yet oil has a higher exchange value on the market.

**Utility** Assessment of the benefit an individual derives from the consumption of a basket of goods. It is a subjective assessment as it depends solely on the subjective preferences of the individual. The concept of utility is the basis of neoclassical theory. The difference from 'use value' (a concept developed in classical and Marxian political economy) is subtle: as mentioned, utility expresses a subjective evaluation of the good; use value, by contrast, is an objective characteristic of the good itself. Water has the property of quenching thirst (and thus has a use value with respect to the objective need for hydration), regardless of the individual's subjective preferences for the different goods that can satisfy this need.

**Visible hand** Principle according to which the conscious coordination of individualistic subjects enables socially superior economic results compared to those achievable through their spontaneous interaction. The expression 'visible hand' is used by Chandler in contrast to the famous Smithian expression of 'invisible hand'.

**Voting impossibility theorem** Impossibility of determining a social objective function from individual preferences consistent with a set of reasonableness and desirability requirements. This theorem, formulated and proved by Arrow, is also known as the 'third welfare theorem'. It shows that in a context of agents with heterogeneous preferences, where the principle 'one head, one vote' applies, any attempt to aggregate individual preferences to obtain a scale of social preferences gives rise to internal consistency problems or leads to violating the Pareto efficiency principle.

**Welfare economics, fundamental theorems** The first theorem states that, under certain assumptions, the competitive equilibrium (when it exists) is Pareto-efficient. The second theorem states, under more restrictive assumptions, that any Pareto-efficient configuration can be achieved through the competitive mechanism as long as market interaction is initiated from an appropriate distribution of resources among individuals. These two theorems are generally presented as proof of the desirability of the market of perfect competition according to neoclassical methodology. In reality, besides the fact that Pareto efficiency coincides with social desirability only under very particular assumptions, the very logic of the two theorems raises conceptual problems. For the third welfare theorem, see: *Voting impossibility theorem*.

# Index

For Product Safety Concerns and Information please contact our EU representative GPSR@taylorandfrancis.com Taylor & Francis Verlag GmbH, Kaufingerstraße 24, 80331 München, Germany